EVERY HAND REVEALED

EVERY HAND REVEALED

GUS HANSEN

LYLE STUART
Kensington Publishing Corp.
www.kensingtonbooks.com

LYLE STUART BOOKS are published by

Kensington Publishing Corp.
850 Third Avenue
New York, NY 10022

First printing: May 2008

10 9 8 7 6 5 4 3 2 1

Printed in the United States of America

ISBN 13: 978-0-8184-0727-7
ISBN 10: 0-8184-0727-1

To Chip Reese—

*Remembering the Ones who left way to soon
but still enrished our lives in many ways*

and My Friends and Family—

Cherishing the ones still among us.

CONTENTS

ABOUT GUS HANSEN

by David "Chip" Reese

I MET GUS HANSEN many years ago before he even started playing professional poker. He was just a young kid who played backgammon in Denmark. I was an accomplished backgammon player and Gus destroyed me when I played him. I was extremely impressed with his quick mind and ability to logically solve a problem. I knew then that if Gus ever took poker seriously he would become a force to be reckoned with. I was right!

Gus Hansen holds three World Poker Tour titles. No one else has done that yet. He also won the WPT Bad Boys Invitational as well as the 2005 Poker Superstars Invitational on the Fox network, and just recently he captured the crown in the highly lucrative Aussie Millions Tourney in Australia.

Gus has done something that is very difficult to do: He's brought original thought to an age-old game. Many of his ideas on how to play poker have made me take a second look at some conventional strategies I thought to be true. I look forward to reading his book and know that I will definitely learn something from it.

Gus is not only a very talented poker player but also a very popular one worldwide. His popularity among women has greatly increased female interest in the game of poker. Not just me but the entire poker community would love to hear what

Gus Hansen has to say about this old but increasingly popular game they call poker.

Chip Reese was a world-renowned poker professional who repeatedly was voted "best cash game player of the year" by his peers. In 2006, he won the $50,000 buy-in H.O.R.S.E. poker tournament at the World Series of Poker—regarded by many as the most prestigious event: the one demanding the most skill. Much to the shock and sadness of the entire poker community, Chip passed away in December 2007.

PREFACE

I WAS UP AGAINST 746 competitors. It lasted five days. It took me 329 hands. But it was all worth it, because I won. Do you wanna know how? I will show you.

Since the beginning of my professional career, I have often been called "the madman" by people believing I am insane, making loose plays with any hand, calling large bets with seemingly unplayable hands, and raising out of position with garbage holdings. There is, however, logic behind the madness. My approach to poker is mathematical and analytical and in my mind this is the only way to win in poker. My aggressive style has nothing to do with being macho at the poker table— it is simply the right way to play the game. Lucky for me, I have five major international titles to prove it.

This book will give you the opportunity to see the hands from my perspective and get a grasp of the basic concepts and principles of my poker philosophy. What you will discover is that my kind of poker requires constantly attacking your opponents, constantly accumulating chips, constantly keeping track of pot odds and winning percentages, and constantly gearing up as blinds and antes increase.

It is the first poker book to go behind the scenes and actually show you what I had, and how I played it during the Aussie Millions Poker Tournament 2007. All the hands that I played are turned face up and every decision I made is explained in my pursuit of the title. The revealing is made possible because of the little tape recorder that I always bring to the tournament tables. After having played a hand, I take a couple of steps away from the table to record the action. In addition to describing the play of the hand, I also take note of my opponents and whether they have displayed any patterns, mannerisms, etc. This is information I can hopefully use in later encounters. Although it takes focus away from the action at hand, it is necessary to capture all the impressions while they are still fresh in my mind. Each and every hand has been recorded and commented on, and the vast majority of them will appear in this book.

Every Hand Revealed is a visit to my world. It is the story of a crazy five-day rollercoaster ride from my first hand—5♠7♠—to my last hand—A♣A♥. It is a story of moves, big laydowns, bad beats, suck-outs, and lots and lots of stealing. Of patience, pressure, and aggression. Of bluffs, reads, and tells.

Welcome to my mind . . .

ACKNOWLEDGMENTS

Special thanks to my manager, brother-in-law and friend Erik Balck Sørensen—without him this book would probably never have hit the shelves. To my sister Tine Marie who is always there to pick me up and support me when the going gets tough.

Thanks to my comrades in the poker world: Abe Mosseri, Haralabos (Bob) Voulgaris, Howard Lederer, and Chip Reese, who assisted me in writing this book, but more importantly have helped me improve and develop my game throughout the years.

Thanks to Kensington for having the patience to deal with a poker player—I know it is not easy.

INTRODUCTION

FOR A LONG TIME I have been searching the market for challenging poker literature. I am a firm believer in listening to and learning from people who have done well but I rarely come across a book that convincingly presents a viable poker strategy based on practice, not theory. Too many books out there are solely theoretical and way too many have a much too cautious view on how to play poker.

My victory in Melbourne in January 2007 provided me with the perfect opportunity and material to write the book I have been looking for myself. It would be an instructional book comprised of real hand examples and extensive commentary extracted from on-the-spot experience. Basically it is like being at the tournament yourself, only you are able to avoid the mistakes and hopefully profit from the successful moves I made. At the same time I get to share my trade secrets rooted in actual holdings, thoughts, and plays without a lot of theoretical and hypothetical mumbo-jumbo. This is the way I would like to learn!

My basic idea was to make the format of this book very simple. After a brief Introduction and a few tips on how to get started in a live high-buy-in tournament, we will get the real action going. Hand after hand after hand . . .

With very few exceptions, all of the hands that I played during the Aussie Millions Championship Event are presented in this book. I decided to take out almost all the hands that I folded without any action pre-flop but aside from that, only minor adjustments have been made to the hands extracted from my little tape recorder. In order to display as much information as possible every hand comes with "hand info" detailing the size of the blinds, my holding, my position in the hand, and the approximate size of my chip stack.[1] These are all important data if you want to thoroughly evaluate the specifics of a hand.

I am a big fan of hand examples with extensive commentary as the poker problems become much easier to extrapolate from and understand. In this case you have a whole book of hand examples guiding you on how to get started, how to play during the first levels, how to pick up speed and be aggressive, how to deal with the different styles of play you encounter, how to fight off tilt, how to progress in short-handed play, how to be a successful closer, and much, much more!

The Outline of the Book

Each chapter takes you on a one-day journey Down Under with thorough lead-in advice relevant to that particular day's action.

In Chapter One all the hands from day one are revealed along with my considerations as to starting in a live tournament. Chapter Two covers day two with special emphasis on how to play high-ante structures. Day three of the tournament is laid out in Chapter Three including my advice regarding short-handed strategy. During Chapter Four we are down to fourteen players battling it out for the final table. In the introduction to that chapter I focus on how to keep the pressure on and at the same time avoid the obvious all-in moves by the short-stacks. In Chapter Five we are finally seated at the seven-

---

1. It should be noted that most chip counts are estimates as I did not have time to count my chips every time I recorded a hand.

handed final table. I discuss final table tactics and the ladder principle before presenting the hands playing down from seven players to three. Chapter Six shows all the hands played between Andy Black, Jimmy Fricke, and myself. The initial advice discusses the dilemma of going for the gold or settling for second. My heads-up battle against Jimmy Fricke can be found in Chapter Seven. Before the actual hand showdown and commentary I explain my heads-up strategy.

All days are fully reported, from the first cards dealt to the bagging of the chips. Each chapter contains several special highlighted hands called crucial hands. All crucial hands will be marked for easy access. There are more than twenty crucial hands highlighted in the book. You will find a list for easy reference at the end of this outline.

Chapter Eight provides you with the stats of my tournament play. The stat charts include how many hands I played, how many top-notch hands I actually had, how many uncontested pots I won, a whole section on bluffing, and lots of other good stuff. I present my final remarks in Chapter Nine.

Although I try my best to reveal *everything* in this book, I am not afraid of the potential repercussions. The most important skill of a successful poker player is to be able to change gears and, thereby, always to keep his opponents guessing. So go ahead and test me—I am always up for a challenge.

CHAPTER 1

AUSSIE MILLIONS—DAY 1

My Advice Before Today's Play

How to Approach a Tournament from the Beginning!

There are many different ways to approach the beginning levels of a tournament.

Some people feel the most appropriate measure is to sleep a couple of extra hours and enter the tournament at their convenience. A few pros actually take this method very seriously, following it almost religiously. Others think that the first couple of levels are the very building blocks of what could be a bright and prosperous tournament. The theories range from A to Z but it's hard to say which one is better. I would say it depends solely on your mood. If you are feeling tired and exhausted from a late-night poker session the day before, it could very well be your best move to get some extra rest. Sacrifice a little equity in the beginning to be on top of your game for the subsequent higher and more important levels! If on the other hand you are in tune and ready to go, no need to skip anything! I have personally fiddled with both and my best results definitely stem from the latter. I will say though that the sample size is too small from which to draw any conclusive result. Obviously for anyone out there for whom stamina never is going to represent a problem throughout five long and grueling days at the poker table—although I doubt if you exist—playing all levels is of course a must!

I have mixed emotions, but my advice to you is clear cut. Show up from the get-go, especially if it's your first major tournament. You don't want to miss anything. Indulge yourself in the atmosphere, control your emotions, feel the crowd, observe your opponents, and last but not least play some poker! These are all the little things that make a poker tournament a truly unique experience!

It is nice to mess around with your sleep schedule, but what's most important is of course: "When I do show up on time, how should I proceed?"

Again we are looking at two completely different approaches.

1. Limping with a lot of hands, trying to see cheap flops.
2. Playing ultra conservative, only entering pots with top-notch hands.

Approach number one relies on superior post-flop play and that someone around the table will make a serious deep-stacked mistake. It is often used by players who believe themselves to have an edge against the rest of the field, which means just about every poker player in the world.☺

Approach number two relies on superior hand-selection! People are not trying to flop a flush with Q♥ 4♥ and double up, although each and every one of us would welcome that scenario. People are looking for pre-flop edges, and for their Kings to hold up against AJ, 66, or 98 suited.

So which one will yield the best results? I wish I knew. I have used them both successfully and unsuccessfully.

I do believe that Hold'em is somewhat of a flop-game, so if you can see three cards relatively cheaply it is generally a good idea. The problem is that sometimes you get raised along the way, and now your speculative hand has turned into an unprofitable one! Another problem with playing mediocre starting hands at the early levels is that it mainly depends on your opponents making mistakes. I personally don't like my game plan to be built too much around other peoples' inadequacies.

Somewhere along the same lines lies this statement: "There is almost no money in the pot. Why bother messing around with inferior holdings?" I can come up with no good answer! I would have a hard time arguing that limping for a 100 at the 50–100 level with 8–7 off-suit in middle position is an obvious moneymaker with 20,000 in front of me. I just *cannot* make that statement! It is way too hypothetical!

Regrettably the conservative approach is not without downsides either. There is one question you should always ask yourself when playing tight: "Is my style too predictable?" More often than not the answer is yes, and it is a considerable downside worth noticing.

If you sum it all up, it may sound like I'm giving the conservative approach the go-ahead. I'm so much of a flop fan that it overrides my other arguments.

Bottom line: I lean toward approach number one, but I'm not convinced. I don't think there is a wrong or a right answer. Remember, this is not an internet tournament where blinds and antes shoot through the roof in a matter of minutes and aggression is the ultimate feature. This is a major tournament with a slow progression of the blinds, allowing much more room for individual style and preference.

Now Let's Shuffle Up and Deal

Hand 1

Blinds	My Position	My Hand	My Chip Stack
50/100	4th	5♠ 7♠	19.85K

The day before the tournament started I was joking with Phil Ivey and Patrik Antonius that we would start out at the same table so that the organizers could hype up the tournament. But with more than 350 players seated on day two we knew that it was highly unlikely to happen.

Obviously I was a little bit surprised to find Phil Ivey as well as Kathy Liebert and Evelyn Ng at my table. Not the best of table draws, but at least Patrik wasn't there. I am not at all a morning person as I am usually a fairly slow starter and not especially keen on risking it all during the first couple of levels. Having one of the world's very best male players and two of the best female players at the table wasn't my idea of a let's-take-it-easy kind of start. One thing was clear—I had to play my very best from the get-go.

Although I definitely would have preferred some more unfamiliar faces at my table, Mr. Ivey's presence did raise a couple of interesting questions:

1. Is Mr. Ivey bringing his deadly "I want to win this tournament" game-face to the table?
2. Is it a more relaxed Phil-version just arriving from the golf course?
3. What kind of interesting side bets are we gonna make?

The answers come in the order received:

1. I hope not, as Phil's A-game will represent a major headache for anyone aspiring to win the trophy.
2. A much more pleasant alternative. No matter who you are, winning a poker tournament takes concentration, dedication and focus. Not saying that a relaxed Phil doesn't have a chance, but he has to kick it into gear before he becomes a real factor.
3. A lot of the pros love to make side bets on a poker tournament. Phil and I both happen to fall into that category.

There are three different kinds of bets: Last Longer, Must Win, and Cross-Booking. As the name indicates, "Last Longer" solely concentrates on outlasting your opponent. "Must Win" means that you must make the money to qualify for winning the bet. For this type of bet there is usually a bonus for making the final table and winning the tournament. For both categories a predetermined amount is wagered, and you therefore know exactly how much you stand to win or lose. "Cross-Booking" is a totally different story. You are essentially betting that your opponent will not make money in the tournament. Whatever he wins you will have to pay and visa versa. Let us for example say that Phil and I cross-book each other and Phil ends up winning the tournament. I would have to pay him an additional first prize, in this case $1.2 million! This type of betting is of course only for hard-core gamblers.

At last year's World Series of Poker, I had "Must Win" bets in two different tournaments. Unfortunately, it was against Sammy Farha who won the Omaha high-low and Chip Reese who won the H.O.R.S.E event. Needless to say, that was NOT a lucrative experience! It was time to make up for my losses. Side bets are usually made before the tournament starts, but since we are at the same table we might still get some action going.

Phil and I discuss the different options, but since Mr. Ivey is a top-notch negotiator, making Samuel L. Jackson look like a 5th grader, we end up settling for the fourth option: No Deal!

Having to worry about how Phil is doing throughout the tournament can also be a slight distraction when trying to play your best, so maybe discarding the side bets is not that bad an idea after all.

This is our 10-handed feature table:

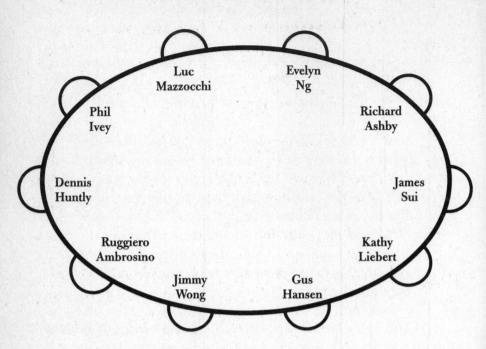

I have started out pretty tight the first round or two and this is actually my first hand of the tournament. Everybody folds to me in fourth position and I decide to limp in with 7♠ 5♠. Jimmy limps along and so does Phil and the two blinds.

Five guys to the flop:

Besides my unlikely back-door flush I guess this is what you could call a "nothing-at-all" flop. An easy check-fold and on with the next hand. The blinds check, I check, and when Phil bets 300 into the 500 pot everybody mucks.

Hand 2

Blinds	My Position	My Hand	My Chip Stack
50/100	BB	8♣7♥	19.75K

Four of my opponents limp for 100 and I tap the table in the BB holding 78*o*. Another five-handed flop:

A very deceptive flop! An open-ended straight draw and an 8-high flush draw to boot. Looks good but in reality not much to cheer for! With four opponents a higher flush draw is highly likely, not to mention that somebody could have a made flush already. I check, hoping to get a free card and complete my straight-draw on the turn. The two initial limpers knock the table but Mr. Sui on the button over-bets the pot with a 600 bet. The SB folds and I immediately follow suit. Besides the fact that I could be drawing completely dead, there are still three guys left to act behind me. This makes it almost impossible for me to call. Everybody folds behind me and Mr. Sui flips over 9♥ 4♥—one of the few hands where I wish I would have called!

Hand 3

Blinds	My Position	My Hand	My Chip Stack
50/100	SB	7♠8♥	19.65K

Everybody folds to my SB and I look down at 78*o* again. Limping and folding are okay but raising is just a lot more fun. Furthermore it is about time I win my first hand. I do as Mr. Wong folds.

Hand 4

Blinds	My Position	My Hand	My Chip Stack
50/100	1 off the button	9♣ 7♣	19.4K

Another hand, another limp! I am 1 off the button with 9♣7♣ and decide to spend 100 on a cheap flop. The button wants to play a little higher and makes 350 to go. The BB calls and I call another 250 to win 850.

The flop comes:

Again not really what I was looking for. The BB checks, I check behind, and the button bets 700 into an 1,100 pot. My hand hits the muck almost as quickly as our BB friend announces raise! The BB makes it 2,200 more and takes down the pot.

Hand 5

Blinds	My Position	My Hand	My Chip Stack
50/100	2 off the button	6♦ 7♦	19.15K

I am back in the saddle in the very next hand. Although my stack has dwindled slightly since we began I am not quite ready to abandon my limping strategy, especially not with a nice suited connector in middle position. I limp 2 off the button with 6♦ 7♦ and with the blinds limping along we have a nice little threesome.

The flop comes:

A no-hitter! Both blinds check and I take a 150 stab at the 300 pot. Small blind folds, but the big blind is waiting for me and quickly raises it 400 more. I muck my Seven high no nothing hand.

Hand 6

Blinds	My Position	My Hand	My Chip Stack
50/100	2 off the button	Q♥ 9♥	18.55K

I open for 300, 3 off the button with Q♥ 9♥. Pretty decent hand with only four players yet to act! Luc Mazzocchi in the BB is my only customer.

The flop comes:

Although I don't really have a clear-cut impression of Luc's style of play I put him in the somewhat conservative category, which means that he is likely to be playing high cards. He checks and I bet 400 to win the pot right there, or if that fails go for plan B—hit an 8 on the turn. Betting the flop after a pre-flop raise is called a continuation bet and trust me, we will encounter a lot of those along the way. He calls. Time for some drawing power to set plan B in motion.

Turn:

No Eight, but a sneaky and straighty Three. He checks again and I convince myself that it is the perfect card to execute plan C. He didn't project a lot of strength before or after the flop, so another bullet on a "four-to-a-straight" board should be enough to finish him off. Nine hundred into a 1,450 pot feels like the right amount. Unfortunately Luc thinks 2,900 is an appropriate amount! My Q-high can't compete against a 2,000 raise so without further ado I muck. Plan A was good, plan B needed luck, and plan C was imaginative. Overall, not my best performance. It is still early though, and I have plenty of time to correct my wrongdoings, but I can't afford too many 1,600 "I-have-absolutely-nothing" moves.

Hand 7

Blinds	My Position	My Hand	My Chip Stack
50/100	BB	2♠3♠	16.95K

I have been laying low for a couple of hands and find myself in the BB. Everybody folds to Kathy Liebert in the small blind who opens for 300. I don't believe she is trying to bully me out of position, so until I've proven otherwise I'll put her on a genuine hand. I still think 2♠ 3♠ is worth another 200 so I decide to call.

The flop comes:

Bottom pair! A hit but nothing to get too ecstatic about. On the other hand there is no straight or flush draw on this totally discombobulated board. I could therefore very well be ahead since it is not an easy flop to connect with. A check on her part would, with a high probability, have confirmed a miss but Kathy bets out 400, not giving me any information whatsoever. I have to decide which path to take:

1. Folding! A bit premature with a pair and a back-door flush draw.
2. Calling! Reasonable to see what the turn will bring and maybe be able to use my positional advantage.
3. Raising! Last legal and viable option. Knocks out any inferior holding and some superior as well. It also gives me some more information as to where I stand in the hand.

I believe it is a close call between options two and three, and as many times before I choose the active route. I raise 900 more but would quickly regret that as Kathy came right back over the top for a total of 4,000. Time to depart with bottom pair.

My raise had cost me 900 and a chance to improve, but that's the price you sometimes have to pay when testing the waters. Kathy clearly had the best hand, so no shame in folding.

Hand 8

Blinds	My Position	My Hand	My Chip Stack
100/200	SB	5♠ 7♠	15.65K

Status check: End of level 1 and my stack is diminished by 20%! Not that I am really worried though, as I still have a little more than 15,000 left in front of me.

The blinds are now 100/200. Everybody folds to my SB and I open for 600 with 5♠ 7♠. I was able to steal Jimmy's blind once before but alas, not this time. Mr. Wong re-raises me an additional 900—a rather small and odd amount! It could be an invitation to call, quite possibly representing a big hand. I almost always respond positively to nice invitations, especially when the odds are so compelling, and this time is no exception. Being up against a potential powerhouse though, my plan is to proceed with caution. I call the 900 and the flop comes:

Well, that was a brief party. I have nada, so checking feels right. Jimmy's 2000 bet quickly ends the hand, and another 10% of my stack has gone missing.

Hand 9

Blinds	My Position	My Hand	My Chip Stack
100/200	BB	A♠ J♥	14.15K

Dennis Huntly opens in third position for 600. Phil Ivey on his left calls and I call as well with A♠J♥ in the big blind. I am not even contemplating a re-raise since I am dealing with two early-position players in a ten-handed game. Although it may sound ludicrous coming from me, folding is probably the second best option. The flop comes:

No help, and my hand's justifying powers run out. I check, Dennis checks, and Phil bets 1,200. You never know with Phil, as he could have any two cards. Playing back at him with Ace high and another player behind me is not on today's menu, though. I fold and Mr. Huntly folds behind me.

Hand 10

Blinds	My Position	My Hand	My Chip Stack
100/200	1st	K♥ Q♥	13.45K

I open for 600 in first position with K♥ Q♥. Everybody folds to Kathy in the big blind, who calls another 400.

The flop comes:

Kathy checks and I make a standard continuation bet—700, just over half the pot. She calls instantly and the turn is:

Kathy checks again and without really thinking about it I fire the second bullet—1625 into a 2650 pot. Again Kathy calls without a lot of hesitation. A King or a Queen on the river would be nice. The river is:

Kathy checks for the third time and I surrender—something I should have done on the turn. 5♠ wasn't a scare card and taking a free card would have been the proper play. Kathy flips over 8♥ 8♦ for top two, and as expected my King-high came in as a nice second-place finisher.

I'm going to hit the ground floor pretty soon, unless I start saving those 1625 bets I have scattered around lately. I barely have 10k left and we are only on the second level—not good!

Hand 11

Blinds	My Position	My Hand	My Chip Stack
100/200	BB	J♣ 9♣	10.22K

I am holding J♣ 9♣ in the big blind and am pleased to see a couple of early limpers. James Sui tries to spoil the party by making it 800 on the button. I would be well advised to fold my hand in this spot, especially after losing too much on the last hand but I guess I am just a little impatient. I call 600 more and the two limpers fold.

The flop comes:

Top pair medium kicker, but I'm not quite sure of Mr. Sui's intentions so I decide to take it slow. I check and James bets 1,200 into a 2,100 pot. I call, waiting to gather some more information on the turn. The turn is:

That is all the information I need! I'm not going to back off this one. My only concern is how to extract another 8,150 from Mr. Sui! Even though there are two flush-draws lurking out there, checking seems to be the right approach. I'm pretty confident he is going to fire again and I see no need to interfere with that kind of behavior. I check and he bets 2,600. That was the signal I was waiting for, so without too much Holly-wood acting I move all-in—5,925 more.

I was expecting a quick call, but either I misread the strength of his hand or else he is making one heck of a read. To this day I'm not sure which one it is, but no matter what, he came up with a well-timed fold. I still pick up a nice profit though—more than 5,000. Funny how perception changes! I started the day with 20,000 in chips and now barely a couple of hours into the day I'm ecstatic to have 15,000 in front of me.

Hand 12

Blinds	My Position	My Hand	My Chip Stack
100/200	1 off the button	K♠ 6♠	15.225K

I open 1 off the button for 750 with K♠ 6♠. Dennis Huntly in the big blind is my only customer, but unfortunately not the kind I was looking for. He re-raises to 2,500, basically asking if I want to be his customer. I didn't have a strong urge pointing in that direction, so folding was easy. I didn't want to keep throwing good money after bad with the worst hand. Apart from one big hand, I hadn't picked up too many winners at this table, so I was delighted to see the floor manager come over and pull me out of my chair.

Hand 13

Blinds	My Position	My Hand	My Chip Stack
100/200/25	Button	A♠ 7♥	14.1K

After a little bit of a debacle at my first table I am very happy to get moved to another seat in the room. It didn't seem like anything was going my way in the beginning but I still manage to have over 14,000 left out of the 20,000 I started with. The fact that I am not at the same table as players like Kathy Liebert, Evelyn Ng and Phil Ivey is another added benefit. Last but not least, I'm of course ecstatic to see the antes introduced for the first time—as they naturally favor aggressive play.

I wait around for a couple of hands just to see who is who out of eight unfamiliar faces at my new table. But after five hands I can't take it anymore.

Four people limp and it felt like the right time to make my first stab. I make it 1,350 on the button with A♠ 7♥. Having an

Ace in my hand didn't really influence my decision. Although Aces are nice to have I had decided to raise no matter what. Raising a bunch of limpers is a very common theme for most of the early big-stack professionals. Players like Antonio Esfandiari, Michael Mizrachi, and Alan Goehring love to represent big holdings, thereby picking up a lot of medium-sized pots. I have always been a little wary of making that move but I am starting to like it.

Everybody folds except one. That doesn't necessarily mean that my attempt has failed as I still have one barrel left. After the usual "check to the raiser" I am gonna fire on the flop no matter what.

The flop comes:

Now I actually have some kind of hand. Second pair, top kicker, not that bad! Unfortunately the limp-caller hadn't read all the conventional poker books. He is supposed to check to the raiser! Instead he leads out 6,000 into a pot containing about 4,000. What's wrong with him?

Needless to say it changes the dynamics of the hand completely. My 2,500 continuation bet in the flop has become totally irrelevant and I am now facing a decision for all my chips. Although a case can be made for calling the 6,000 and then later on making an educated decision for my last 8,500, that is *not* how I play! It is either 14,500 or zero! And most likely zero!

What could he have? AJ suited, QQ, or maybe K♠Q♠ come to mind. Not a lucrative spot for an A7o. After contemplating for a bit it seems like this is a pretty easy fold. And so I do.

Hand 14

CRUCIAL HAND 1: Doubling Back into the Tournament

Blinds	My Position	My Hand	My Chip Stack
100/200/25	1st	K♦ 9♦	12.6K

I open in first position for 600 with K♦ 9♦. My nemesis from the previous hand tries to interfere once again and calls the 600 1 off the button—and so does the table chip leader in the BB.

The flop comes:

King high flush draw and two over cards—what more could you want? The BB checks and I bet 1,200. Nemesis calls 1,200 and surprisingly the BB raises 2,000 more to a total of 3,200. I don't see how I can fold this hand, leaving me with two options:

Calling—hoping for a call behind me
Moving all-in—hoping everybody folds

I think it is a close call with both plays having some significant upsides. But being the tight player that I am I choose the conservative route . . . I call and Nemesis calls behind me. The turn brings:

What a beautiful diamond and what an ugly pair!

This could end up being one of those situations where you put your last money in the pot drawing completely dead. Nemesis could have me beat with the Ace high flush and the BB with a full house. A sad farewell if you go out like that but I am getting too old to fold my King high flushes.

BB checks. Since I considered moving all-in on the flop with a King high and diamond draw it should be obvious for everybody that all-in is the right move now that I actually made my flush. I spend a minute or two thinking it over—as it is a decision for all my chips—but no matter how much time I spend I can't come up with a different answer. All-in it is!

Nemesis—who afterward said that he folded the Queen high flush—took a couple of minutes of his own before he folded. In general you should not believe the stories you hear at the poker table but if in fact he did fold the Queen high flush, I have to compliment him! I am not sure I would have been able to make that play. Analyzing the hand away from the table, though, it all makes a lot of sense.

What could I possibly have, apart from an insane bluff?

Remember I did open in 1st position, I did bet on the flop in a three-handed pot, I did call a check-raise with a guy who had already shown some strength behind me, and when the third diamond hit I did push all-in. All in all, the Queen-high flush didn't look that enticing anymore.

Action is back to the BB who also goes into the tank. After a while I am absolutely certain that I have the best hand and therefore I'm wondering, "What could he call me with?"

I think the rest of the world probably thought the same when he turned over his hand. He ended up calling and after I showed my flush he reluctantly displayed J♣ 8♠! *Wow!* I guess he put me on the insane bluff variation.

The river blanked out—2♠—and I doubled up into the 30k range.

Great fold, strange call, weird hand!

Hand 15

Blinds	My Position	My Hand	My Chip Stack
100/200/25	4th	7♦ 7♥	28.85K

I open in middle position for 650 with two Sevens. My opponent sitting 1 off the button makes it 2,300, the blinds fold, and I call 1,650 more. The flop comes:

I check, he bets 2,000 and I fold. Couldn't have imagined a worse flop—three over cards in a straight formation.

Hand 16

Blinds	My Position	My Hand	My Chip Stack
100/200/25	Button	A♦ 6♦	26.1K

Everybody folds to my button and I make a standard raise with A♦ 6♦. The blinds fold and I pick up 500.

Hand 17

CRUCIAL HAND 2: Doubling Up Again—Flush vs. Set

Blinds	My Position	My Hand	My Chip Stack
100/200/25	2 off the button	J♣ 5♣	26.6K

Having doubled up a couple of hands ago I feel a bit more confident about the whole enchilada. The 27,000 also gives me more room to maneuver. I open for 600 two off the button with J♣ 5♣, the button click-raises to 1,200, and I call. It is almost like he is inviting me to call since he is giving me very lucrative pot odds of 5:1. And who am I to decline an invitation like that? Even against two Aces it is right to call. I will of course have to proceed very carefully as it is very possible I am up against a big hand. On a side note this is one of the first hands I have seen this guy play since I joined the table, so for starters I have him in the tight category.

The flop comes:

Even though I flopped a flush draw I am gonna stick with my initial game plan—proceed carefully. I check and surprisingly he checks behind me. The turn brings the:

I have made my flush and hopefully I can extract a bit of money from my seemingly tight opponent. I bet out 2,000, and another surprise comes along as he quickly makes it a total of 6,000.

What now?

What kinds of hands fit into the patterns displayed so far?

Click-raising before the flop, checking the flop behind me, and then suddenly raising the turn after I lead out! Theoretically A♣5♣ seems like a possibility but then again I don't believe this guy would make a move like that. Only KK and 99 seem to fit all the criteria with a slight edge to KK. This was the most certain read I had made all day but I still wasn't sure how to proceed. It did make things quite a lot easier, though!

Whichever set he had didn't make a whole lot of difference to me since it was impossible for him to make a bigger flush than I would with the K♣ on the board.

After at least calling the 4,000 more the pot would contain 15k and I would have exactly 19,375 left. Should I shove the rest of the money in or wait?

The obvious play: moving all-in knowing I have the best hand and giving my opponent the wrong pot odds to call. Upside: Doubling up 77% of the time when he calls. Downsides: 1. I don't take advantage of the fact that I know exactly what he is holding. 2. He might correctly fold. 3. Going broke 23% of the time when he calls.

The call: Only calling his 4,000 raise might seem a bit odd with what is knowingly the best hand, but there are a couple of good reasons why. Upside: Avoid going broke on the hand if the board pairs on the river. Downside: Failing to double up when a club comes on the river.

Let's take a closer look at the math:

There are forty-four remaining cards that can be divided into three categories:

Twenty-seven blanks
Seven clubs
Ten cards pairing the board

All math examples are used with the assumption of perfect play on my part and a high level of curiosity on my opponent's part:

1. I double up when a blank hits.
2. He calls a medium-sized value-bet when a flush card hits.
3. I lose no more money when the board pairs.
4. He always calls my all-in move on the turn.

Assuming perfect play is always a far stretch, but this is a very specific situation and can of course only be used in such instances.

Calling the Turn (Keeping the All-in Move in Reserve)				The All-in Move on the Turn		
			Result			Result
Cards left	44			44		
Blanks	27	61.4%	54,000	34	77.3%	54,000
Pairing the board	10	22.7%	19,800	10	22.7%	0
Clubs	7	15.9%	42,220*			
Equity			44,350			41,727

*My opponent calls a 8,000 value bet on the river

So my average chip stack after the all-in move would be 41,727 and 44,350 after the waiting play—a 2,600 edge.

It looks like the "safe" play, taking full advantage of my knowledge, comes out ahead in the spread-sheet, but giving a couple of style points for the more aggressive play, and adding in the fact that it is always dangerous to assume anything at the poker table, it is very close indeed.

Just calling would be my preferred play after having figured everything out away from the table, but failing to sort it all out right then and there, I decided to go all-in for 19,375 more. He calls, shows a set of nines, and we are down to the skill-card.

The river is the:

A beautiful card, which keeps me alive in the tournament. I am now above average with almost 54,000 in chips.

Hand 18

Blinds	My Position	My Hand	My Chip Stack
150/300/25	2 off the button	K♦ Q♠	53.2K

Blinds have gone up to 150/300 but unfortunately for me the ante stays at 25. I fare a lot better the higher the antes are compared to the blinds.

The player in first position limps and I limp along 2 off the button with K♦ Q♠. Normally I would raise but it doesn't hurt to see a cheap flop once in a while. The BB, whom I labeled as a "crazy Italian" player on my tape recordings, checks his BB. The flop comes:

They both check and I decide to check behind, not really fearing any turn cards except maybe an Ace. The turn comes:

The crazy Italian now bets 500, the early limper makes it a total of 2,000. When checking the flop I was hoping to get some action on the subsequent streets but I hadn't quite expected a bet and a raise! Still believing that my top pair, second kicker, has a good chance of being the best hand I make the 2,000 call. No need to raise as I don't want to get *too* involved with a paired board and the Italian lurking behind me.

The Italian gets out of the way and we are down to heads-up. The river brings:

He bets 3,000 into a 6,000 pot and it is time to stop and think. I know for a fact that when I check the flop in position people put me on "absolutely nothing." On the other hand I did call a bet and a raise on the turn, which indicates I must at least have something. So I have sent out two contradictory messages, which I guess makes it hard to put me on a certain hand. When I am facing a decision where I am a little bit in the dark as to my opponent's whereabouts I like to bet and let him make the decision. I guess he liked the idea because that is exactly what he did! Bet out and put me to the test!

I am not so sure of his whereabouts either as his actions were a little funky as well. The two Deuces on the board didn't scare me at all as I was up against a first-position limper. It was much more likely that he could have AA, AK, or a set of Sixes, none of which I could beat. Searching for beatable hands, the heart flush-draw was the obvious choice. The 2♥ on the turn had brought two hearts on the table and it was very possible that he was making a play with A♥x♥.

Three thousand to win 9,000 seems like a reasonable investment! At the time I thought it was about 50/50 whether I was up against one of the big hands or a busted flush-draw.

I call. He turns over A♥ 5♥ and I win the pot.

Hand 19

Blinds	My Position	My Hand	My Chip Stack
150/300/25	4th	A♣ 4♣	59.6K

Another first-position limper and again I choose to limp along, this time with the A♣ 4♣. The SB and the BB join the party and we take a four-handed flop:

The blinds check and the initial limper bets 800 into a 1,425 pot. I have a gut-shot, a backdoor flush-draw, and Ace high. It doesn't seem to be quite enough to justify a call with two people behind me yet to act, but then again it is only eight hundred. I call and the blinds both fold. The turn brings:

He bets 2,200, leaving himself with seven thousand. I have to call 2,200 to win 5,200, which means I need approximately 30%

winning chance. My back-door flush draw has been upgraded to a nut flush draw giving me nine flush cards, three straight cards, and possibly three Aces. My initial read is that I am up against a very strong hand so it seems wise to discount the three Aces when counting my outs. I might even have to rule out the two clubs pairing the board, leaving me with seven clubs and three Threes—a total of ten sure winners. Ten out of forty-four remaining cards only gives me 22.7%, indicating that I should fold but . . . if I do hit I think I will be able to win my opponent's remaining 7,000, catapulting my odds into easy call territory!

I call. The river comes:

No hit! He bets 5,000, strengthening my belief that I would have gotten all his money had I made my hand. As it was, I of course quickly folded.

Hand 20

Blinds	My Position	My Hand	My Chip Stack
150/300/25	2 off the button	J♣ T♣	55.7K

I open for 1,000 with J♣ T♣, 2 off the button. The BB—a presumably very tight player—calls. The flop comes:

Good flop! He checks, I bet, 1,200, and he calls.

Turn:

He checks again. There is now 4,800 in the pot and my opponent is left with 12,000. I am not quite sure what his check call on the flop meant. Could he be flushing? Straighting? Pairing? I guess they are all possible. I do believe my two Jacks is the best hand right now, so it is time to pull out my preferred play of all time—all-in!

Instead of trying to extract more money from my opponent, picking up the 4,800 is my main priority. Only betting 3,000 on the turn could leave me in a very tough spot facing a 9,000 bet when the K♦ shows up on the river. Whatever he is drawing to I know he has outs to beat me and I want him to pay top dollar if he wants to make that attempt.

I would obviously have proceeded differently had my opponent had 40k left but with only 12k in his stack I was ready to gamble.

I bet 13,000 and I guess "top dollar" wasn't in his vocabulary since he quickly folded.

I happily pick up the 4,800.

Hand 21

Blinds	My Position	My Hand	My Chip Stack
150/300/25	1st	5♣5♥	58.2K

I limp in first position with two fives. The crazy Italian, with about 12,000 in his stack, makes it 800 and everybody folds. I of course call the 500 more. The flop comes:

I check, he bets 1,000, and I call. Continuation bets have become pretty standard nowadays and I thought my 55 still had a pretty good chance of being in the hunt. The turn card is the:

In case I was leading after the flop I know I am not in front anymore when the Ace shows up. I check and he quickly checks behind me. By now I should obviously have realized that he dislikes the Ace more than me. The river card is:

Again I check, he checks behind, and turns over two Jacks for the winning hand.

SOME REFLECTIONS

Limping: Fine
Calling the continuation bet: Fine
Checking the turn: Fine
Planning to give up when he bets the turn: Fine
Giving up when he didn't bet the turn: Horrible!

My opponent was eager to bet the flop but was disgusted when checking the turn. Failing to pick up on tells like that is plainly and simply unforgivable. I even get the added security of a King on the river making it just about impossible for him to call with his JJ or QQ. On the river I should have led out with a pot-sized bet and taken down the pot. I cannot afford to miss out on such obvious bluff opportunities in the future!

Hand 22

Blinds	My Position	My Hand	My Chip Stack
150/300/25	BB	A♣ 8♥	55.7K

The button makes it 1,200 and the SB calls. I have A8o in the BB and believe it is time to pick up a little speed. I have not been re-raising a lot pre-flop, making it more plausible that I have a big hand. Now that I think about it, it might actually be the first time I do so. In addition I could very well have the best hand since we are talking about a button raise.

I make it 4,300 to go and they both fold. Nice pickup instead of having to play the flop out of position.

Hand 23

Blinds	My Position	My Hand	My Chip Stack
150/300/25	2 off the button	K♠ Q♦	58.1K

I open 2 off the button with KQo for 1,000. The big blind calls, leaving him with 6,600. The flop comes:

Just about as good as it gets for a no-pair flop! He checks and I see no reason to prolong the inevitable! I bet 6,600, putting him all-in. He quickly folds and I pick up the 2,400 in the middle.

Hand 24

Blinds	My Position	My Hand	My Chip Stack
200/400/50	BB	5♦ 4♥	59.3K

Blinds increase to 200/400 but the antes double! The ante is now 25% of the small blind and adds a lot of value to stealing the blinds and antes. A lot of times you can pick up 1,050 (400 + 200 + [9 × 50]) for a 1,200 raise.

The player in third position opens for 1,200. The SB calls and I call in the BB with 54o. Not my favorite hand against an early-position raiser, but with the small blind in there as well I only have to call 800 more to win 3,200. Even if I am up against KK and AT I get the right price. The flop comes:

SB checks, and I check hoping the original raiser will make a substantial bet. He doesn't, so it is checked around. The turn comes:

The nuts! The SB checks again, and I bet 2,200 only to see four cards immediately hitting the muck! @#$%&%$#%—too

quick on the trigger. Don't you just hate when that happens? You patiently wait around for something good to happen and then your opponents have absolutely zippo.

I shouldn't blame the rain, though. It was a bad bet on my part. The original raiser obviously had two high cards and the small blind whatever. This was not the time to chase both of them away. I should have checked one more time as they were both drawing completely dead.

I might have been able to pick up a bluff or somebody could have improved to the second best hand had I let them see the river for free.

Hand 25

Blinds	My Position	My Hand	My Chip Stack
200/400/50	BB	K♣7♦	61.5K

A new player at the table opens for 1,300, 1 off the button. I am in the big blind with K7o and decide to give him a warm welcome. I re-raise to 4,500 and he folds. I'm starting to be a tad more aggressive with late-position raisers, and so far it has worked pretty well.

Hand 26

Blinds	My Position	My Hand	My Chip Stack
200/400/50	Button	5♣4♦	63.1K

A young guy makes it 1,200, 2 off the button. He looks very indecisive and I read it as sheer weakness. I re-raise to 4,600 on the button with 5♣4♦ planning to win it right there.

The blinds and the raiser fold. I overhear the blinds' conversation of whether they should have called my re-raise with AQo and ATo respectively. Had I known an AQ was still out there

I would definitely have been a lot more reluctant to re-raise. As it was it worked out anyway and I am starting to feel more confident about my reads. Mind you—my read had nothing to do with the blinds but was only focused on the initial raiser. Obviously it was a small but significant mistake on my part not paying enough attention to the two guys behind me. Had I been more alert I probably would have stayed away from this one. Luckily for me the blinds weren't quite strong enough to fight the double-raise.

Hand 27
Hand 28
Hand 29

Blinds	My Position	My Hand	My Chip Stack
200/400/50	Button	J♣ 7♥	64.3K
200/400/50	1 off the button	A♠ 3♠	65.3K
200/400/50	3 off the button	Q♦ Q♣	66.2K

An entire round goes by without me playing a hand—I didn't even defend my blinds. This is not to my liking at this otherwise lucrative ante level! I'm determined to pick up the pace as well as blinds and antes.

Hand 1: On the button I don't need a lot of excuses to play—especially not after a 9 hand drought! I find a Jack and a 7, two different suits, exactly what I was looking for! I raise to 1,250, no callers, profit 1,000.

Hand 2: 1 off the button I need a little bit more—J8 I would say! A♠ 3♠ is more than enough and I push repeat! Raise 1,250—no callers—profit 1,000.

Hand 3: Folding a hand so as not to blow my cover seems appropriate, but I don't want to overdo it. After my short break I raise to 1,250, 3 off the button. This time there was a little more meat behind it—two Queens! It is always nice to pick up some real substance a couple of hands into a rampage. You never know when somebody might want to put an end to it—this time I was prepared. It could have been nice if somebody tried to make a move, but no such luck and I had to settle for a three-peat. Raise 1,250—no callers—profit 1,000.

I guess it all adds up!

Hand 30

Blinds	My Position	My Hand	My Chip Stack
300/600/75	1st	A♥Q♠	66.7K

Again the blinds and antes have gone up but this time proportionally.

I open in first position for 1,850 with A♥Q♠. The short-stacked guy in fourth position moves all-in for 11k and I call. He flips over A♣5♣.

Showdown

My Hand   **My Opponent's Hand**

So far, so good. Turn and river:

I come in a nice second! Short-stacked guy doubles up.

Sometimes I wonder why people wait around *so* patiently only to go crazy at some point in time with Ace-rag hands, against a first-position raiser.

Hand 31

Blinds	My Position	My Hand	My Chip Stack
300/600/75	2 off the button	A♣ T♦	54K

I open 2 off the button for 1,800 with A♣ T♦. Usually I don't get too many customers, but this time around both the button and the big blind showed some interest. There is now 6,450 in the pot and we are off to a three-handed flop.

Top pair, top kicker, but no spades! I have to admit I wasn't too excited about the prospects of this hand with two callers, but things are looking up. After the expected big-blind check, I bet 4,800. The button calls and the big blind folds. Turn is:

Very ugly! It felt like I was ahead on the flop, but that card could very well have turned things around. I give it the man-datory study before I check. John Doe checks quickly behind me and I'm sensing the Eights wasn't that terrible after all.

River:

A blank on the river was exactly what the doctor ordered! Apart from completing a straight for the unlikely 97-holding, the 6♣ didn't change anything! Although I'm not certain, I like my chances of having the best hand and therefore a medium-sized value bet seems to be in order. I bet 6,300 and without any hesitation he calls. I didn't like the speed and the ease with which he put in the 6,300, but little did it matter, because my pair of Tens, Ace-kicker, was the best hand. Maybe I could have bet a little bit more on the end, but then again . . . I wasn't too confident about the whole situation, so all in all I'm pretty happy about the outcome.

Hand 32
Hand 33

Blinds	My Position	My Hand	My Chip Stack
300/600/75	SB	K♣9♦	68.8K
300/600/75	3rd	8♥8♠	69.8K

I fold my big blind without a fight, but make a quick comeback in the small. Everybody folds to me and with a 1,900 raise I regain my chips from the previous hand.

Along the same lines! I make it 1,850 to go with 88 from middle-early position, only to see six guys muck their cards almost simultaneously.

Hand 34

Blinds	My Position	My Hand	My Chip Stack
300/600/75	BB	5♣7♣	71.3K

A very quiet guy opens in second position for 1,800 and I call in the BB with 5♣7♣.

The flop comes:

I check my 7 high with no plans of ever putting any more money in the pot. He bets 3,000 and I fold.

Hand 35

Hand 36

Hand 37

Blinds	My Position	My Hand	My Chip Stack
400/800/100	1 off the button	5♣3♠	69.3K
400/800/100	3 off the button	Q♦J♣	71K
400/800/100	2nd	A♠J♥	73K

The main difference between cash games and tournament play is the always increasing blinds and antes. We are now on level seven, last level of day one, playing 400/800 with 100 ante. The 4:1 ratio between the SB and the ante makes it very enticing to steal, and I am eager to pick up at least my fair share.

Every time we jump to a new level I take a minute or two

to figure out how I want to proceed at this exact level, calculating the ratio between the blinds and the different stack sizes around the table, and of course considering whether the ante is high enough to go into hyper-aggressive or just aggressive mode.

With a cost of 2,100 per round and an at-the-moment average stack size of 40k I felt it was a good time to pick up some pots. The fact that my table was a little low on chips and a couple of guys were in let-me-at-least-last-till-tomorrow mode just made it more obvious.

So here we go!

Hand 1: I open for 2,200, 1 off the button with 53o. Everybody folds.
Net Result: +2,100

Hand 2: I open for 2,200, 3 off the button with QJo. Everybody folds.
Net Result: +2,100

Hand 3: I open for 2,200 in 2nd position with AJo. Everybody folds.
Net Result: +2,100

Picking up 6,300 with no contest whatsoever is not bad for a round's work!

Taking advantage of people's mindset and doing it at a time when it actually adds some bite to your chip stack is, in my opinion, mandatory.

Hand 38

CRUCIAL HAND 3: Making the Wrong Read— Folding Top Pair

Blinds	My Position	My Hand	My Chip Stack
400/800/100	2 off the button	J♣ 3♣	73.4K

New round, same procedure. Or maybe not?

I make it 2,500, 2 off the button with J♣ 3♣. The BB ponders for a while but finally decides to call. It felt like he was thinking about the re-raise and not the fold so my instinct tells me that my J3 is probably not the best hand.

The flop comes:

Top pair, ridiculous kicker, but top pair nonetheless!

He was supposed to check but instead he decides to fire out 6,000. What was that all about? It is not very often that I am facing a substantial lead-out bet when I am the initial raiser and therefore I wanted to take my time to make sure I made the right decision. My opponent had another 14k in front of him, which meant my maximum downside from this point on would be a total of 20k. Maximum upside, 26k.

Options:

Folding: Seems very odd now that I finally flopped top pair.
Calling: Putting in 6,000 and awaiting his next move.
Raising: Shooting 20k into the middle hoping my J3 is ahead.

Three very different approaches, and which one to take is gonna be decided solely on my read on the situation.

Reads:

He looked eager to re-raise pre-flop—not a good sign.
He led out 6,000, which is a significant part of his stack— not a good sign.
He looked mighty confident about the situation at hand— not a good sign.

I can remember three times in my career where I raised pre-flop, flopped top pair, and folded facing a single bet! Was this going to be the fourth?

The only holdings that made some kind of sense to me were the AJ, the QQ, and hands of similar strength. The more I thought about it the more confident he looked, and in the end I saw no other choice than to muck my hand! I folded.

Because of my very curious nature I showed the Jack face-up, as I was certain he was going to turn it over if he had bluffed me. Don't worry—he did! He turned over two Tens displaying his victory to the table, or should I say, my ridiculous fold.

Where did I go wrong? My initial read about him wanting to re-raise before the flop was correct. Re-raising pre-flop with TT would be the normal play. My read on his confidence level after his lead-out bet was also correct. I think taking my time made my opponent certain that his TT was the best hand because how could I ever be taking that long with a Jack in my hand? My read on his lead-out bet was incorrect—I took it as a sign of strength where it was in fact meant as a stab to take down the pot if I didn't hit the flop.

I made an informed decision based on all the facts I had available at the time. I came to the wrong conclusion but that is bound to happen when you sit for more than ten hours at the

poker table. Maybe I should think twice next time I am about
to fold top pair on the flop.

Hand 39

Blinds	My Position	My Hand	My Chip Stack
400/800/100	SB	T♥ 9♥	69.6K

Table change. Now facing one of the young guns, Jeff
Madsen. I have to admit I liked the old table a little bit better.
I am sure that the youngest double WSOP winner ever is not
just gonna let me control the table without a fight.

Jeff Madsen opens in early position for 2,400; I call in the SB
with T♥ 9♥. The BB also calls. The flop comes:

A beautiful straight flush draw! The big end, I might add,
also giving me two over cards!

There is 8,000 in the pot and the respective chip counts are:

Me	68k
Jeff Madsen	50k
BB	65k

Although I only have Ten high, there is no way I am going to
fold my hand in the near future. I have 43% against a set, 57%
against an over pair, and 69% against A8. This is my kind of
gambling hand.

I have a number of options on how to proceed with a potent
hand like this, but I do believe leading out to be the superior
play. 1. I don't want to give a free card to hands like A♣ Q♣,
hands that I am fairly certain Jeff will check behind me. 2. The

pot-size in comparison with the stack-sizes plays well into a three-bet scenario. Let me explain:

Example 1: I bet 5,000, Jeff or BB raises to 18,000, I move all-in for 49 more. A very nice rhythm and might knock out a lot of hands that potentially could get me in trouble.

Example 2: I check, Jeff or BB bets 5,000, I raise to 18,000, now I become the victim of an all-in move. Easy call, but still! Also one of them could smooth-call when I check-raise. In case a blank hits, I might have to put in 40k on the turn with only one card to come. I could of course check-raise all-in on the flop, but it doesn't have the same sting as in the first example.

Leading out clearly has the best feel to it, and so far I haven't come up with anything to convince me otherwise. I lead out for 5,000 but nobody wants to come along for the ride and I pick up the 8,000 in the middle. As his cards hit the muck, Jeff mutters "Do you have to bluff all the time?" Seeing no reason to shy away from the truth, I quickly respond "What do you mean? I had at least Ten high." From our little conversation it was obvious to me that Jeff would have liked to get a free card—reassuring me that leading out was the superior play. It is always nice to have your opponents subconsciously confirm your theories.

Hand 40

Blinds	My Position	My Hand	My Chip Stack
400/800/100	3rd	A♥J♥	74.8K

We are closing in on the final hand of day 1, and I'm in the mood for a last-minute sprint. I open for 2,600 in third position with a very respectable A♥J♥. The small blind, let's call him Jasper Parnevik as he has that Scandinavian-golfer look, calls. Big blind is out, and the flop comes:

Not a whole lot to cheer for. "Mr. Parnevik" has been playing rather tight, and therefore I think it is safe to assume that if he didn't have me beat before the flop he probably has me beat now! He checks and I check it right back. Turn:

"Jasper" checks again. Maybe I misjudged the situation, maybe I do have the best hand, maybe I should just bet and get it over with? I convinced myself that a 4,200 bet was perfect for the conditions—4,200 it is. It didn't take "Jasper" long to add another 12,600 to the equation thereby making the total bet 16,800! Beautiful trap-play, "Mr. Parnevik"! I had see-sawed back and forth from right to wrong, guided by a sly Swedish maneuver, only to cost myself an additional 4,200. Needless to say I was done with the hand, and for all I cared, done with the day! I glanced at the clock and fortunately there were only a couple of minutes left till I could rack up my chips.

End of Day 1

• Recap, Day 1

End of day one and it is time to recap the day's events. My early limping strategy didn't prove very successful this time, but it hasn't completely discouraged me. I'll be back on the limping wagon before long—but remember, only for the early levels. I did have a lousy beginning at a tough starting table but fortunately it didn't last all day. A lucky hand and a beautiful seat change helped me to get back on my feet. I felt more in control at my new table. Of course my improved batting average helped me take charge of the situation. No matter how you look at it poker is inevitably much easier to play holding some decent cards. My increased aggression, once the antes reached a significant level, also played an important part in my respectable finish.

Looking around at some of the other tables, the most impressive stack is in the hands of Mr. Patrik Antonius—315k! I don't know how that is possible, but I do know that right now Patrik is the overwhelming favorite to win it all. My somewhat-above-average stack of 66.7k looks a little bleak compared to his, but taking it one step at a time, I'm at least still in the hunt. For now all I can hope to do is avoid any Finnish players at my table tomorrow. Following is a brief look at some of tomorrow's big stacks.

TOP TEN AFTER DAY 1A AND 1B

Patrik Antonius	315,400
Dennis Huntly	246,200
James Mogan	229,300
Nebil Soner	201,400
Christopher Chronis	178,100
Xen Xenofontos	172,200
Thariq Ahmad	159,200
Jimmy Fricke	139,100
Kristy Gazes	133,900
Mark James	132,600

CHAPTER 2

DAY 2

My Advice Before Today's Play

How to Play During High-Ante Structures

High-ante structure—you gotta love it! A feast for the aggressive player, resurrection of the maniac who has blown most of his money at slower levels and the slow death of the "rock."

Before I get too ecstatic let's start out by determining what I consider a high-ante structure. The measuring stick is the ratio between the small blind and the antes. In most tournaments you will encounter ratios ranging from 6 to 1 to 3 to 1. I believe anything lower than a 4 to 1 ratio between the small blind and the antes should be considered a high-ante structure, with a 3 to 1 ratio being the highest. As you can see, if the ratio goes down the ante structure goes up. So far so good! Now I'll try to explain my opening statement!

Once the antes show up, we have reached a turning point in the tournament. It's a new ballgame! Usually antes of 25 are added at the 100–200 level—a 4 to 1 ratio. Instead of having a dry pot with 300 (100 + 200) in it, there will now be 300 + (10 × 25) or 550 in the pot at a ten-handed table. The added money just makes it much more enticing to play and much more lucrative to steal. If your game plan is to attack, antes are your best friend, but if your game is called patience, the antes could very well be your worst enemy. Another reason I'm so excited about the antes is the fact that I don't believe most people take the appropriate measures against an ongoing assault. Let's continue the example from above. You are in the big blind facing a standard 600 raise. Without the antes you have to call 400 more to win 900—not bad! But out of position facing a tight opponent it could definitely also be better. A 31% winning chance, which is exactly what you need getting 9 to 4, is probably right on the nose, and therefore there is no reason for you to go out of your way to defend when there is not much to defend. Let's add a little spice—250! With the antes the math is as follows: 400 to win 1,150 equals 26% winning chance, not a big difference, but it all adds up! Oops, I forgot to mention something. This time you are up against me and not some tight player. The quality of my starting hands is, in case you haven't noticed, on average quite a bit lower than John Doe's. Where defending before was optional, it now becomes clear as daylight!

What I'm getting at is this: With antes in the middle, pot odds go up. Pot odds go up, people steal more. People steal more, starting requirements go down! It is easy to deal with each parameter separately, but obviously much harder to make the proper connection between the three. If somebody fails making the right assumption and doesn't defend enough you should do whatever possible to exploit it.

Let's look at the ante situation from a different perspective: Whether the antes are at a 3 to 1 or 4 to 1 ratio, they represent a noticeable part of your contribution to the pot. If for example we are at a nine-handed table playing 600–1200 with a 200 ante, a round of play will cost you 1,800 in blinds and 1,800 in antes—a 50–50 proposition. The sneaky little antes are not so insignificant anymore and should not be taken lightly. Still, I have a feeling nobody takes them seriously enough. There is an unwritten rule lurking around out there that says the standard raise should be three times the big blind. A reasonable assumption, but if you ask me, a little flawed! It seems like the rule forgot to take antes into account. Raising the same amount with and without antes is plain and simply off balance. My recommendation is raise to proportionally more when antes arrive!

As you will see I love to be hyper-aggressive during high-ante structures. I see no other approach that comes close in results, fun, or accumulative aspects. *Certain* is a word that I usually refrain from using in my poker vocabulary, so let me put it this way instead. I am *fairly sure* that the best way to deal with large antes is: attack, attack, attack!

Back to the Table

Hand 41

Blinds	My Position	My Hand	My Chip Stack
500/1000/100	BB	T♦ T♣	66.7K

After an episode of "24" and a good night's sleep I am ready for hopefully another good twelve-hour session.

A table with a lot of unknown faces and one familiar one, Jeff Madsen, greets me (see page 52).

Looking forward to get started I pick up TT in the BB. Unfortunately everybody folds and I just pick up the antes and the small blind. On a positive note I am very pleased to get a walk indicating that they are not going to mess around when I am in the BB.

Hand 42

Blinds	My Position	My Hand	My Chip Stack
500/1000/100	SB	7♥ 7♦	68K

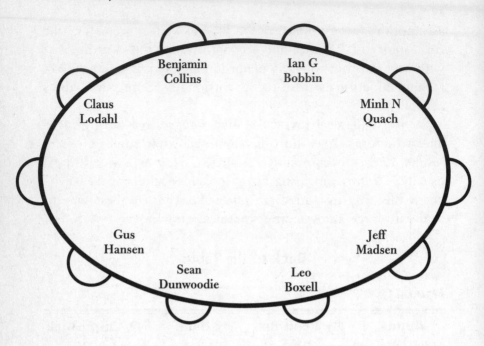

Sean Andrew Dunwoodie—presumably a local—raises on the button to 4,000. I am in the SB with 77. I am a big fan of re-raising a late-position raiser and this time I actually have a hand to do it. Although it is not a monster it is a solid, above-average hand and should therefore be treated as one. I re-raise to 12,600 and Sean goes into the tank.

Unfortunately he comes out of the tank with an additional 41,300 going all-in for a total of 45.3k. Now it is my turn to stop and think: thirty-three thousand more to win 60k. That translates into at least a 36% winning chance for the call to be profitable. Let's state the obvious—I have about 18% against an over pair and about 55% against hands like AK, AQ. 36% is right in between 18% and 55%, so which way to turn? I think it is more likely to be the over pair than the two high cards, making "the fold" my preferred play. At this point in time, I also need a very good reason to put such a substantial part of my stack into the middle. Curiosity won't cut it anymore, and I couldn't come up with another compelling argument to call.

I fold and he picks up the pot.

Later Mr. Dunwoodie played a hand or two in a very uncharacteristic fashion, leading me to believe that my 77 was stronger that it appeared at the time.

Hand 43

Blinds	My Position	My Hand	My Chip Stack
500/1000/100	Button	9♠ 4♣	55.3K

Hating the fact that I put 12,600 in the pot without ever seeing a flop, I decide to try to make it back in a hurry.

When everybody folds to my button I see no other option than to open for 3,300 with 94o. The blinds oblige and fold.

Hand 44

Blinds	My Position	My Hand	My Chip Stack
500/1000/100	1 off the button	K♣ 7♦	57.5K

I am still stuck 10,200 on the two previous hands and hope to get another crack at this one. Everybody is still folding and this time I am 1 off the button when I make it 3,300 with my K♣ 7♦. Again I pick up the blinds and antes.

Hand 45

Blinds	My Position	My Hand	My Chip Stack
500/1000/100	3rd	4♥ 4♣	59.6K

After raising a couple times this round already, I thought it was time to change the pace. I limp in with 44 in third position. Limping also fits the nature of the hand! I am in early position and I don't want to face a re-raise, forcing me to put way too much money in pre-flop. Keeping the pot small and hopefully getting another couple of limpers is much more up my alley.

Notice that contrary to most of the other hands that I play where I am trying to pick up the blinds and antes, in this hand I am aiming at a completely different target. Here I am hoping to flop a set and hopefully win a big pot against a guy with top pair, top kicker, or maybe two pair. Depending on position and stack size you should be ready to play your small pairs in many different ways. Sometimes aiming for a multi-way pot and sometimes going for the quick pickup.

Jeff Madsen is the only customer as he checks his BB option. The flop comes:

A hit! I flopped my set, but unfortunately I don't think there are enough people in the pot to have hit top pair. My sole hope relies on Jeff Madsen. Jeff checks as expected and I check behind him, giving him a chance to catch up. Looking at it now I am not sure I agree with my check as Jeff was in the BB and I therefore had absolutely *no* idea which two cards he was holding. The downside of giving a free card to a random Deuce or Trey seems bigger than the potential upside of trapping the J7o. The turn is:

He checks, I bet 1,600, and he folds.

Hand 46

Blinds	My Position	My Hand	My Chip Stack
500/1000/100	BB	Q♦ 8♠	61.6K

A tight player opens in second position for 3,000 and I call in my BB with Q8o. When will I ever learn? Calling raises with Q8o in the BB when a tight player opens in early position is just not gonna get the money. The flop comes:

I check, he bets 7,000, and I fold. A lot of smart people might say I lost 2,000 too much in that hand!

Hand 47

CRUCIAL HAND 4: To Value-Bet or Not to Value-Bet with AA—That Is the Question

Blinds	My Position	My Hand	My Chip Stack
500/1000/100	3rd	A♣A♥	57.6K

I open for 3,100 with AA and Jeff Madsen calls in the BB. AA is of course the ultimate starting hand in No Limit Hold'em, but also the hand where I see the most people go broke in silly two out situations. I did so myself in the Doyle Brunson North American Championship two months ago and I wasn't planning on doing it again.

The flop comes:

Jeff checks, I bet 3,600, and Jeff calls. The turn card is:

Jeff checks again and I check behind. The river is a:

Jeff bets 13k, I call, and he quickly mucks his hand.

Let's take it from the top:

Pre-flop: Raising with AA is the best play.

On the flop: A standard continuation bet, a little bit in the low end but not a big deal.

The turn: With possible straight and flush draws out there a bet seems in order, but what I really wanted was to control the size of the pot. Facing a check-raise on the turn would put me in a tough spot and I simply would not know what to do. Therefore I wanted to avoid the situation. If Jeff checks the river I am of course gonna make a very substantial value bet. Checking the turn has another potential upside. It could induce a bluff on Jeff's part as my check indicates weakness.

The river: After another beautiful queen, Jeff suddenly bet out 13k leaving me with two viable options—call or raise.

♦ *Calling:* Weak, tight, and timid, as I can only be beat by the improbable KK and the fourth Queen

♦ *Raising:* A much better poker alternative. My play so far had concealed the actual strength of my hand and now it was time to reap the benefits. Raising 20k more would for sure get called by a King and maybe even by some weaker full houses. I was of course scared of the ugly re-raise scenario where I would be put to the test for all my chips and again I wouldn't know what to do. I know for a fact that Jeff could make that play with two random cards.

All in all, checking the turn worked out good for me as Jeff was obviously bluffing on the river with some kind of busted draw.

As for the river, I chose the timid route—I am not proud of it, but I guess that hand from two months ago was still lurking in the back of my mind.

Hand 48

Blinds	My Position	My Hand	My Chip Stack
500/1000/100	Button	8♣ 6♣	76.6K

A tight player opens 2 off the button for 3,500 and I call on the button with 6♣ 8♣. Notice the difference between this hand and the Q8*o* a few hands ago. Here I have position but most important, I am facing a late-position raiser. The flop comes:

He checks and I bet 4,600 into a 9,300 pot. It is a small bet of less than half the pot but I had a feeling that it would be enough to push him out of the pot if he hadn't connected. On the other hand, if he did connect and played for the "dirty" check-raise I would have saved a couple of thousand as I would be done with the hand.

He ponders the call but ends up folding. I think it is very likely that he was holding two high cards. It is of course always nice to hit the flop but my pair of sixes was fairly irrelevant for the actions that took place. My bet depended solely on the fact that he checked in front of me and I would still have bet had I completely missed the flop.

Hand 49

Blinds	My Position	My Hand	My Chip Stack
500/1000/100	3rd	3♥ 3♣	82.1K

Another small pair and another limp! Again trying to flop a set in a multi-way pot. A three-handed flop, as the blinds limp along. The flop comes:

The SB bets out 3,000. Jeff and I fold.

Hand 50

Blinds	My Position	My Hand	My Chip Stack
500/1000/100	2nd	K♥ J♦	81K

I open for 3,100 in second position with K♥ J♦. GR—the Green Rock (green because of his bright green shirt)—at the table, who hasn't played *any* hands so far, calls and Jeff Madsen calls in the SB. The flop comes:

I knew there was no way I had the best starting hand with GR in the mix, so I was prepared to give it up unless I really liked the flop. I didn't. Jeff checks, I check, GR bets and eventually wins the pot against Jeff with another bet on the turn. I put him on something like two Jacks. Sometimes you just have to give up!

Hand 51

Blinds	My Position	My Hand	My Chip Stack
500/1000/100	SB	A♣ K♦	76.6K

A tight player opens in second position for 2,900. I have A♣ K♦ in the SB and take a quick peek at the two relevant chip stacks. The BB has about 15k left and the initial raiser about 12k. Nobody can seriously hurt me, leaving me with one obvious choice: all-in!

I re-raise to 16k and they both fold. Note that with different chip stacks I might have taken a more conservative route.

Hand 52

Blinds	My Position	My Hand	My Chip Stack
600/1200/200	2 off the button	7♥ 8♥	81K

We are now at the all important steal-as-much-as-you-can level. With blinds at 600/1200 and a super high ante of 200 it is of utmost importance that you move to the edge of your seat and start raising some hands.

There is 3,400 in the pot and a normal raise of three times the big blind (3 × 1,200) is 3,600 which means close to a 1:1 ratio. Getting away with stealing the blinds and antes 50% of the time is a break-even proposition. On top of that there is the added benefit of actually hitting a hand and maybe winning a monster pot. Really, there is *no excuse* for playing conservatively at this level.

Our table has been moved to the TV room.

A young guy opens for 3,600 and I call 2 off the button with 8♥ 7♥. Jeff Madsen decides to ride along and calls 2,400 more in the BB. The flop comes:

Jeff fires 5,300 into the pot. The opener calls and although I might have to catch up, I call, too. After all I am getting over 4:1.

Turn:

That was the kind of catch I was looking for. Jeff checks and the initial raiser checks as well. I have to consider how to proceed with my trip Eights. I obviously have a powerhouse and my opponents are probably drawing somewhere from slim to dead. Therefore, I want to try and extract as much money as possible without knocking everybody out of the hand. On the other hand, I don't think slow-playing is the right idea either with a possible flush-draw lurking out there. I bet 13,200—a little less than half the pot. Jeff quickly folds his hand and it is now up to my last remaining opponent. He ponders for a while and eventually mucks his hand. I win the 29k pot.

Determining the correct bet size is always very tricky not to use the word "impossible." Maybe this time I could have bet a little less and thereby won me a bigger pot, but at the time 13k seemed appropriate.

Hand 53

Blinds	My Position	My Hand	My Chip Stack
600/1200/200	3rd	A♠J♥	100.6K

Sean Dunwoodie, with about 90k in chips, opens for 3,600 in second position. I have 82,500 in front of me and decide to call with A♠J♥. Jeff Madsen calls as well in the BB. The flop comes:

Jeff checks, Sean bets 10,500, and I call with top pair, Jack kicker. I wasn't quite sure exactly where I stood in the hand so I wanted to tread carefully until I had a better grasp of the situation. Madsen folds. The turn is:

Sean checks and I am starting to like my hand. I bet 16,600. He calls. The river is:

Sean checks and for some weird reason I check behind him. I show my AJ and Sean mucks his hand. I win the 70,000 pot. Although a third club came on the river, value-betting my

Aces seems like the normal play. The best explanation I can come up with is that I had very limited experience with Mr. Dunwoodie's play and check-calling with an AK AQ could definitely have been part of his repertoire. In retrospect I was happy to take down an already substantial pot, but I definitely should have been more forceful on either turn or river!

Hand 54
Hand 55

Blinds	My Position	My Hand	My Chip Stack
600/1200/200	1 off the button	A♣ Q♥	133.5K
600/1200/200	2nd	A♥ Q♦	136.5K

Trying to keep up my ante-stealing average I raise twice in the same round. The fact that I had AQ both times makes it easier to pull the trigger of course, but it didn't really matter as I won both hands without contest.

3,400 a pop adds up.

Hand 56

Blinds	My Position	My Hand	My Chip Stack
600/1200/200	1st	7♠ 5♠	136.3K

We lost a player and for a while we have been playing seven-handed. I open in first position for 3,600 with 7♠ 5♠. Three players call: Minh Quach, Jeff Madsen, and the BB. The flop comes:

No need to try anything crazy with my Seven high so I check. Surprisingly everybody checks. The turn is the:

Attempting to steal the pot entered my mind but I wanted to hear the truth from everybody one more time before I tried. Everybody checks again and my plan now is to make a medium-sized bet if a blank hits the river. The river is the:

Not exactly the blank I was looking for. I guess I am not going to steal it after all. We all check to Mr. Quach, who goes all-in. Everybody folds and he shows A8—the absolute nuts.

Hand 57

Blinds	My Position	My Hand	My Chip Stack
600/1200/200	BB	K♠ Q♥	132.5K

Two players limp for 1,200 and now suddenly the SB raises to 5,100. This usually means significant strength coming from an unknown player. I decide to call anyway in the BB with K♠ Q♥ and the initial limpers fold. The flop comes:

He checks and, taking his supposedly pre-flop strength into consideration, I check behind. The turn is the:

SB leads out for 5,500 and I fold. There is absolutely no hand I can beat and even though I probably have a couple of outs it is not worth it.

In hindsight I think I should have folded pre-flop! For some reason I am a really big fan of KQ. Admittedly, it is a very respectable starting hand, but this time around it just wasn't a good matchup against a presumably topnotch hand. As far as my post-flop action goes I have no regrets. I have a feeling that his post-flop check was one of those funky plays with either top set or two Aces.

Hand 58

Blinds	My Position	My Hand	My Chip Stack
600/1200/200	Button	K♥ 8♣	126.4K

We are still seven-handed, when Jeff Madsen limps in second position. I hadn't raised for at least three hands, so it was time to kick it into gear. Jeff hadn't been making any of the limp re-raise kind of plays and he didn't seem particularly strong this time either, making me a solid favorite to pick up the pot.

I raise to 5,200 on the button with K♥ 8♣. A successful attempt, as everybody folds. I pick up 4,400.

Hand 59

Blinds	My Position	My Hand	My Chip Stack
600/1200/200	Button	7♥ 6♠	127.4K

I open for 4,600 with 7♥ 6♠ on the button. A local player calls in the BB. The flop comes:

He checks, and I decide to stray away from my usual continuation-bet strategy. I check. Turn card:

He checks and I continue my weird maneuver and check behind. River card:

He checks for the third time and I think it is fair to say that I gathered all the information I need. My opponent has absolutely nothing! His nothing beats my nothing, though, so I obviously have to bet. I bet 8,000 to take down the pot.

Hand 60

Blinds	My Position	My Hand	My Chip Stack
600/1200/200	2 off the button	9♣ 9♠	133.6K

One of my younger opponents opens in early position for 3,800 and the player next to him flat calls. I am 2 off the button holding two Black Nines and have to select one of three options:

1. Folding—Nope.
2. Calling—Hate to try and flop sets when I don't need to.
3. Raising—Could be an instant winner?

That settles the silent argument. I re-raise to double rainbow—13,200. For those of you who don't play a lot of live poker, rainbow is one chip of each color. Double rainbow is therefore two 5,000 chips, two 1,000 chips, two 500 chips and two 100 chips. Luckily the rainbow scared everybody away and I pick up a nice little 10,000 profit!

Hand 61

Blinds	My Position	My Hand	My Chip Stack
800/1600/200	BB	A♥ 7♥	143.4K

The blinds have gone up once again and we are now playing 800/1600 with 200 ante. Usually I like to step it up a notch at the beginning of a new level. Very uncharacteristically I have been laying low for a couple of hands but that doesn't mean I haven't been watching the action.

There have been a couple of interesting bluffs lately, mainly by Jeff Madsen but also Minh Quach has joined the ranks of three barrel-bluff masters. On a very interesting note, all bluffs were made very quickly and furiously when the final blow was delivered. In English, both Jeff and Minh were usually taking their time when contemplating a river bet. When they were bluffing they fired out instantly. Hopefully I will be able to use that knowledge at a later stage in the tournament.

Back to the action! One of the short stacks moves all-in for 11,700 in first position. Everybody folds to my BB.

The raiser has so far been playing very tight, indicating a strong hand, but time and time again I have seen presumably tight players go berserk. They simply cannot take it anymore! No hands for hours and hours and every time they have something resembling a hand some young buck has already raised or re-raised when the action gets to them. Slowly getting blinded away, they have to make a move sometime, eventually sticking it all-in with a wide range of hands.

I am in the BB with A♥ 7♥ and have to call 10,100 to win 15,700. Close to 3:2 or 39% to be exact.

I don't like to fold in these spots. As mentioned above there is a wide variety of hands in play and I am not quite sure of my opponent's state of mind. On the other hand it was a first-position move.

I decide to go with it. I call and he flips over JJ. Definitely a mistake against that hand as I only have 32%. But hey, I have won plenty of those before!

Not this time, though. I hit a seven on the flop but no more help so my opponent doubles up.

Hand 62

Blinds	My Position	My Hand	My Chip Stack
800/1600/200	Button	K♣ Q♣	130.5K

I open for 3,200 on the button with K♣Q♣. Both blinds fold.

Hand 63

CRUCIAL HAND 5: Taking Out Two-Time WSOP Winner Jeff Madsen

Blinds	My Position	My Hand	My Chip Stack
800/1600/200	2nd	A♣ Q♣	133.5K

Sean Dunwoodie in first position opens for 6,100 and I call in second position with A♣ Q♣. Minh calls in the SB and Jeff Madsen moves all-in for 37,600 more in the BB.

The initial raiser folds instantly and just as instantly I call. Mr. Quach gets out of the way and it's time for the . . .

Showdown

My Hand   **Jeff's Hand**

So far, so good! Turn:

Ouch! Jeff hits his miracle card and I am left with three outs. River:

Oops! Miracle right back!

A little too much excitement but luckily I prevailed. My stack is getting bigger and one of the toughest competitors at the table is no longer there. All in all a great development.

Let's take another quick peek at my two decisions made during this hand:

1. Calling the opening bid: Probably as optional as anything. Call, fold, and re-raise are all legitimate plays, folding being the least legitimate as far as I am concerned. But I am sure there are people out there advocating this type of play against a first position raiser.

2. Calling Jeff's all-in move: With Mr. Dunwoodie out of the way it is a totally different ballgame. He was the only one I was really worried about as his 100k stack could really hurt me. Minh Quach behind me is fairly irrelevant as there is about a Chinaman's chance that he has me beat. The math is simple: I have to call 37 to win 57— approximately 39%. If I could call in the previous hand needing 39% with A♥ 7♥ this seems like the easiest call in the world with A♣ Q♣. Of course a case could be made for the fact that Jeff was re-raising the entire field and therefore undoubtedly had a strong hand. But then again, mine was pretty decent, too! Before calling I put myself in the 50–50 range, making a fold absolutely and totally ridiculous!

Hand 64

Blinds	My Position	My Hand	My Chip Stack
800/1600/200	3rd	T♥ 9♦	187.2K

I raise to 5,600 in third position with T♥ 9♦. Everybody folds and I pick up the blinds and antes.

Hand 65

Blinds	My Position	My Hand	My Chip Stack
800/1600/200	BB	6♦ Q♣	190.4K

The button raises to 4,600 and I call with Q♣ 6♦. The flop comes:

I check with the intention of folding my hand as quickly as possible. He won't let me as he checks behind. The turn card is the:

Same intentions, but again he refuses to take what is his as it goes check, check. River:

A delayed hit! Unless I am facing the super-duper-double trap my pair of Sixes is a sure winner. It is time for a value bet. I bet 8,000 into a 12k pot and he folds.

Passive play is not gonna win tournaments! Giving me a couple of extra chances to hit my hand was a big mistake on my opponent's part. At least he didn't make the double mistake—checking the best hand twice and calling my river bet once he was beat. So give the guy some credit for folding.

Hand 66

Blinds	My Position	My Hand	My Chip Stack
800/1600/200	SB	K♣9♦	197K

In a Scandinavian battle of the blinds I am holding K♣9♦ in the SB. My Swedish opponent in the BB has played just about zero hands in the last couple of hours and I am therefore expecting to pick up the blinds and antes with a standard raise.

I make it 4.5k and a little surprisingly, he calls. The flop comes:

King high and a gut-shot but unfortunately I think we are in Swedish territory. I check and he immediately bets 10k. When he called my initial raise I thought I was beat—now I am almost certain. No reason to fight City Hall—I fold.

No continuation-bet out of position!?! Not something I usually refrain from doing, but this time I chose to go with my read.

Hand 67

Blinds	My Position	My Hand	My Chip Stack
800/1600/200	SB	6♣7♥	189.5K

I have been playing much more intuitively during this tournament, something I have been neglecting the last couple of months. Trusting the vibes and going with my reads has already earned me a handful of pots—and I wasn't about to stop right here.

Minh opens for 5,500, 1 off the button, and I was just sensing he didn't really have anything. Nor did I, I might add! I was sitting with 6♣ 7♥ and went for the re-raise. I made it 16.6k and Minh quickly folded.

Hand 68

Blinds	My Position	My Hand	My Chip Stack
800/1600/200	1 off the button	A♥ 8♣	197.6K

I open with A♥ 8♣ for 5,000, 1 off the button. An Australian gentleman calls in the SB. The flop comes:

He checks and I bet 6,600. He folds.

I don't know if I had the best hand but I was fairly certain that he was gonna fold unless he had a pair of some sort. Switching back and forth on whether or not to make a continuation bet has proved a successful strategy so far. Sometimes picking up the pot with nothing, but also cutting my losses when my opponent showed too much interest in the hand. This time betting seemed like the best approach.

Hand 69

Blinds	My Position	My Hand	My Chip Stack
800/1600/200	1 off the button	5♣ 6♣	201.6K

One round later I open for 5,000, 1 off the button with 5♣ 6♣ and again the Australian gentleman calls in the SB. The flop comes:

He checks. I bet 5,600 and he folds.

I have had good success with my continuation-bets as I have been able to take down a lot of pots with very mediocre holdings. The fact that I am not betting 100% but only 80% of the time has added a little bit of credibility toward the strength of my hand—ultimately making it easier for my opponents to believe the stories I'm trying to tell. Before I get too far ahead of myself I have to admit that there is a more substantial factor, easily outweighing my storytelling abilities, with regard to my high post-flop pickup ratio. The main reason for my successful continuation-bets is of course the fact that my opponents have had jack-shit, zippo, absolutely nothing!

If you are able to pick up all the pots when both of you have nothing, you'll do very well in No Limit Hold'em tournaments.

Hand 70

Blinds	My Position	My Hand	My Chip Stack
1000/2000/300	1 off the button	7♣ Q♣	205.6K

We have been moved from the featured table and are now back in the main room.

With an ante of 300 and blinds of 1k/2k, I am looking forward to raising a lot of pots, and hopefully add a significant amount to my chip stack. I open 1 off the button for 6,500 with Q♣ 7♣. The "Green Man" (named for his green outfit) calls in the BB. The flop comes:

A good flop for me since I will probably win it if Green Man doesn't have a King! He checks. I put him on a wide range of hands, a lot of them beating my Q7, but that doesn't change the fact that I am going to bet. I bet 6,600 and he folds after long deliberation. Unless his thought process was a complete act, he definitely had me beat, but as mentioned above, no king—no call.

Hand 71

Blinds	My Position	My Hand	My Chip Stack
1000/2000/300	Button	A♣ T♦	210.6K

After an early limper, my "right-hand man" makes it 8,000. I am on the button with A♣ T♦. Normally I wouldn't hesitate to raise with this hand but here there has already been substantial action before it is my turn. My AT doesn't look so appealing anymore and I think the proper play is to fold. I fold and the raiser wins the pot.

This illustrates very well the difference between *being* the initial raiser and *facing* a raise. As an initial raiser I am prepared to play just about any two cards dealt to me. If somebody has raised in front of me my hand selection becomes much more conservative and otherwise decent raising hands just go straight to the muck.

Note that even though I have re-raised with some rather suspicious hands earlier on in the tournament it has always been because of a specific read of the situation. Here I felt it was genuine strength that urged my right hand man to raise and therefore AT was simply not good enough.

Hand 72

Blinds	My Position	My Hand	My Chip Stack
1000/2000/300	1st	A♠ K♣	209.4K

I open in first position for 6,200 with A♠ K♣. Everybody folds to the BB, who raises an additional 8,000. A very tiny re-raise! Even though I have come to the conclusion that more and more people use the mini-raise as kind of an information raise instead of the old-fashioned I-have-two-Aces trap, I have a feeling this raise is for real. Suspecting a rather strong hand from my opponent, I'm not looking to invest too much money in this hand unless I improve dramatically. Of course I am not gonna fold but re-raising is not even part of my vocabulary under these circumstances.

The flop comes:

He instantly bets 25k into a 32k pot and I surrender. I see absolutely no reason to alter my pre-flop read and since I didn't connect it was an easy fold.

Hand 73

Blinds	My Position	My Hand	My Chip Stack
1000/2000/300	BB	9♣ K♣	194.9K

Very next hand, same opponent. Everybody folds to the SB who makes it 8,000. Controlling my strong urge to re-raise, I just call in the BB with K♣9♣. Although he had just beaten me in the previous hand I wanted to keep my composure—after all, there was no reason to make it personal. The flop comes:

He checks, not seeming too ecstatic about the flop. I wasn't too crazy about it either but at least I had a gut shot and a backdoor flush draw. Acting more on his indicated weakness than the actual strength of my hand, I felt this was a good opportunity to grab the 18k in the middle of the table. I fire 10,200. He folds, claiming a big Ace. Going back to the previous hand, it all seems to ring true. Re-raising a first position raiser showed definite strength. The follow-up continuation-bet was just the icing on the cake—my AK was the second best hand! Next hand—the pre-flop strength, the missed flop, the check-fold. This guy wasn't about to risk his entire tournament with less than top pair.

Having the worst hand two hands in a row, but winning one of them, is not that bad.

Hand 74

Blinds	My Position	My Hand	My Chip Stack
1000/2000/300	SB	8♦ 8♠	199.9K

We have just lost a player and are down to playing seven-handed. Whether there are seven or eight players around the table may not seem that important but as far as I'm concerned it is a big deal!

In every team sport losing a player is devastating, as each player represents a high percentage of the total team. In soccer going from eleven to ten players is bad, but going from five to four in hockey is terrible! So, the lower the number of players, the bigger impact losing one will have. Going from three-handed to heads-up is of course the biggest jump, but going from eight to seven should certainly not go unnoticed.

Even though I have to admit it is not the best comparison of all time, this emphasizes the fact that losing players at the poker table should have a significant impact on the *quality* and *number of hands* you play. I'm not saying that you should go completely berserk just because somebody got knocked out, but a slight increase in aggressiveness will definitely be the right approach.

Personally I will kick it up a notch as I'm not so sure anybody else at the table will.

Minh Quach opens in second position for 8k. I look down and find two Eights in the SB, a very playable hand at this "short-handed" table! I now go through my usual routine of counting down the relevant chip stacks. Figuring out how much you can lose, or how much you want to lose before entering a pot is a crucial element in good tournament poker.

In this case the BB has 45k left and Minh about 40k for a total of 48k.

Note how this somewhat limits my possibilities, as a standard re-raise to about 24k leaves me pot committed—making the all-in move a superior raising option.

So where do I want to go with this hand? Do I have the best hand? Do I *think* I have the best hand? How does my hand play post-flop vs. pre-flop?

Let's take it from the bottom. There is no doubt in my mind that medium pairs play much better pre-flop than post-flop. Apart from the 1 in 8 where you actually flop a set, you will be facing over cards in 7 out of 8 instances, making it almost impossible to know how to proceed. Calling is a bad choice!

Although I do not know, I think there is a very reasonable chance that I have the best hand. Folding is out of the question!

I just gave a long speech about going into aggressive mode when losing a player, so there you have it. Raise! Being aware of my opponents' chip stacks and thereby choosing the superior raising option actually makes this an easy play!

I re-raise to 50k and leave it up to my opponents to make their decisions. Nobody wants to tag along, and I can add 12,100 to my stack as they both fold.

Hand 75

Blinds	My Position	My Hand	My Chip Stack
1000/2000/300	2 off the button	K♣ 3♣	211.4K

Continuing my aggressive play I open 2 off the button for 6,000 with K♣ 3♣. The short-stacked small blind moves all-in for about 16k. This gives me almost 3:1 on the call and I can't remember the last time I folded under these circumstances. I call and he shows A8o, giving me 40%.

The flop comes:

This leaves my opponent without much hope. The turn and river are:

I win the pot and knock out another opponent.

Hand 76

Blinds	My Position	My Hand	My Chip Stack
1000/2000/300	2 off the button	A♥ 2♣	226.4K

I open for 6,600, 2 off the button with A♥ 2♣. I actually had a feeling that the BB was rather excited and therefore I should have just laid my hand down. Too late now, as I watch the BB move all-in for a total of 10k. I have to call 3,400 more, which of course only requires two napkins. He has JJ, giving me a 29% winning chance.

The flop comes, a third Jack, and I am drawing completely dead.

I should have paid a little more attention as I think I could have avoided this little uphill battle.

Hand 77

Blinds	My Position	My Hand	My Chip Stack
1000/2000/300	2nd	3♠ 3♦	215.4K

I limp in early position with my favorite limping hand, the small pair. The SB calls and the BB checks. The flop comes:

They both check and I see no reason to give more free cards. I bet 3,300 into an 8k pot with my two Treys. They both fold.

Hand 78

Blinds	My Position	My Hand	My Chip Stack
1000/2000/300	SB	4♠ 4♥	219.3K

This is the last hand at this level and as always I strongly urge my opponents *not to go broke before the break.* Everybody folds to my SB and I look down to find another small pair. My opponent in the BB has 33k left and blinds are 1000/2000.

I could limp, try to flop a set, and maybe bust him this way but that is kind of a long shot. The standard raise to about 6k could win the pot right there but also leaves me vulnerable if he decides to take a flop with me. If re-raised I think I would have to play it for his entire stack as my two Fours are likely to be in front.

Then there is of course the "biggest club in my bag"—the all-in move! It seems rather insane to shoot in 33k to pick up 5k, but at least it is an option.

I contemplate for a bit and decide, "If I am not gonna fold to his re-raise anyway, I might as well do it myself." I will admit that I have seen some mighty big lay-downs over the years when people are facing elimination.

I raise to 40k and as everybody else is leaving for the break, the BB goes into the tank. I suppose his urge to stick around a little longer was too strong compared to his eagerness to double up. He finally folded his hand face up—revealing two black Sevens!

It's a serious victory for the all-in play as I am not sure I would have fared as well with any of the two other plays, and I'm a tad bit lucky that the BB wasn't in a gambling mood! This is understandable, since calling big all-in raises with medium-small pairs has never been a lucrative No Limit Hold'em strategy.

Hand 79

Blinds	My Position	My Hand	My Chip Stack
1200/2400/400	Button	3♦ Q♠	223.4K

Back from the break, everybody folds to my button. I open for 7,200 with my Q♠ 3♦ and both blinds fold, a nice way to start a new level with 6,400 extra in my stack.

Hand 80
Hand 81
Hand 82

Blinds	My Position	My Hand	My Chip Stack
1200/2400/400	Button	K♠ 7♦	223.4K
1200/2400/400	SB	J♥ 4♣	225K
1200/2400/400	3rd	A♠ K♥	229K

During the last two rounds I have had very poor starting hands, even for my standards. Nonetheless I have still managed to steal a couple of blinds and antes raising with K7o and J4o. Keeping yourself afloat during a dry spell is very important especially at a time when the blinds and antes can put a serious dent into your stack.

When I finally had a hand—in this case A♠K♥—the BB called me for his last 6,500 with T6o. A King on the board and that was it for him.

Hand 83

Blinds	My Position	My Hand	My Chip Stack
1200/2400/400	2nd	J♦ Q♠	239.4K

I open in second position for 7,200 with Q♠J♦. The BB makes a funky re-raise to 20k—not that that in itself is strange but for some reason he leaves himself with only 7k. To play out the all-in scenario I have to put another 20k in the pot to win 40k. It's one of those 2:1 deals that I just can't refuse. I go all-in and he quickly calls. There's a not-insignificant 58k in the pot!

He turns over A♥ 8♠ giving him a 57–43 advantage.

Showdown

My Hand   **My Opponent's Hand**

Now I suddenly have an 80–20 advantage.

The turn is:

Oops! And the river is:

I can't beat a full house! He wins the pot.

Hand 84

CRUCIAL HAND 6: A 290,000 Pot with
Ace High on the Flop

Blinds	My Position	My Hand	My Chip Stack
1200/2400/400	BB	A♣ K♦	211.4K

John Doe in first position limps and it is folded around to the SB. He ponders for a while whether to raise or not but ends up just calling. I wake up with A♣ K♦ in the BB and raise it 11,200 more to a total of 13,600. The limper folds and the SB calls. The flop comes:

Not quite what I was looking for but it also makes it very hard for my opponent to have hit anything.

He checks, I bet 16,600, and he check-raises me to a total of 45k. Although unpleasant, it was not totally unexpected. The SB had definitely come to play and this seemed like a good spot to make a move. I reconstruct the entire hand and play it over in my head a couple of times.

Bottom line:

1. I was expecting a move.
2. I didn't think he started out with a pair.
3. In case I was wrong and he actually did have something like two Sixes, he would be hard-pressed to call 90k more.
4. In case he should decide to call with a flush-draw it would be a 50–50 deal.

5. Math says he only has about an 8% chance of holding a
   Nine, and my read said that I could eliminate those 8%.

All-in all, barring the ugly Nine scenario, the all-in move was
starting to make a lot of sense to me.

I convinced myself that it was gonna be hard for him to call,
and even if he did I was ahead anyway, so I pulled the trigger.

135k on A-high! I was either a fool or a hero!

The SB went into thinking mode, which had me scared for a
bit. Had I completely overplayed my hand, my read, everything? After a while I calmed down as I was back into he-is-
going-to-fold-anyway mode. But no!

He finally shoved the rest of his chips in the middle, and
needless to say I wasn't happy about it. I reluctantly turned
over my beautiful no-pair no-draw. At least I could still claim
A-high top kicker.

It was good!

Maybe I hadn't totally lost my mind after all. It wasn't like
I was home free, but I was definitely in the hunt. The SB turned
over Q♥ T♥ for a queen-high flush draw and two live cards. I
was in front but still a small underdog with about a 45% winning chance.

Turn:

Exceptionally good card! I now only have to fade the hearts,
and not the A♥, I might add. Being an 81–19% favorite I'm
starting to feel good about the hand.

River:

Pheew! I had knocked out my worst competitor at the table and added significant spare change to my stack.

In retrospect, normally this was way too much money to put in the pot with Ace high. Were there really enough mitigating circumstances to justify my "crazy" play? Hmmm . . . ?!?

All I know is that I went with my read, and put in some serious money to back up my opinion.

Hand 85

Blinds	My Position	My Hand	My Chip Stack
1200/2400/400	3rd	7♠ 5♠	359K

I just got rid of one big stack with my experimental AK play and I now have about 360k. Unfortunately as in the old saying "When you chop off the dragon's head two new heads pop up," two new big stacks appeared at my table. They both have approximately 150k and even though I have them easily covered, they have caught my attention.

Despite the new challenge I am still gonna stick to my aggressive approach.

I open in third position for 7,200 with 7♠ 5♠ and everybody folds.

Hand 86

Blinds	My Position	My Hand	My Chip Stack
1200/2400/400	BB	5♣ 5♦	365K

The two new guys have unfortunately been fairly active at the table, taking away some of my play.

Again one of them, better known as Patrick Fletcher, opens in middle position for 7,000. I call in the BB with 55 as I see no reason to go crazy against a 180k stack. The flop comes:

I decided to play it small pre-flop and without a Five on the flop I am going to continue that way. I check, he bets 12k, and I fold.

Timid play on my part. I could have re-raised pre-flop, led out on the flop, but both plays are very optional and for once I just chose the conservative route. With absolutely no read on Mr. Fletcher it is sometimes better to be safe than sorry!

Hand 87

Blinds	My Position	My Hand	My Chip Stack
1200/2400/400	SB	7♣ 7♥	358K

Minh Quach opens for 11k, 2 off the button. I have two Sevens in the SB. I re-raise to 50k, which is enough to cover both the BB and Mr. Quach. Note that there is a humongous difference between the former hand and this one. I am not at all interested in risking 180k with two Fives but 50k with two Sevens is much more reasonable.

The BB thinks for a long time before finally folding his hand. Minh calls his remaining chips and flips over A♠ T♥.

Showdown

| **My Hand** | | | | **Minh's Hand** |

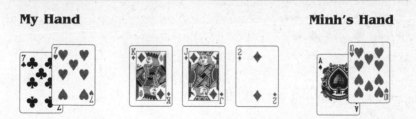

I am now a 60–40% favorite. Turn:

70–30%. River:

100–0! I win the pot.

A cry suddenly sounded from the BB as he disgustedly told the table about his 99, now resting safely in the muck.

Hand 88

Blinds	My Position	My Hand	My Chip Stack
1200/2400/400	Button	T♥ 9♠	411K

I open for 7,200 on the button with T♥ 9♠. The SB folds as usual, but one of the new guys in the BB calls!

The flop comes:

He checks and I bet 9,800. He folds.

Hand 89

Blinds	My Position	My Hand	My Chip Stack
1200/2400/400	BB	T♠ T♥	421K

Patrick Fletcher opens again—this time for 7,000. Eager to put a stop to my only real pre-flop-raising competitor, I hope to find a good hand in the big blind. TT seems to fit the criteria very well. I re-raise 19k more to a total of 26k.

I know a lot of people like to play two Tens more cautiously especially when facing the second chip leader at the table, but that is just not my style. By merely calling you just delay the inevitable question: "Do I have the best hand?" By waiting you also sometimes get the answer a tad bit late, as he has already outdrawn you on the flop.

Patrick Fletcher responds promptly: "I have the best hand!" Or at least he indicates so by re-raising to 57k. Do I believe him? It goes against my curious nature to fold my hand but here I could be facing some serious repercussions with what was at best a coin flip.

I decided to fold and move on to the next hand. The subsequent table talk led me to believe that I was indeed way behind.

Hand 90

Blinds	My Position	My Hand	My Chip Stack
1200/2400/400	1 off the button	6♣ 4♠	393K

I open 1 off the button with 6♣ 4♠ for 7,200 and Patrick Fletcher calls in the BB. Lately he has been the main reason I haven't dragged down as many pots as usual. The flop comes:

He stands in the way again—this time with a lead-out of 11k. I consider the single-raise to 22k but I really don't have anything to support that move with. A fold is in order.

Mr. Fletcher wins another one.

Hand 91

Blinds	My Position	My Hand	My Chip Stack
1500/3000/500	3 off the button	K♣ 9♥	385K

All the 100 chips have been taken off the table as we are now anteing a whopping 500. Blinds have gone to 1,500/3,000, which adds up to a starting pot of 8,500 at our eight-handed table. That is a lot of money considering the average stack size is 150k.

As always I like to aim for the first pot of a new level. I open 3 off the button with K♣ 9♥ for 10k. The crew-cut guy 1 off the button makes it 45k. There are only two guys at the table who can really hurt me—this is one of them. Not a lot to think about. I fold. Crew-cut takes down the pot.

Hand 92

Blinds	My Position	My Hand	My Chip Stack
1500/3000/500	BB	A♥ K♦	374K

Everybody folds to the SB, who limps for 1,500 more. I make it 13k from the BB with A♥ K♦. He calls. The flop comes:

He checks. Praying for a fold I bet out 16k. He obliges.

The lower the cards on the flop, the more important it is to just close your eyes and make a continuation bet. So far in this tournament it has worked out pretty good.

Hand 93

Blinds	My Position	My Hand	My Chip Stack
1500/3000/500	SB	5♣ 2♥	391K

Everybody folds to my SB. I am holding 52o and decide to let it go. I love to raise against only one opponent but sometimes it is too much of an uphill battle. Furthermore, on the rare occasion that I do fold my SB in this spot, I like to make the whole table aware of what a tight player I am!

Hand 94

Blinds	My Position	My Hand	My Chip Stack
1500/3000/500	3rd	A♦ 9♦	386K

I open for 11k in 3rd position with A♦9♦. Kevin Atkins calls the 11k on the button and both blinds fold. Flop:

Still the same A-high, but with a pair on the board I can afford a 22k continuation bet. Kevin quickly calls and I'm starting to dislike the prospects of this hand. Turn:

With a Queen showing up, I see absolutely no chance of me having the best hand and after the mandatory Hollywood act I tap the table. Kevin checks behind me and we are off to the river:

Didn't change anything. I'm definitely beat but his check on the turn gave me a boost and I therefore thought it was okay to try some idiotic bluff. I bet 44k but Kevin beat me in the pot and I immediately muttered "good call." Kevin turned over two Kings and while contemplating my poor decision to bet, I looked down at my hand one more time. A♦9♦! Oops, I think I made a flush. A little embarrassed by my sudden discovery I sincerely apologized to Kevin for my distasteful slow-roll. No matter what, I had won the hand and could pocket a nice little 85k profit.

Hand in hindsight: This was probably my poorest performance so far in this tournament. Trying a hopeless bluff where all the ammunition I had was a turn-check from my opponent was obviously a mistake. Not knowing what cards I had in my hand was absolutely unforgivable! I still won the hand but for a split-second it was aimed at the muck. Furthermore had I known I was holding the nut-flush I would have made a serious value-bet in the 80k range. Paying attention could have earned me 40k more and unless I want to play the rest of the tournament blindfolded I better start opening my eyes!

Hand 95

Blinds	My Position	My Hand	My Chip Stack
1500/3000/500	SB	J♥ 5♠	467K

An early limper, myself in the SB, and the BB take a three-handed flop. I am holding J♥ 5♠. The flop comes:

I lead out 6k into a 13k pot with my top pair. The BB folds and the limper calls. The turn is a:

At least not an over card but a little too straighty for my taste. I decide to check and see what my opponent is up to. He checks behind me.

The river is:

Having a bad feeling about the hand I check again. He bets 12k into a 25k pot and I stop to think. In a cash game this would be an easy call for me. This is *not* a cash game, and so far I haven't encountered too many river bluffs. People tend to be a little more careful about splashing around with their precious tournament chips, making this call far from trivial. Unfortunately, my not-so-well-known nickname is "Curious George"!

I call the 12k only to realize that I was drawing completely dead on the turn. My opponent had checked the nuts behind me, obviously to trap me for a river bet. He shows KQ for the King-high straight.

Hand 96

Blinds	My Position	My Hand	My Chip Stack
1500/3000/500	1 off the button	K♥ 5♠	445K

I open for 10k, 1 off the button with K♥ 5♠. Patrick Fletcher calls in the BB. The flop comes:

Top pair, lousy kicker, and no clubs! Patrick makes another annoying lead-out bet—this time 10k. This wasn't the first time Mr. Fletcher had bet right into my face and I should have treated it more as a probe bet than a sign of actual strength.

Therefore the right play is to raise in order to either win the pot right there or gather some more information. I failed to do so, which turned out to be a big mistake on my part. Instead I just called the 10k, leaving me in the dark and Patrick with the initiative. The turn is:

Patrick keeps the pressure on with a 16k bet. Knowing even less about what is going on but feeling my two Kings still have a fighting chance, I call. This was another lost opportunity to define the hand more precisely with a well-timed raise!

The river is:

The pot has now reached significant heights with about 75k in there.

Patrick bets 13k, which is almost the same as saying, "Raise, please raise me." This was my third and final opportunity to take a crack at the pot, so surely I wasn't gonna miss the boat again. Wrong! Again Curious George left his footprints on the sand as I threw away another 13k with the second-best hand.

Patrick flips over J♠ 9♥ for two pair and wins the 100k pot.

Not one or two, but three times I could have taken down this pot with a good straightforward poker play, none of which I took advantage of. Instead I allowed Mr. Fletcher to control the pace and subsequently outdraw me on the river, forcing me to call his tiny value bet. This could all be described in one sentence: I played this hand like a novice, a fish, an idiot!

According to my tape recorder I was seriously on tilt after this hand. And trust me, I was. Luckily for me the break wasn't too far away, as I could surely use some time off.

Hand 97

Blinds	My Position	My Hand	My Chip Stack
1500/3000/500	1st	9♣9♥	394K

I open in 1st position for 10k with 9♣9♥. I tend to vary the size of my pre-flop raises depending on the direction in which I am headed. In this case I am not looking for any customers. I would much rather win the 8,500 right here than see a flop with two random over cards on the board. Therefore my pre-flop raise is somewhat bigger than usual.

A very tight player calls in the SB. The flop comes:

He now bets 10k in a 23k pot catching me completely by surprise. That is the only reasonable explanation I can come up with to defend my call. I should of course have processed the information at hand and mucked my middle pair. The turn is the:

He bets another 10k and I finally come to my senses. Not one, but two stabs, from a tight guy, in the SB, out of position—I mean, does it get more obvious?

I fold. He shows A♣ Q♣.

Hand 98

Blinds	My Position	My Hand	My Chip Stack
1500/3000/500	BB	J♦ 8♣	373K

Keith Sexton has arrived at the table and fires right away. He opens for 9.5k in first position and it is folded around to me. I make one of my questionable calls with J♦ 8♣ putting another 6.5k in the pot. Flop comes:

A double belly-buster, but not a pretty one! I have no diamonds in my hand and even if I should be so lucky to hit a King there is no guarantee I am going to win a big pot. People tend to freeze up when there is a four-straight on the board. I check and Keith bets 20k into a 24k pot. I would like to take one off, but the price is a little steep, considering my implied odds are not very good. I don't want to get too entangled in this pot. Best way to avoid that: fold.

I fold. Keith wins the pot.

Hand 99

Blinds	My Position	My Hand	My Chip Stack
1500/3000/500	SB	K♥ Q♥	363K

Very next hand I have K♥Q♥ in the SB. Everybody folds to me and I raise to 11,500. Keith folds.

Hand 100

Blinds	My Position	My Hand	My Chip Stack
1500/3000/500	Button	A♦2♦	370K

One off the button opens for 11k, and I have the "super-optional" hand: A♦2♦ on the button.

I don't care what anybody says, there is no wrong or right in this situation. It all depends on your mood, your read, your chip stack, etc. I felt there was some meat behind the raise, so the re-raise was quickly discarded. I don't think anyone would blame me if I folded, but a mix of position, curiosity, and being the overwhelming chip leader at the table lead me to call.

Both blinds folded, and the flop comes:

He bets 18k, and I am down to one option: fold.

Hand 101

Blinds	My Position	My Hand	My Chip Stack
1500/3000/500	SB	K♣7♣	352K

A tight player limps in first position. I can't remember any hands that he participated in, therefore it is probably safe to assume he has a reasonably strong holding. I have had good success with my limps so far—being able to pick up a couple of small pots whenever my opponents missed the board. With a tight opponent I feel I have a good chance of gauging where he is, thereby making good decisions later in the hand. I limp along with K♣ 7♣. Another limper and the blinds make it a five-handed pot.

The flop comes:

Top pair, but since this was a multi-way pot, I wasn't about to go crazy. Both blinds check and the early limper bets 20k into a 19k pot. That should be enough to scare just about anybody away. Unfortunately I wasn't anybody—or should I just say that part of my brain definitely wasn't working at full capacity. I had flopped a pair of Kings, but considering the circumstances it was about as bad a top pair as I could imagine. There is just no way Mr. Tight would lead into four people with anything inferior to my K7! I had twenty-eight perfectly good reasons to fold, but I went the other way and called the 20k. Just to make matters worse I still had three players behind me. They all fold, so we are down to heads-up.

The turn is:

Mr. Tight fires again but this time he only bets half the pot—30k. Still mumbling about my idiotic call on the flop, I now see a little light at the end of the tunnel—a flush-draw!

I had given up all hope of having the best hand, but a club

on the river could change things around. Nine clubs, maybe two Kings, maybe three Sevens, a total of 14 cards, getting 3 to 1 and the river-bet belonging to me—I kinda like those odds. I call another 30k planning to muck instantly unless one of my 14 friends decides to show up. River is:

Mr. Tight checks, and I tap the table behind, happy to get a chance to see what I was up against. He turns over K♥Q♥, and I get another chance to tell myself how bad I played. Just to re-cap: My call on the flop was horrific, but calling the turn was the right play considering my implied odds. A Seven on the river would have cost me some, but the nine clubs would have turned my initial bad play into a nice little money-maker!

Key factor in this hand: *The more players, the stronger holding you need to take down the pot.*

Hand 102

Blinds	My Position	My Hand	My Chip Stack
1500/3000/500	2 off the button	J♦Q♠	299K

Still fuming about the last hand, I open in middle position for 11,000 with Q♠J♦. Everybody folds and I make back 8,500 of the 53,000 I threw away last hand.

Hand 103

Blinds	My Position	My Hand	My Chip Stack
1500/3000/500	BB	5♦3♥	306K

Everybody folds to the SB who makes it 15k, a rather substantial raise considering the going rate was more in the 9k range. I guess he is aware of the fact that I am prone to call with just about any two cards facing a standard raise, especially in position.

He obviously did not want any customers, just making me more eager to call. But calling 12k more with 53o is a little steep even for me. I fold.

Hand 104

Blinds	My Position	My Hand	My Chip Stack
1500/3000/500	SB	A♠8♥	303K

Lately people have been unusually inactive when I'm in the blind. I assume it is a mix between bad cards and unwillingness to tango with the "crazy" big-stack. It has been lucrative for me, so I have no complaints.

A♠8♥ in the SB looks like the best hand and as usual I attack the BB. I raise to 11,500. Keith folds.

Hand 105

Blinds	My Position	My Hand	My Chip Stack
1500/3000/500	Button	8♣2♥	309K

Last hand before the break. Another excellent opportunity to pick up 8k! Three guys are looking for the bathroom, two guys are looking for their girlfriends, one guy is looking for the bar, leaving just little ol' me to steal the blinds and antes. 8♣2♥ on the button should be just enough to accomplish the mission. I raise and everybody folds. Pretty sweet!

Hand 106

Blinds	My Position	My Hand	My Chip Stack
2000/4000/500	BB	Q♥ T♦	316K

The price has gone up. We are now playing 2000/4000 with a 500 ante. I am in the BB and the button raises to 11k. I am holding Q♥ T♦, which in my opinion is worth at least a call from a button-raise. I am sensing a little weakness and have to consider which way to go.

Going by the old saying, "If you can call, you can raise," I decide that re-raising is my best option. It also gives me an excellent chance to win it right here. I make it 35k and the button mucks.

Noticing that your opponent might be out of his comfort zone allows you to make some moves with a very high probability of success. It also lets you to control the game much better as your competitors will be more reluctant to raise you, fearing the big re-raise.

Hand 107

Blinds	My Position	My Hand	My Chip Stack
2000/4000/500	SB	6♠ 5♠	333K

Next hand, same guy! He raises to 12k, 1 off the button. I call in the small blind and the BB folds. I am holding 6♠ 5♠ and I guess I could have made another move, but this time it seemed like he was a little bit more confident about his hand. In spite of that, I still felt that my suited connector was good enough to warrant a call.

The flop comes:

Bottom pair and countless backdoors! Enough to bet? Without a doubt!

I bet 16k into a 32k pot, which is a little bit in the low end. On the other hand, if he indeed did raise pre-flop with a big hand—as I kind of expected—I might be saving myself some money by keeping my bet to a minimum. He calls.

Because of my rather small bet I am not quite sure where he is, as I thought he would be capable of calling 16k with just two over cards.

Turn:

Gin! Not necessarily, but I'm starting to really like the possibilities. Two pair and no flush-draws to worry about! There are two scenarios playing out in my head right now:

1. He has an AK type of hand. Checking is the right play as he is drawing dead, and the only way to win more money is to let him catch up.
2. He has a big pair and slow-played it on the flop. Checking is more optional as all the money should be aimed at the center no matter what I do.

Just to keep everybody up to date, there is 64k in the pot, my opponent has approximately 95k left, and I have him easily covered.

According to my at-the-table analysis, checking is the superior play, and so I do. He checks behind me, and I am now routing for an Ace or a King, hoping that he would improve to what is known as "the second best hand."

River:

Full house! It is now time for the "big bluff." It is of course not a bluff, as there is somewhere in the range of 0% chance that he has me beat. But he might perceive it as a bluff. I want to extract as much as possible, and am therefore leaning toward a pot-sized bet. On the other hand I don't want to go for his entire stack as it seems like people tend to tighten up when their whole tournament is on the line. Pot-sized, but not the Full Monty, 65k seems appropriate.

I bet 65k and he starts to think. I didn't really expect a call, as I thought Ace high was his most likely holding. Fortunately it looked like I was wrong.

He thought for a long time before putting in another 65k, but seemed very unhappy with his decision as I turned over Fives full.

Post-hand gossip: He later told me that he had two Queens, and that he felt he had misplayed it on the flop. I had to agree, but I really couldn't blame him for calling the river. Checking the turn behind me could be described as a little funky too, but probably ended up saving him money.

Hand 108

Blinds	My Position	My Hand	My Chip Stack
2000/4000/500	1st	Q♠ A♠	431K

The exit of one of the players at the table means we are back to seven-handed.

I open for 12k in first position with A♠ Q♠. Nobody wants to play and I take down the pot.

Hand 109

Blinds	My Position	My Hand	My Chip Stack
2000/4000/500	BB	4♣ T♣	439K

The very next hand I'm in the BB with T♣ 4♣. Keith Sexton opens in first position for 12k. Even though I have told myself I should stay away from those early-position raisers when all I have is garbage, I decide to call.

Flop comes:

The flop could easily have missed Mr. Sexton if he is holding two high cards! In case he has a big pair I still have a fair amount of outs unless of course it is two Tens. I'm not really looking for that second scenario, but the first one—picking up the pot with Ten high—is mighty interesting.

I lead out for 19k, and Keith puts on his thinking cap. Throughout the tournament he has been very methodical, taking his time on important decisions, trying to process all the available information.

After long deliberation he ends up folding and I win the 30k pot. I guess he was holding two high cards and couldn't muster up a call.

Hand 110

Blinds	My Position	My Hand	My Chip Stack
2000/4000/500	SB	9♦ 6♥	457K

The button moves, the dealer shuffles, and I'm now in the SB. Everybody folds, I limp for 2,000 more with 9♦ 6♥, and Keith checks behind me.

The flop comes:

Second pair and an obvious spot to bet! My goal is to pick up the 12k in the middle. I am not looking for some fancy check-raise move, which would just over-commit me in a pot where I originally had very little invested. Betting also has the advantage of knocking out hands like J7 and T8. Personally I would feel pretty silly giving a free card, losing to 83*o* when an Eight hit the turn. Remember Keith has two totally random cards in his hand as it was checked to his BB.

I bet 6k and Keith calls. It feels like he has a Deuce, and my plan is to bet again on the turn.

The turn is:

I bet again thinking I'm still ahead. Thirteen thousand is enough to win the pot as Keith folds.

Apart from stopping the free card, my bet on the flop also allowed me to get a better read on the situation. Imagine if I had checked and Keith bet! It would be much harder for me to assert what he was holding. Did he bet just because I checked? Was it a deuce, a queen, or a Six with a better kicker? Not much to go by. Not that my lead-out bet assured me what he had 100%, but it surely helped to define it!

No matter what, I was on a roll: three hands dealt, three hands played, three hands won!

Bubble Time—Exploiting People's Fear of Getting Knocked Out Before the Money

Let us take a small time out to dwell on the situation at hand and see what's in store for us the next hour. Apart from a slower pace of play, which really should have no effect on the outcome of this tournament, it is crunch time for different reasons.

It is the end of day two, the bubble is approaching, and slowly a picture is forming of who is who, and which way they are going.

♦ The Survivors—Basically haven't played a hand for days! The few they play are with *premium* hands!

♦ The Accumulators—Basically haven't folded a hand for hours! The ones they fold are *really* unplayable!

♦ The Regulators—My own homemade category inspired by Warren G and Nate Dogg! These players have a couple of tricks up their sleeves.

So who has the right idea? I'll step out on a limb and say the accumulators, although it really depends on your goals. If you are in "top gun" mode and are convinced that there are no points for second place, you belong with the accumulators. If this is your first major tournament, you won the entry on Full Tilt poker, you would love to make the money and the $15,000 you earn for making it to the top eighty would really hit the spot, it is a whole different story. Clinging to your small stack should be top priority, as survival is the only thing that matters. Be cautious, though: Surviving might fit your purposes right now, but true survival can only be obtained by sacrificing some equity when folding otherwise playable hands. If the survivors are sacrificing overall equity it should be clear to everybody that there is money to be made at this hour! The accumulators do their best to grab hold of that money by constant aggression.

But what about the accumulators—don't they make mistakes? Or have they just found the perfect way to approach this game? Well, remember this brief little intermezzo is only a guideline for play around the bubble. As long as the rest of the table let them accumulate in peace they have got a pretty good thing going. But their tactics can be exploited as well. The accumulators obviously play way too many hands, and as a regulator you should regulate. Exploit the survivors, but don't stop there. Come over the top on the accumulators and you will surely make a killing!

It all sounds very simple, straightforward, and easy but you still have to figure out who fits in which category. Knowing who you are up against at the poker table is important information, but at bubble time it is absolutely crucial to know before you proceed! There is such a big difference in everybody's agenda and therefore also in their style. What would be considered a serious blunder against an accumulator is an absolute must against a survivor and vice versa. You have to be able to put a label on your opponent in order to be effective at this hour.

If you are still in the tournament you have had plenty of time to evaluate your opponents, so there is no excuse for not knowing what is going on. I only hope that I can utilize the available information better than the rest of the table!

Back to the action!

Hand 111

Blinds	My Position	My Hand	My Chip Stack
2000/4000/500	Button	6♠ 6♦	470K

The tournament director has just informed us that we will be playing hand for hand until we reach the money. I wish there was a different way to deal with the bubble situation, but so far nobody has come up with a better solution. The play will be very slow for a while, but I guess it gives me time to walk around and observe some of the other remaining players.

It may slow down the pace, but it ain't gonna slow me down, as I'm planning to kick it up a notch! I actually already did but sometimes it helps my agenda that everybody around the table is fully updated. What I mean is that it is a lot easier for me to steal the blinds and antes when the tournament director has told everybody that it is OK to let me steal. By announcing bubble time, he made everybody aware of how important it is NOT to get knocked out. The fact that everybody knows just makes my job easier.

I'm on the button with 6♠ 6♦ and what better way to start bubble time than with a raise. Everybody folds to me, I make it 14k and the blinds quickly surrendered. In seconds flat I have picked up the blinds and antes and can safely add 9k to my stack.

Hand 112

Blinds	My Position	My Hand	My Chip Stack
2000/4000/500	2 off the button	A♦ K♦	479K

My right-hand man opens for 13k, and even though I'm aware of his tight approach especially at this point in time, my A♦ K♦ is aimed at the all-in button. I make it 55k, and as expected nobody wants to see the flop. Another 22k in the right direction!

Hand 113

Blinds	My Position	My Hand	My Chip Stack
2000/4000/500	1st	Q♥ J♦	500K

Q♥ J♦ is not a powerhouse in first position, but under these circumstances it's absolutely playable. After all, we are only seven-handed, and three of them put on their survivor shoes. We haven't seen a flop for about a round, and this deal was no exception. Everybody folds and yet another 9k is added to my account.

Hand 114

Blinds	My Position	My Hand	My Chip Stack
2000/4000/500	BB	9♠ 6♠	509K

Finally we should get to see a flop. I'm in the big blind with 9♠ 6♠ and needless to say I'm going to defend. But there's not much to defend when nobody attacks, so I have to settle for a 5k stack increase!

Hand 115

Blinds	My Position	My Hand	My Chip Stack
2000/4000/500	Button	A♦ 9♥	512K

I reluctantly fold my small blind, but come right back with A♦ 9♥ on the button. My hands have definitely been above average the last couple of rounds, but I'm not sure it has made a big difference in the outcome since nobody wants to tango. No dancing partner this time around either. Fold, fold, fold, fold, 14k, fold, fold! Nothing new under the sun. The only thing changing around here is the size of my chip stack—usually in beautiful 9k intervals!

Hand 116

Blinds	My Position	My Hand	My Chip Stack
2000/4000/500	2nd	Q♦ Q♣	520K

I open for 14k in second position with two Queens. I'm hoping that someone has noticed that I'm playing more than my fair share of hands and wants to put an end to it. Not really, as the only one even paying attention is the big blind. He does put another 10k in the pot, so with 34k in there we get to see a flop. The flop comes:

He checks and I . . . *no!* Once again somebody just led right into me from the blind—25k. I will say I have encountered more than my fair share of lead-outs today. Very atypical, and sadly I have to admit that I haven't really been able to deal with them properly. This time it was going to be different! I just could not imagine John Doe having me beat in this spot, so I was already eyeing his chip stack. Mr. Doe had about 125k left, and I wanted it all. I announced raise and moved a big pile of chips toward the middle. He immediately got the message, but wasn't a big fan of the idea. We had slowly closed in on the 81–82 mark, and fighting a big uphill battle right here hardly seemed like the right approach. From the looks of his face it looked like a big Jack! No matter what it was, it hit the muck, and I could add another 44k to my stack. Nice to keep going in the right direction, but this time I had a feeling that I could have done a lot better. Just calling might have enabled me to get that 125k on the turn. I wasn't going to fold anyway, so maybe giving him a free card was the right idea.

Hand 117

Blinds	My Position	My Hand	My Chip Stack
2000/4000/500	Button	9♣ 7♦	556K

Nothing lasts forever! After six consecutive deposits into my chip bank, something was bound to give. I even folded both my blinds to show my good intentions, but it didn't help. I open for 14k on the button with 9♣ 7♦, but Keith Sexton in the small blind was not going to let me take another one without a fight. He re-raised enough for me to lose all interest in the hand, so I quickly folded.

Hand 118

Blinds	My Position	My Hand	My Chip Stack
2000/4000/500	1 off the button	9♠ Q♠	542K

I open for 13k, 1 off the button with Qs 9s, and again I meet resistance from the small blind. This time it's only a call, though, so it's much easier to deal with. The flop comes:

Open-ended straight draw with an over card—pretty good if you ask me. As the flop hits the table we receive some very important information—we are now down to eighty players! Unless my opponent wants to split eightieth place with some random John Doe, he'd better sit very still for the remainder of the hand. His chip stack is no real threat to me and I have a solid playable hand. I move all-in and it seems like he is almost happy to let it go. The day is over and everybody can safely go to sleep knowing they will be back for more action tomorrow.

End of Day 2

Recap, Day 2

All in all a very good day! I have avoided most big stacks, being able to control the situation as chip leader at my respective tables. A good table draw is worth a lot and I will have to say I have been fairly lucky in that department. I have been on cruise control most of the time and with the exception of a couple of big shootouts, I have been able to play mostly small pots where I could control the tempo. Picking up blinds and antes has been the main contributor, but a couple of well-timed maneuvers have also played a part in my increasing stack! Bubble play also turned out very well for me, but I can't really say that came as a surprise. The bubble tends to favor aggressive play, and if you are the chip leader at the table, you should be in for nice little stack increase.

On the negative side I have to admit that I lost my composure for a second or two due to Mr. Fletcher's erratic play. He caught me off guard, but I'm planning not to let that happen again. Keeping the pressure and avoid going on tilt seem to be fitting goals for day three.

The observant reader would notice a big disparity in the number of hands played on day one compared to day two—forty hands as opposed to seventy-eight hands during the same number of levels. Did I really have that many good hands on day two? No—the reason is very simply the increased blinds and antes. Whereas the slow pace of the first three levels of day one called for more conservative play, all levels on day two were at a fast-pace structure.

TOP TEN AFTER DAY 2

Haralabos Voulgaris	634,500
Gus Hansen	562,500
Jimmy Fricke	535,500
Jan Suchanek	516,000
Emanuel Seal	514,000
Andrew Black	501,500
Patrick Fletcher	484,500
Paul Wasicka	451,500
Chris Chronis	416,000
Michael Ismael	400,500

I ended the day with 562k in chips, only surpassed by my very good friend Haralabos Voulgaris. It seemed like he really took advantage of everybody the last hour and catapulted himself into first place. As for yesterday's chip leader, Mr. Antonius, it was the roller-coaster ride of a lifetime—up to 550k, down to 140k, up to 425k, down to 2,800, up to 380k, only to end at 236k! It is not a misprint! He was down to 2,800 and three hands later he had over 50k. Still mind-boggling how that happens!

A good night's sleep and I'm ready for tomorrow.

CHAPTER 3

DAY 3

My Advice Before Today's Play

Full Table vs. Short-Handed

The first time I encountered a planned six-handed structure was at the Shooting Star tournament at Bay 101 in 2005. With thirty-six players remaining it turned into six six-handed tables and stayed with a maximum six players at a table until the end. It was well received back then, and more and more tournaments are nowadays experimenting with short-handed structures because it creates a more exciting format for both players and viewers. But it does a lot more than just add a little excitement. It creates a whole new universe!

It is like playing baseball with only four outfielders. Singles turn into doubles, doubles turn into triples, and bunting might be a very effective weapon because of the lack of defenders. In case you don't like baseball it can also be compared to going from one-on-one in basketball to five per side. You change the number of players playing the game, you automatically change everything. Different skill-sets become important as your involvement goes up or down due to an increase or decrease in the number of players.

Enough sports analogies, let's get back to poker! Somebody once said, "Patience is a virtue" and I'm sure he was right. All I know is he definitely wasn't talking about short-handed tournament poker. Too much patience will end up ruining you, as the fast-paced nature of the game will take its toll. In a nine-handed game patient hand-selection and watching the world go by is a very reasonable approach, but those virtues come up a tad bit short when we are down to six players. Six-handed is more of a brute force environment where aggressive behavior and constant pressure is the nature of the beast. With nine players around the table you can quietly pick your spots, but as the number of players goes down and the intensity goes up sometimes the spots pick you! So before you sit down make sure you got the right head count. It is not enough to fine-tune your arsenal if you are bringing the wrong guns.

It should be obvious to everybody by now that I bring a totally different approach to the table depending on how many chairs are left. I'm basically trying to emphasize how important I think it is to distinguish between the two completely different tasks at hand. Trust me, it is two different worlds! For example: If you are a tight, solid, good player in nine-handed surroundings but fail to make the proper adjustments going into a six-handed structure, chances are you will leave the tournament in the middle of the pack without ever really making a run at the title. You need to adjust. The best way to do so is to kick it into gear and take the highway! It may sound trivial to pick up speed and indeed it should be, but I still see a lot of players getting stuck in a nine-handed mode, thereby drastically diminishing their chances of making it to the Promised Land. I can understand that it may be hard for someone to completely change their otherwise very selective starting requirements and start playing marginal hands—hands they never even considered could be money-makers. But it is a necessity if you want to make a serious impact in the final stages of a tournament. Just try to imagine that you have five opponents thinking in their same old conservative ways, and you are the only one willing to make a change. Most likely you will be controlling the pace, grabbing hold of what's yours, and of course taking a little bit of theirs.

Let me give you another example: Going by tight nine-handed standards, you might be playing approximately 15% of all hands dealt to you. Transfer those percentages into a six-handed environment, where you have six players each playing 15% of the hands—15% multiplied by 6 is 90%. Something just doesn't add up! Who is going to win the last 10% of the hands? Let me tell you—I will!

There is a lot of extra money floating around out there, and not seizing the opportunity to add them to your stack is a grave mistake. I know the example is a little bit home cooked, since it assumes that nobody will ever call a raise and therefore that there is only one player per hand. That is of course not the case, but if you think about it, it actually only makes the example stronger. Assuming on average two players per hand it is actually 200% that needs to be dispersed between the six players.

What I am trying to say is: I believe the right percentage of hands to play in a six-handed game is somewhere in the neighborhood of 30%. You should of course add or subtract from that number depending on your opponents, but if you ever go lower than 20%, you will put yourself at a major disadvantage.

If you are still not convinced let me give you a list of my final compelling arguments.

1. The blinds come around much faster.
2. Your average cost per hand has increased.
3. The number of opponents has decreased.

As you can see, each and every one of my arguments point in the same direction: Play more hands and make more moves!

Back to the Table

Hand 119

Blinds	My Position	My Hand	My Chip Stack
3000/6000/500	Button	A♠ Q♥	562.5K

It's Wednesday morning and we are back in action. Some might call it afternoon but since I just got up it feels like morning. The tournament directors have spent the night reshuffling the tables and apart from Keith Sexton there are six new and unfamiliar faces at my table:

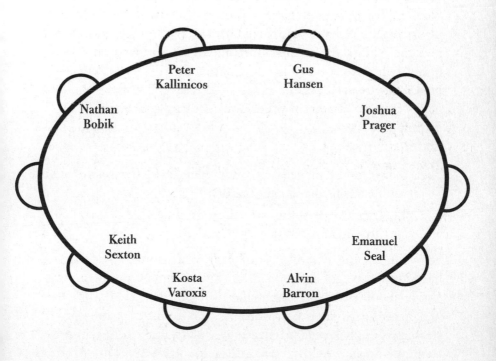

It looks pretty good since I am looking at four short stacks, two mediums, and only one guy, Emanuel Seal, in the 500,000 range. The structure is as slow as it has been for a while. Although the blinds have gone up to 3000/6000 the ante has stayed at 500. A 6:1 ratio between small blind and ante is probably as low as you will ever see in a major tournament. This means that the correct strategy is probably to sit back a little, thereby giving myself some time to evaluate my opponents. I am of course not going to follow that advice! Looking back on day two, much of my chip stack has come from constant aggression so why not keep up the heat?

In the very first hand everybody folded to my button and I find A♠ Q♥. I raise to 18,000 only to have Emanuel Seal in the BB pop it to 56,000. Under normal circumstances I think my hand is worth a re-re-raise. A button raise from me only confirms that I still have two cards in my hand, which means that a re-raise from one of the blinds might be a move and doesn't necessarily indicate a big hand. After all there are only four hands that really have me beat—AA, KK, QQ, AK.

There are a couple of other considerations, though.

1. This is the first hand of the day and people usually don't come out swinging, let alone re-raising.
2. I have never played with Emanuel Seal before, so I have no idea what he is capable of.
3. Emanuel Seal is the *only* guy at the table with a chip stack to worry about.

So what does it all add up to? Following some advice that I have from my good friend and chip-leader Haralabos Voulgaris—I call. Having a somewhat different style than mine it is beneficial for both of us to discuss and analyze various poker strategies. He has been advocating "call and take a flop in position" whereas I tend to re-raise a lot pre-flop. This time it seems prudent to go with his approach.

The flop comes:

Mr. Seal bets 100k and I fold.

To this day I have no idea what I was up against. I have a feeling that he might have taken this one away from me, but on the other hand I don't want to throw it all away on some crazy re-raise the first hand of the day on some vague hunch. Folding was fine.

Hand 120

Blinds	My Position	My Hand	My Chip Stack
3000/6000/500	1 off the button	6♦ Q♣	506.5K

On the very next hand I choose to discard my general rule to lay low for a hand or two after I've just lost a big pot. I open 1 off the button with Q♣6♦ for 19k and again the BB pops me. This time it is Alvin Barron who moves all-in for 65,500, giving me precisely 2:1 odds, or 33.33%.

I call.

As it turns out I have a 36% winning chance against Alvin's A♠J♦. It was right to call but I probably should have followed my own advice and stayed away from this hand. The flop comes:

I need another Queen or a Six but there's no help on the turn and river, and Alvin takes down the pot.

Two hands dealt, two hands played, two hands lost! I have lost 123,000 or more than 20% of my stack right off the bat—not what I had envisioned.

Hand 121

Hand 122

Hand 123

Blinds	My Position	My Hand	My Chip Stack
3000/6000/500	3rd	K♠ 6♠	440K
3000/6000/500	1 off the button	Q♥ 9♦	441K
3000/6000/500	Button	Q♣ T♠	441K

Eager to make some of my lost money back I try to find any excuse to raise a pot and steal the blinds and antes. I haven't really had too many chances since one of the guys at the table has been experimenting with a lot of all-in moves, but . . .

What has happened is that the focus has shifted away from me to the crazy all-in guy providing a perfect cover. I have quietly, without anybody noticing, managed to steal two sets of blinds and antes in one round. K♠ 6♠ and Q♥ 9♦ were good enough to twice add 13,000, or a total of 26,000, to my stack.

Back on the button I open for 19,000 with Q♣ T♠. Emanuel calls in the BB. The flop comes:

Top pair, decent kicker—an obvious spot for a continuation bet! Surprisingly I don't get the chance. Mr. Seal leads out for 25k. Even though I still have to worry about his big chip stack, there is no way I am going to let him boss me around! I re-raise

44,000 more to a total of 69,000. I think a re-raise in the 90,000 range would have been more appropriate since my tiny re-raise almost invited him to mess around. It didn't matter anyway as he folds after some deliberation.

Hand 124

Blinds	My Position	My Hand	My Chip Stack
3000/6000/500	1st	7♠ 6♠	490K

I open in first position for 20,000 with 7♠ 6♠ only to have Mr. All-in perform his trick all over again. He makes it a total of 120,000, which is a little steep for my pocket. On top of that it seems like he is very eager for me to call, making my fold even easier.

I fold and he confirms my read by showing Q♠ Q♣.

Hand 125

Blinds	My Position	My Hand	My Chip Stack
3000/6000/500	Button	4♠ 4♥	460K

Nathan Bobik, with about 100,000 left in his stack, opens 2 off the button for 21,000. I have 4♠ 4♥ on the button and mysteriously decide to call. With only 80,000 left in Nathan's stack either re-raising or folding seems like more normal options. Calling turned out to be a much better choice than the aggressive re-raise. The SB, Josh Prager, pumped up the volume with a 150,000 all-in move and Nathan immediately called. A good spot for two Fours if they are both holding a big Ace but a *really* bad one if anyone is paired up. I, for one, did not like the spot and quickly folded.

Josh showed A♠ J♥ and Nate turned over Q♥ Q♦.

Josh hit a Jack but it was not quite enough. Nat doubles up.

I still can't explain my more than out-of-the-ordinary strange call. Some would probably even consider it a bad call and I don't have the proper arguments to disagree. Only thing I know is I lost 21k more than some, but lost somewhere around 79k–129k less than a lot of people. Weird, weird hand!

Hand 126

Blinds	My Position	My Hand	My Chip Stack
3000/6000/500	3rd	J♠ 6♥	437K

Last hand before the break and once again everybody at the table is preoccupied with everything else but poker. Not me! I raise to 17,500 with J♠ 6♥ and both blinds fold. Easy peazy.

Hand 127
Hand 128
Hand 129
Hand 130

Blinds	My Position	My Hand	My Chip Stack
4K/8K/1K	4th	T♥ 8♥	448K
4K/8K/1K	BB	6♦ 3♣	467K
4K/8K/1K	SB	9♠ 5♦	458K
4K/8K/1K	Button	K♣ 9♦	453K
(all 8-handed)			

We are a new level, an eight-handed table, 4,000/8,000 blinds, 1,000 ante. My chip stack remains status quo after the first round of the new level. I steal the blinds and antes one time with T♥ 8♥ in early position and decide to fold two rather crappy hands in the blinds.

I am back on the button with K♣ 9♦ and make my standard raise of 22,000. Both blinds fold and I pick up 19,000.

Hand 131

Blinds	My Position	My Hand	My Chip Stack
4K/8K/1K	2nd	T♦ T♠	469K
(8-handed)			

I open for 22,000 in 2nd position with T♦ T♠. Kosta Varoxis moves all-in on the button for 130,000. There is not much to think about. I have to call 108,000 more to win 172,000, which means I need to win 39% of the time. Folding medium-big pairs with those kinds of odds is *not* recommended! Most of the time I'm up against two over cards, making me a small favorite! Sure, he might have QQ but 88 is just as likely! He turns over A♣ Q♣. I have 54%.

The flop comes:

I am up to being a 72–28% favorite. The turn:

An 86 % favorite and counting.

Ouch! Kosta wins the 280k pot.
No reason to dwell too much on this hand. Both Kosta and

I played the hand very straightforwardly and coin flips are an inevitable part of tournament poker.

Hand 132

Blinds	My Position	My Hand	My Chip Stack
4K/8K/1K (8-handed)	Button	Q♠J♠	323K

After an early position limper I decide to make it 28k on the button with Q♠J♠. Both blinds fold but the limper is a little more tenacious. He calls and the flop is:

Q-high and some backdoor spades—just enough to test the waters if he checks and fold if he bets. He checks, so I bet out 38k. I start to regret my actions since it looks like my opponent is pulling out the big machinery. Fortunately it is only for show and instead of raising he merely calls the 38k.

Unless it was reverse-reverse psychology, first used by Garfield in 1982, I'm pretty sure he had just handed me a lot of information. He did NOT have a big hand. At best some kind of funky draw. I should be able to take advantage of that knowledge on the turn. Turn:

Perfect card! Definitely didn't complete any draws, so I should be safe. He checks as expected and it's time for another well-timed bullet. No need to exaggerate though. Unless I had completely misjudged the situation, 48k should be plenty to take down the pot—especially with this kind of board. Luckily I was right. He folded and I could add another 85k to my stack.

I don't know if he was trying to be cute or wanted to get a reaction from me when he messed around with a big pile of chips facing my continuation bet. No matter what his intentions were it didn't work out as planned. He gave away more than he received.

A friend of mine is a big fan of trying to extract information from his adversary with fancy head fakes, hand gestures, chip manipulation or some simple table talk. I don't really do too much of this mumbo-jumbo myself, as I prefer to stay calm and collected. On the other hand, I can't really discard the technique as flawed simply because I don't have enough experience in working that way.

I am undeniably aware of numerous occasions where my friend's table-tricks worked out beautifully—as he of course is very quick to point out his brilliant footwork. I just have a feeling he forgets to tell me about all the times his little routine fails and he is the one coming up with the short end of the stick.

What I'm trying to get at is this: the most important factor is to keep your cool and not give away an inch. If you can stay calm and gather information at the same time—perfect. Just make sure you collect more than you give away! Going back to the actual hand, I definitely came out ahead. The exchange of information worked well in my favor and his fooling around might very well have been the main reason for my second bullet on the turn.

Hand 133

CRUCIAL HAND 7: Biggest Hand So Far— Busting the Defending Champ

Blinds	My Position	My Hand	My Chip Stack
4K/8K/1K (8-handed)	SB	A♣ Q♠	389K

Defending champ Lee Nelson has been moved to the table. He opens in middle position for 24,000 and I decide to just call with my A♣ Q♠ in the SB. The BB folds! The flop comes:

I think it is fair to call it an above-average flop!

I check and as expected Lee bets 44,000 into a 64,000 pot. Having flopped three Queens with top kicker, or as some would say, a monster, I have a couple of different options:

1. Calling, trying to trap Mr. Nelson, would be more tempting with no flush draw on the board. Another drawback is that calling simply fails to put more money in the pot. For it to be a real trap, I would have to check the turn as well and could thereby easily give Mr. Nelson two free cards. I don't like it!

2. The mini-raise, doubling his 44,000 bet to about 100,000, trying to keep Lee in the loop but forcing him to put a little more money in the pot. It might also be interpreted as a cheap steal-attempt, thereby inducing Mr. Nelson to make a move. I like it!

3. Standard raise to about 150,000. Put even more money in the pot, but this might force Lee out of some marginal hands. Has some merit!

As you can see I prefer the mini-raise.

After some deliberation I make it 100k. Now it is Lee's turn to think. Surprisingly quickly he goes all-in, putting a total of 326,000 toward the middle. As I'm pretty happy about the development I don't hesitate to call. After all, I am holding the third nuts or more likely "the nuts" since Lee would have played it a little slower if he was holding either Q4 or 44.

There is now 716,000 in the pot, so the next two cards are very crucial for the outcome of this tournament. The defending champ is all-in and I am left with less than 50,000 in front of me. Whoever wins this pot will be well on the way to the final table and the other guy will be headed—or more or less headed—to the sideline.

Showtime:

Lee: K♣ 9♣
Me: A♣ Q♠

Winning percentage before the turn:

Lee: 23.1%
Me: 76.9%

Turn:

No club but now he has a gut shot as well. His winning percentage stays the same.

River:

Nice. I win the 700,000+ pot.

So what really happened here? How did we get 700k in the middle at this stage in the tournament? Let us take it from the top.

Lee's opening raise from middle position with K♣ 9♣—a play that has my utmost sympathy. My call in the blind with AQo is definitely not mandatory and I would generally lean toward the re-raise. Being out of position, facing a tough opponent with a big chip stack, I opted for the more conservative call.

Checking the flop—very straightforward as Lee will most likely take a stab with any two cards.

Flop bet by Lee—good solid play! Continuation bets is a big part of winning tournament strategy and should be performed a very high percentage of the time, especially this time when he actually has a flush draw to back it up!

My mini-raise—described earlier in the hand.

Lee's all-in move—*oops*. I do *not* agree with this play.

A much better option would be to just call and see what develops. Lee is in position and has the luxury of awaiting my next move. If I had an air ball there is a very good chance that I would give up and he would be able to take it away with a medium-sized bet on the turn. On the other hand, if I had a Queen I would probably move all-in on the turn and Lee would be able to get away from the hand without losing all his money.

Don't forget, if a club comes on the turn we would get all the money in with me having the drawing hand.

As you can see Lee would have gained a lot of information by flat-calling. Not only would he have a better idea about the strength of my hand but he would also get to see whether a club showed up or not.

Furthermore, contrary to what people think I am actually a very tight player ☺, at least in some situations. Very rarely do I check-raise a big stack on the flop with absolutely nothing. I was in a comfortable position and not especially looking for a spot to pull off a big bluff. Analyzing the hand again and again, I have come to the conclusion that my most likely holding is a random Queen with the Ace high flush draw next in line, none of which the K♣9♣ fare well against.

I am not quite sure why Lee opted to move all-in but I have a strong feeling that my reputation played a big part in his decision.

Hand 134

Blinds	My Position	My Hand	My Chip Stack
5K/10K/1K (6-handed)	2nd	9♥9♠	750K

We are down to thirty-six players and there has been a re-draw for seats. It is going to be six tables of six players each. I love this format! We do it every year in the Bay101 Shooting Stars tournament and it seems like more and more tournaments have picked up on the fact that a lot of players like this format toward the end of the tournament. What it means is that there will be no more leaning back, no more waiting for the nuts—only aggressive play will be in charge. And trust me, I am ready for some kamikaze plays.

Blinds are 5000/10000 with a 1,000 ante, so the cost of living is 21,000 per round. I have about 750,000 in my stack with the next in line having about 300,000. I decide that it is time to go in all-in mode.

Some of you might have watched the final round of Poker Superstars Invitational (PSI) 3 where I needed to win the last heat in order to qualify for the last sixteen. Only first place would do me any good and because of the high blind structure I felt that the all-in strategy was the right way to go. Twenty-seven all-ins in a row! Luckily for me it added up to twenty-four wins and three ties and I went on to win the heat.

The blind structure that we are playing now is somewhat comparable to the PSI and I felt I could put some serious pressure on my five opponents with some well-timed all-in moves.

The first hand dealt I am in second position with two beautiful Nines. A perfect fit for my pre-determined strategy! All-in it is! Of course I wasn't risking my entire 750,000 since nobody could afford more than 300,000. Both blinds folded and I picked up 20,000.

Hand 135

Blinds	My Position	My Hand	My Chip Stack
5K/10K/1K	SB	A♣ 4♦	758K
(6-handed)			

I am in the small blind with A♣ 4♦. Everybody folds to me and I have an easy all-in play against Ross Boatman's 212,000 stack. For some reason unknown to me, I only make it 32,000. Ross calls, and the flop comes:

Perfect flop . . . at least for a guy in maniac mode! With 70,000 in the pot and Ross having 180,000 left I'm getting ready to fire. There is a good chance that Ross didn't hit the flop and even if he did he still might not be that eager to put the last of his money on the line with the 6♦7♦. Therefore it is very easy for me to correct my pre-flop mistake by putting him all-in.

I bet 200,000 and after considering the pros and cons he decides to fold. I win the pot thinking that the second-best hand probably won this one.

Hand 136
Hand 137

Blinds	My Position	My Hand	My Chip Stack
5K/10K/1K (6-handed)	2nd	A♦ 5♣	795K
5K/10K/1K (6-handed)	1 off the button	A♣ 6♥	814K

During the first round of play I have had a fair number of Aces in my hand, not meaning AA but A*x*. Changing gears a little bit, I stray away from the pre-flop all-in move, raising to 32,000 instead. Both times, with A6*o* and A5*o* respectively, nobody wants to play and I pick up 20,000 a pop.

Hand 138

Blinds	My Position	My Hand	My Chip Stack
5K/10K/1K (6-handed)	SB	A♥ 5♦	822K

Another Ace in my hand, with A5*o* in the small blind and only Ross Boatman in the BB to worry about! He still has somewhere around 190,000 in his stack and I choose to go back to the "Allen Iverson" move: 200,000 toward the middle, and Ross quickly folds.

Recap: ten hands dealt, three all-in moves, two standard raises—90,000 profit.

Hand 139

Blinds	My Position	My Hand	My Chip Stack
5K/10K/1K (5-handed)	SB	7♥ 7♣	828K

A player has been knocked out at our table, unfortunately not by my hand, but nonetheless we are down to five-handed.

First position opens for 35,000. I am in the SB with 77 and I am wondering whether the opener would like to put his remaining 385,000 into the middle. Based on my read, it didn't seem that way. I move all-in to see if I was right.

A bit surprised by the magnitude of my raise, he rolls his eyes and shakes his head before finally deciding to fold. A nice 50,000 pick-up!

Some might call it a rather insane 50,000 pickup but I felt this was the right time to apply maximum pressure. So far I had increased my stack from 770,000 to 910,000 with these vulgar kinds of plays and until somebody proved me wrong I was going to continue.

Hand 140

Blinds	My Position	My Hand	My Chip Stack
5K/10K/1K (5-handed)	Button	4♥ 4♦	887K

The very next hand Paul Wasicka opens 1 off the button for 25,000. I am on the button with 44, still riding the maniac wave. Before I make my move I just want to make sure that I don't run straight into a brick wall in the blinds. None of the blinds seem particularly interested in the hand and therefore I am ready to go!

Paul Wasicka only has 245,000 left so in case anything goes wrong I would still have more than 600,000 left. I move all-in and as expected both blinds fold. Action is back on Paul, who is not happy about the situation. He goes through a couple of Yes/No/Maybe motions before finally calling the floor person to the table. An unexpected turn of events, but all Mr. Wasicka wants to know is whether our table is the next one to break. He is obviously not very keen on having me breathing down his neck every time he looks at his cards—or to put it another way, he wants to get the f— out of Dodge.

Personally I really hope that we are the next table to break because I *never* want any callers when I move all-in with two Fours! Unfortunately it isn't so. I guess I should have tried to bribe the floor person.

The floor person's message cleared things up for Paul Wasicka, who decided he had to make a stand at some point against my constant aggression. Now was the time! He calls and flips over 7♠ 7♥. *Ouch!*

Showdown

My Hand	Paul Wasicka's Hand

No Four in sight, and Paul takes down the 555,000 pot.

A few of you might be asking: "Is Gus on drugs?" Not at all! This was the way I had been playing, taking down pot after pot without ever showing a hand. This time I ran into a rather unfortunate matchup but that is sometimes the price you have to pay. Had Paul instead called me with AJ and failed to connect, everybody would say, "What is he doing calling with AJ anyway?" It is not always the result that matters. Although I will admit that my recent plays have been ultra-aggressive, I don't regret any of them. Keep in mind that Mr. Wasicka came very close to folding his hand, in which case I would have just added another 45,000 to my stack.

Hand 141

Blinds	My Position	My Hand	My Chip Stack
5K/10K/1K	BB	A♠ 6♥	604K
(5-handed)			

Ross Boatman goes all-in for 150k in first position and everybody folds to me. Remember that we are only five players at the table so this should not be treated as a first-position raise but as a 2-off-the-button raise. I have to call 140k more to win 165k, which means I need about 45%.

A♠ 6♥ could be the best hand, but I think the Six is a tad bit too low to make a stand. Somehow I convince myself otherwise. I call and Ross turns over A♠ 9♣. A bad matchup for me! I only have 31.4%, quite a bit less than the 46% I was aiming for.

Showdown

My Hand				Ross Boatman's Hand

Running Sixes looks like my best chance. A Queen and a Five finish me off and I'm now down under the 500k mark. What should I have done?

My call was very debatable! My stack had taken a big hit against Paul Wasicka a couple of hands ago, and to preserve my table chip lead, I should have let this one go.

Hand 142

Blinds	My Position	My Hand	My Chip Stack
5K/10K/1K (5-handed)	Button	J♣ 8♣	447K

Having lost about half my stack, or to be more precise, 420k on two pre-flop all-ins, it seems like a good time to slow down. Especially considering that I only had 19.4% and 31.4% winning chances in the two hands respectively. If I keep up the same pace I could be headed for the rail in a matter of minutes. That is not at all part of my plan and hopefully I can avoid it by going back to my successful nip-and-tuck style of small pots and small stabs, slowly but surely building up my stack!

I open for 32k on the button with J♣ 8♣. BB, who has about 400k left, calls.

The flop comes:

A gut shot, but apart from that not much to brag about!

BB checks as expected, and for once I am considering just checking it back.

I would hate to get check-raised out of the pot, thereby losing the opportunity to hit my gut-shot draw. On the other hand I love to take the first stab, so . . . let's see what he says.

I have spent a lot of time this entire tournament taking a good look at my opponents, especially in crunch-time situations. Even though this might not be the most crucial hand, there is still 74k in the pot that I would love to add to my stack. My first impression of my opponent is the classic "Please don't bet, I really want to see a free card." I spent about thirty seconds contemplating my decision, and in that period of time I saw nothing that made me want to change my mind. He did *not* want me to bet—therefore, I bet!

I bet 48k and he folds.

You could argue that this was just another standard continuation bet, and I would be hard-pressed to disagree, since in essence that is exactly what it was. I still like to think of it as a little bit more than that because of my methodical scrutiny of my opponent's behavior. It was not just a totally blind continuation bet with no regard for the circumstances. My opponent seemed uncomfortable with the prospects of putting more money in the pot, making him an easy target.

Adding a little bit of reading ability into your continuation bets will vastly improve your cost-benefit chart at the end of the day!

Hand 143

Blinds	My Position	My Hand	My Chip Stack
5K/10K/1K (5-handed)	1st	Q♣ T♣	487K

Still playing five-handed at my table, I open in first position for 32k with Q♣ T♣. The button calls as well as Paul Wasicka in the big blind.

Flop comes:

Top pair, decent kicker. Paul checks and I bet 75k into a 106k pot. The button calls and Paul folds.

Turn:

Decision time! There is 379k left in my stack, 315k in my opponent's and 256k in the middle.

My main priority is to pick up the 256k! Am I prepared to risk losing 315k in the process of obtaining my main goal? I'm not quite sure. Let's stop for a second and see what I know about his hand. He called pre-flop and post-flop with guys behind him yet to act, so he probably has a little bit of something. Enough to beat QT? Another question I don't know the answer to. With a lot of doubt creeping into my mind I like to stay on the aggressive path, or to quote my old friend Kurgan from *Highlander*: "I've got something to say. It's better to burn out than to fade away!" What that means is, move all-in and let your opponent make the big decision. It seems like a very reasonable approach, because I know I wouldn't want to be in John Doe's shoes facing a 315k bet with QJ or Q9. It is not an enviable spot to be in. What would you do with those two hands? Is there anybody out there good enough to call with QJ and at the same time fold Q9? Personally I don't think so! If my 315k bet can steer up some noise, and create a tough guess for my opponent, it will definitely have served its purpose.

No way around it—I move all-in. My opponent thinks for a while before finally letting it go. To this day I have no idea what I was up against.

I achieved my goal of picking up the 256k in the middle, putting me right back in the 650k range!

Hand 144

Hand 145

Hand 146

Blinds	My Position	My Hand	My Chip Stack
5K/10K/1K	BB	7♣ 2♥	635K
5K/10K/1K	SB	9♣ 4♦	624K
5K/10K/1K	1st	K♥ 3♣	616K
(all 5-handed)			

Once again it is big blind time. With blinds at 5k–10k and antes at 1k, Paul Wasicka makes it 25k on the button. Small blind folds and I fold 72o. On my tape recorder I mention that I probably should have called. Risking 15k to win 45k facing a button-raise should more or less be an automatic call, but since we are talking about the dreaded 72*o* I guess the fold is acceptable. Needless to say I am only folding low, unsuited, unconnected cards getting 3:1 before the flop!

Next hand everybody folds to my small blind. Ross Boatman is the only one standing between me and the 20k out there so I am quietly preparing to raise. Looking down at 9♣ 4♦, I decide to change my mind. So far I had been raising every time given the same circumstances, and it was time to let one go. I of course waste no time in telling the table that I only raise with "good" hands. The timing turned out to be perfect as Ross, with a disgusted look on his face, turned over A♠ Q♠.

I open in first position with K♥ 3♣. It is not a play I recommend anyone to copy, but the fact of the matter is we are playing short-handed, blinds and antes are very high, everybody is playing very tight, and especially the big blind has shown some remarkable talent for folding his hand. When you add it all up, raising seems like a reasonable alternative. This time it was a successful steal attempt as everybody folds.

Hand 147

Blinds	My Position	My Hand	My Chip Stack
5K/10K/1K (5-handed)	Button	A♦ J♦	618K

My right hand man opens for 27k and I look down at A♦ J♦ on the button. I have noticed my opponent has been a little more eager to join the action lately so this seems like a reasonable spot to try and quiet him down. As if it were the most natural thing in the world, I re-raise to 76k, the blinds fold but somewhat unexpectedly the original raiser calls. With 172k in the pot we are ready for the flop.

I would have preferred a lot of diamonds, but I guess I can't complain. My opponent checks and for some reason I follow his lead and check behind. I wasn't quite sure what to make of his pre-flop call and therefore wanted to proceed with caution. Anyway, it is good to throw a curveball once in a while and on top of that the check did not look particularly dangerous. If indeed I was behind pre-flop versus AK or AQ I had just lucked out and my opponent would be down to three outs. Against middle pairs like 88 or 99 we are talking about two-outers. Giving a free card seemed harmless and would also keep the pot at a manageable size. I did not want to get check-raised by this specific adversary, thereby getting entangled in a huge pot facing hands like A♣Q♣ or possibly even stronger holdings. Check it is.

Turn:

You don't find them much uglier than that. I'm hoping for a check since a substantial bet would leave me in a precarious situation. He checks and I take 20 Hollywood seconds before checking it right back. River:

Again he checks and it is time to go through the hand once more. Three checks in a row usually means: "I'm telling you the truth and I'm not too proud of my hand." Unless he is trying to copy Johnny Chan from the 1998 WSOP with a very devious triple-check check-raise, I think it is safe to believe he has something mediocre. I am not holding a powerhouse but I do have a very respectable second pair.

I know players who subscribe to the idea of just checking it down and taking the pot, but if you have ever seen Phil Ivey in action you will know that it is not the right way to play poker. He is a true master of the value bet and will punish you for having inferior hands and maybe, just maybe, bluff you out of the best one.

I for one don't think I can look myself in the eye if I don't bet this hand. Re-raising before the flop, flopping top-pair, top-kicker and then checking it down should not be allowed. I count down the pot an end up betting a rather timid 99k. Without too much hesitation my opponent calls but my AJ proves too strong. Before mucking his hand he quickly flashes his cards toward me showing either TT or 99.

I took an unusual path this hand but I doubt I could have won any more using a different route.

Hand 148

Blinds	My Position	My Hand	My Chip Stack
5K/10K/1K (5-handed)	BB	T♣2♥	810K

Everybody folds to the small blind, who limps for 5k more. Last hand he folded T6*o* in his big blind to one of Paul Wasicka's mini-raises. I have a feeling he is not too eager to play this hand either, so a small raise seems appropriate. The actual strength of my hand is a minor concern, since my projected pickup vig* heavily outweighs any other factors. As it turns out I have Doyle Brunson's favorite hand, T2o, but again that is not going to stop me from making what I consider to be the best equity play. I raise 22k more to a total of 32k and the small blind quickly folds. A small but nice pick-up solely based on my perception of my opponent and not the cards in my hand.

Hand 149

Blinds	My Position	My Hand	My Chip Stack
6K/12K/2K	1st	A♠ A♥	816K
(5-handed)			

We have now moved up to my favorite tournament level of all time. It is the beautiful 6000–12000 level with a 2,000 ante. One might ask: "Is there any particular difference between this level and the 600–1200 level?" At first glance they seem very comparable, but there is a little more to it than first meets the eye.

As we are moving closer to the final table, the audience is bigger and louder, the pressure is more intense, and the prize money has increased. Those players who happen to be here for the first time will unavoidably be affected by the situation.

Some will lean back and hope for everybody else to get knocked out, thereby climbing up the prize ladder. Some will try to avoid making any stupid mistakes with everybody's eyes on them. Some will be playing 6000–12000 for the first time in their life—and just the mere thought of that will have them trembling. Whatever it is that makes their hearts pound faster and faster, it has a tendency to lead their poker game in the same direction. They will all tighten up. I like to do the oppo-

*Vig = juice, slang for gain or edge.

site. Players tightening up at your table means there are more chances to steal the blinds and antes, and that is exactly what I'll do!

With everybody guarding their chips with their lives I like to aim at what is already in the middle. Since there is a whopping 28,000 in the pot to begin with, this is the most lucrative level to be hyper-aggressive!

We are still playing five-handed. I open in first position for 38,000 with AA. I close my eyes and dream of a re-raise and an all-in move before it is back to me. Unfortunately I wake up to the sound of four hands hitting the muck almost simultaneously! The four quickest releases I have ever seen in my entire life! I guess I shouldn't complain about winning the blinds and antes but I have to admit I was hoping for a little bit more.

Hand 150

Blinds	My Position	My Hand	My Chip Stack
6K/12K/2K (6-handed)	BB	J♦9♠	842K

Everybody folds to the SB, who limps for 6,000 more. Same scenario as last round, where I raised with T2o. This time I have J♠9♥ so I definitely have to raise this one, too. On the other hand I have a hunch that the SB is getting very tired of the limp-fold play and might be in trapping mode. Afraid of getting check-raised, I tap the table. The flop comes:

The SB checks and I cautiously check behind. It seems a little atypical for me to check behind with a pair and an open-ended straight-draw, but for some reason I wanted to keep this pot small. Furthermore, there are only two cards I don't want to see on the turn and that is an Ace and a Jack. An Ace is the only over card that doesn't make me a straight and although the Jack gives me two pair it also puts a four-straight on the board. Turn:

Not really what I was looking for. The small blind bets 15,000 and I call. Even though I have been very careful with this hand I am not ready to give up just yet.

River:

My opponent bets another 30k and I fold. At this point I can't really see what hand I could beat. I put him on a strong hand pre-flop and although I hit a good flop, my pair of Nines didn't improve and it is therefore time to let it go.

Hand 151

Blinds	My Position	My Hand	My Chip Stack
6K/12K/2K	BB	8♣8♥	797K
(6-handed)			

Everybody folds to my opponent in the SB, who limps in. I have 8♣8♥ in the BB and make it a total of 48,000. He folds.

So why did I raise to 48,000 instead of the standard three times the BB 36,000?

I have a tendency to raise a little extra with medium or small pairs because of the difficulties they represent in post-flop play. I would much rather win the pot right here instead of facing some tough decisions later on in the hand and the 12,000 extra usually allows me to win it right there on the spot.

Hand 152

Blinds	My Position	My Hand	My Chip Stack
6K/12K/2K (6-handed)	SB	A♣ 4♥	817K

The guy in second position raises to 30,000 and I fold my A♣ 4♥ in the SB.

Everybody around the table, except me of course, has been playing pretty tight, which means that I have to give them a little more credit for an actual hand when they do decide to raise. I have an Ace but apart from that not much to brag about. It does not seem like a good spot to fight an uphill battle, and furthermore I still have to worry about the big blind, who is yet to act. All in all a reasonable fold!

Hand 153

Blinds	My Position	My Hand	My Chip Stack
6K/12K/2K (6-handed)	Button	2♣ 4♣	809K

I have 2♣ 4♣ on the button and I extend my deepest apologies to Daniel Negreanu for folding this hand. I know I am not supposed to and under normal circumstances I probably wouldn't have done it.

The BB is down to about 110,000, which represents a serious problem should I decide to raise. With a standard raise to 36,000 I am of course hoping to pick up the blinds and antes but if the BB should decide to move all-in I would be left in an ugly spot.

Let's take a brief look at the math. I raise to 36,000, small blind folds, the BB calls the 36,000 and moves all-in for 74,000 more. At this point there is exactly 162,000 in the pot (antes: 10,000 + SB: 6,000 + my 36,000 + BB: 110,000). I would have to call another 74,000 to win 162,000. I need 31.4% and I just hate to lay down suited connectors with those kind of odds. Against most of his hands I would have approximately a 37% winning chance.

To put it another way, I would call, he would turn over the best hand, and most likely I would lose the unfair coin flip.

Bottom line: No need to waste 110,000 on Four-high.

Hand 154

CRUCIAL HAND 8: Calling Paul Wasicka's All-in with Ace High

Blinds	My Position	My Hand	My Chip Stack
6K/12K/2K (6-handed)	2nd	A♥ 6♦	807K

I open in second position for 39,000 with A♥ 6♦. Small blind folds and Paul Wasicka calls 27,000 more. We are off to the flop with 94,000 in the pot. The flop comes:

Paul checks and I bet 52,000. Paul thinks for about forty-five seconds before bringing out the Big Bazooka. A 386,000 all-in move! Not quite what I had expected.

My first instinct was to fold since a call and a loss would severely cripple me. My second thought was to call since I was up against Mr. Paul "Crazy Bluff" Wasicka. With my two first thoughts ending in a tie I had better take a good look at the math before making my decision.

532,000 in the middle − 334,000 to call − 38.6% winning chance is what I need!

As mentioned earlier, Paul Wasicka *loves* the big bluff. The bad news is I can hardly beat a bluff. The good news is that I definitely have some outs since I can't picture Paul having a made straight already.

Let's cut to the chase—what do I really put him on?

POSSIBLE SCENARIOS

His Hand	Comments	My Winning Chance (%)
K9♠, Q9♠	gut shot semi-bluff	74
K6♠, Q6♠	6, worse kicker	70
J9♠, T9♠	Open ended semi-bluff	61
TT	Over pair	40
98♠, 97♠	Pair and gut shot	35
99	Over pair with blockers	32
87♠, 75♠, 85♠	Two pair	31
A8♠, A7♠	Pair, Ace kicker	30
A9♠	Gut shot, Ace kicker	28
66	Sixes	28
56♠, 67♠, 68♠	Pair with a six	25
88, 77, 55	Set	25

As you can see I have absolutely no idea what he is holding. With a connected flop like this, there are too many possibilities to figure it all out at the table. It could be a strong hand like two pair or a set or, even more devastating, a pair and six tying up my straight-draw.

On a positive note, though, I think there is a lot of semi-bluffs lurking around, where I could possibly have best hand, best draw! Anyway I have to make a decision, one that could easily have a significant impact on the outcome of this tournament. My winning chances against Mr. Wasicka's various holdings seem to be in the high thirties, which happens to be right on the nose according to my pot odds, so no help there. One specific factor that I haven't mentioned so far leads me in the direction of calling. Table presence, table control, uncertainty—call it whatever you want, but if I fold this hand and Mr. Wasicka shows me a total air-ball, I will definitely lose some momentum.

If he elects not to show his hand with a little smirk on his face, uncertainty will creep into my mind and it might take me a while to regain my composure and table presence. If I call and he has a strong hand I will have taken a little bit of the worst of it, but he will know not to mess around too much.

What I am trying to say is Paul Wasicka is a great player and if you let him get away with too much, he will slowly but surely take control of the table and I really did not want that to happen.

Although I am not very happy about playing such a big pot, with a very mediocre holding at this point in time, I elect to make the call. And boy was I in for a surprise!!!!

Rail was saying set versus over pair, straight versus Aces, but it couldn't have been further from the truth. First phrase that came out of Paul's mouth was a sad "You got me!"

I quickly responded, "I don't think so."

Back to Paul: "No pair."

I started to like my call, and with a smile on my face I said, "Me neither."

Paul looked pleasantly surprised and turned over A♠ J♠!

Wow, wow, *wow!*

Rail was in shock, and I heard a couple of voices behind me saying, "That Paul guy must be crazy." As for myself, I was also, to say the least, taken by surprise. All my neat calculations were in vain. I had expected some gut-shot semi-bluffs, but two over cards with no drawing potential apart from a back-door flush-draw and the classic pair-draw was a shocker! When I turned over my A♥ 6♦ I got the same speech from the rail, "Crazy, unbelievable, how, why?"

No matter what, the two crazy guys had gotten themselves entangled in a 900k pot with a couple of Ace-high holdings. As for my winning percentages, they were right on the money, 38.7%!

Turn:

Great turn! Not gin, but Paul is down to three wins and eight ties. I am now an 84%–16% favorite.

River:

Straight! For both of us! It's a split pot, which seems like a reasonable outcome for two kamikaze pilots.

The aftermath: Betting on the flop seems like a natural play after having flopped an open-ended straight-draw. The only consideration is whether I should have bet more or less. Fifty-two thousand into a 94k pot, or about 60% of the pot-size, is very standard, but after ending up calling Paul Wasicka's all-in move anyway, maybe I should have moved all-in myself? The result would definitely have been different as Paul quickly would have folded his AJ to a 386k bet.

All-in over bets are dangerous paths to take! You risk a lot for a little, and it can sometimes lead to a quick exit out of the tournament. On the other hand it has some merit as it allows you to pick up a lot of small uncontested pots. Which way to go is not a question of right or wrong, but more of a style issue. Remember this is poker, there are no absolute truths.

Calling the 334k raise was without a doubt a bit of a stretch. If it hadn't been for Paul Wasicka sitting at the other end of the table my hand would have hit the muck rather quickly. Taking Paul's bluffing frequency into account, the call seemed more appealing. Seeing the two cards he turned over, I'm almost about to give myself a pat on the back and say, "great call." Unfortunately, when I replay the hand looking at all the different scenarios my call never comes out better than "questionable"!

As for Paul Wasicka's method of playing this hand, I will start out by calling it different! Not to re-raise Gus Hansen at a five-handed table in a high blind-structure with AJ suited could at best be described as optional! The best play is to re-raise and if possible win the hand right there. Slow-playing, trapping, whatever Paul's intentions were, I really don't think this was the appropriate time for such a maneuver.

Paul's post-flop play deserves some attention as well. "Boom! Maximum pressure!" are some of the words that come to mind. I will admit I would have chosen a slightly different hand to exercise such violence, but when push comes to shove you gotta give the guy some credit. He wasn't afraid to pull the trigger. He put me to the test.

He could have been a hero making me fold AK or AQ, he could have been an idiot losing all his money to two Queens or a set of Sevens, or as it turned out he got all his money in being a 61–39% favorite. A lot of possible outcomes, and I think the best way to describe Paul's play is innovative, gutsy and forceful!

I will refrain from passing any judgment on an all-in check-raise move like that, apart from saying: "It is fun and I like it!"

Hand 155

Blinds	My Position	My Hand	My Chip Stack
6K/12K/2K	1st	6♠6♣	813K
(6-handed)			

It is the very next hand after my battle with Wasicka, and I would usually stay away from this one to collect my thoughts. Even though I feel that is a good piece of advice to calm down after a big shoot-out, I am not about to throw away medium pairs.

I open for 38k in first position with 6♠6♣. Ross Boatman next to me contemplates for a while before finally deciding to call. Everybody else folds and we are heads-up.

Flop comes:

Great flop! Sets aren't easy to come by and I'm hoping that Ross hit something to fight back with. I'm already eyeing Ross's entire stack as my main objective has now shifted from winning the pot to extracting as much as possible from Mr. Boatman. Checking is a reasonable play to allow him to catch up a bit, but I usually prefer to go for the throat right away. A check from me might also arouse some suspicion on Ross's part, and I really don't want him to escape too cheaply.

I decide to lead out with a small bet. Forty-four thousand into a 104k pot is lower than my normal continuation bets, but hopefully not so low that he smells a rat, and hopefully not too big to scare him away.

All my careful considerations were totally in vain as Ross

declares all-in after 2.7 seconds. I call instantly, and Ross is left with little to no hope against my three Sixes. He turns over A♦T♦ for top-pair ten-kicker, but is down to a mere 7.1% against my set.

Turn brings an off-suit Four and it is all over for Ross Boatman. So what happened here? Should Ross have been more careful or is it just one of those hands you can't get away from? With Ross's chip stack the result was inevitable! Whether I checked, bet small, bet big, or moved all-in, his chips were going toward the middle and so were mine. There is no way around it. At this stage of the tournament it was a plain and simple cold-deck. Luckily for me I was on the right side.

Much more interesting is the pre-flop play. Last hand I was wondering about Paul Wasicka's pre-flop play and discarded it as optional at best, with a strong inclination to call it inferior. And yet the very next hand, the same kind of scenario is displayed right in front of my eyes. I open in early position at a short-handed table, only to get called by a "way above average" hand.

What is going on here? I consider both Paul and Ross to be strong tournament players. Yet they both almost simultaneously pulled a stunt I would be hard-pressed to agree with.

There is one significant difference between the two calls, though. Paul Wasicka was last to act and therefore did not have to fear a big hand behind him. He only had to worry about me, and as you might know by now I rarely have anything. Ross had three players behind him, putting him in a much more precarious situation. Still, I would tend to put the two hands in the same category.

Bottom line: Either I re-raise too much or they re-raise too little; I leave that up to the reader to decide! One thing is certain, I'd better start upgrading my calling requirements when re-raised! Going by the last two examples it seems like people only bring the really big guns to the re-raise party.

I just crossed the one million mark.

Hand 156

Blinds	My Position	My Hand	My Chip Stack
6K/12K/2K	SB	Q♣ 8♣	1.059 million
(5-handed)			

Paul Wasicka opens for 32k one off the button. Hans Martin Vogl, who was recently moved to my table, calls on the button. I call 26k more in the small blind with Q♣ 8♣.

Flop comes:

Bottom-pair, gut shot, and back-door flush-draw! A little bit of this and a little bit of that.

As the small blind I have to come out with an opening statement, and what better way than to take the first stab? Leading out gives me a chance to win it right here, but it also forces my opponents to respond, giving me a better idea of where they are than if I let one of them initiate contact. A case could be made for checking, just to see if it is a bet and a raise before coming back to me. Folding would then be the only reasonable option, and I would be able to save my initial bet. But then again, this is Hold'em. If you assume that your opponents always hit the flop you are going to handcuff yourself, and you will never be able to play good aggressive poker!

I lead out for 66k into a 118k pot, and before you can say, "Phil Hellmuth" they both folded!

I was probably up against something like A7♠ and 55. Checking the flop would have given them a chance to hit their presumably five outs for free, and there is definitely no reason to do that.

Hand 157

Blinds	My Position	My Hand	My Chip Stack
6K/12K/2K (5-handed)	BB	J♠5♦	1.135 million

Barry Bonds, here I come! I get a walk. With an average of 257 walks a year I am slowly but surely catching up to Mr. Bonds himself, aiming to be the all-time walk-off leader in ten to twenty years from now.

Nobody at the table seems particularly interested in butting heads with me and I have to admit that it is pretty nice to pick up 16,000 uncontested. By the way, I was holding J5o.

Hand 158

Blinds	My Position	My Hand	My Chip Stack
6K/12K/2K (6-handed)	Button	7♣3♦	1.149 million

After having played five-handed for a while we are back to six-handed. Everybody folds to my button and with two fairly tight players in the small and big blind I am going for the steal just about 100% of the time.

The starting pot contains 30,000 and with a standard raise to about 36,000 I am laying 6:5 to win it right there. That seems like a very reasonable deal against two conservative opponents and even though I am holding 7♣3♦ I am going to test the waters.

The fact that the small blind has already displayed a certain disinterest in the hand makes it even more compelling. I raise to

38,000 and the small blind mucks instantly. Unfortunately the BB had other ideas as he quickly moves all-in for 334,000. I can't come up with any good reason to call 296,000 more with seven high so I fold.

Hand 159

Blinds	My Position	My Hand	My Chip Stack
6K/12K/2K (6-handed)	1 off the button	4♠ 5♠	1.109 million

The very next hand I limp for 12,000, 1 off the button holding 4♠ 5♠. The button and the SB fold and the BB taps the table. I guess I could have won the pot with a pre-flop raise but I was a little afraid of waking up the "all-in specialists." Last hand I opened with a standard raise and folded to an all-in move. If I follow the same pattern this hand it might motivate some of my opponents to interfere with all my steal attempts. And that is the last thing I want to happen!

The only hurdle left in this hand is to have the BB miss the flop, after which I should be able to pick it up with a small bet. The flop comes:

BB checks and I bet 18,000. Mission accomplished. BB missed the flop and I take down the pot.

Hand 160

Blinds	My Position	My Hand	My Chip Stack
6K/12K/2K (6-handed)	2nd	A♠ J♦	1.137 million

I open in second position with A♠ J♦ for 38,000. The small blind stops for a second before re-raising 100,000 more, leaving him with just about 242,357. Everybody else folded and it was back to me.

Two hands ago the same guy moved all-in for 334,000. All of a sudden he has a specific reason only to raise 100,000 more? I was prepared to call an all-in move almost instantly but something wasn't right about this one. It feels like he is leading me on, trying to entangle me in a much bigger pot than my cards can justify. It may sound kind of strange that I am prepared to call a 378,000 all-in move, yet I get very discouraged when he tries to chop off one leg at a time with a 100,000 raise.

I guess it is an opposite world but in poker I see that over and over again. The bigger the hands, the more they try to trap. Going back a couple of hands I myself was in trapping mode when I flopped a set of Sixes. I did not want to scare Ross Boatman away and therefore my lead-out bet was somewhat smaller than usual.

Bottom-line: For all you *Twin Peaks* fans, "The owls are not what they seem." Something just doesn't feel right. I don't like my hand anymore and the only reasonable course of action is therefore to throw it away.

Hand 161

Blinds	My Position	My Hand	My Chip Stack
6K/12K/2K (6-handed)	1 off the button	T♣ 6♦	1.071 million

I open 1 off the button with T♣ 6♦ for 36,000. Luckily nobody wants to get in the way and I take down the 28,000 profit.

Hand 162

Blinds	My Position	My Hand	My Chip Stack
6K/12K/2K (6-handed)	BB	J♣ 9♠	1.095 million

Funky Playing Guy opens in first position for 46,000. Everybody folds and I decide to call 34,000 more in the BB with J♣ 9♠. I have said it before and I'll say it again: in general I should be more careful calling first position raises but I can rarely suppress my curious tendencies. The flop comes:

Even though I flopped a pair I am not too excited about the prospects. I check and he checks behind me. I am not quite sure what to make of his check but I have a feeling I am still behind.

The turn is:

I check again and this time he bets 75,000. If indeed I was behind on the flop I am now more or less drawing dead once the second Queen arrived, making my departure with the hand an easy one. I fold and he takes down the 110k pot. It may seem strange that I'm so quick to depart with a pair of Jacks, and usually I wouldn't. Funky-playing-guy's check on the flop just didn't ring true. If I am correct in my assumption, I would be throwing perfectly good tournament chips after bad as I would at best have two outs. I don't like two-outers!

Hand 163

Blinds	My Position	My Hand	My Chip Stack
8K/16K/2K (6-handed)	SB	Q♣ 5♦	1.026 million

We have moved tables, moved up a level, and are now playing 8k–16k with a 2k ante. I tend to play extra-aggressively whenever moved to a new table, so for the next round or so we are going to follow the play hand by hand.

Everybody folds to my small blind, and I decide to limp for another 8k with Q♣ 5♦. Emanuel Seal in the big blind checks, and the flop comes:

Top two! Emanuel is most likely drawing very slim, so giving a free card seems fairly harmless. I check and he bets 45k. If he had checked behind me he would probably have been drawing dead but his bet indicates a different scenario. For all I care he could have a straight-draw, a flush-draw, one pair, or two pair—whatever it is I'm pretty sure that I'm ahead. He probably has somewhere in between 0 outs with hands like Q3 J5 and 14 outs with 3♠4♠. The problem is I don't know which ones to look out for. I do not like to slow-play against unknown opposition, where some bad judgment on my part could end up costing me a big pot. Check-raising seems like the best play, and who knows, maybe we will get all the money in right here and now.

I call the 45k and raise another 90k. Emanuel goes into the tank, but unfortunately ends up throwing his hand away.

Afterthoughts: Maybe I could have extracted more money from Emanuel, playing the hand a different way, but poker is not an exact science, and you have to choose which way to go. I'm pretty happy with my at-the-table analysis, and therefore I have no regrets about the path I took.

Hand 164

Blinds	My Position	My Hand	My Chip Stack
8K/16K/2K (6-handed)	Button	A♥ K♣	1.097 million

Next hand the last standing Full Tilt qualifier, Robert Goldfarb, limps 2 off the button for 16k. I have A♥ K♣ on the button and re-raise to 80k. Neither Mr. Goldfarb nor the blinds wants to tag along, so I take down the pot for a 50k profit. Very straightforward play, and given the stack sizes surrounding me I was ready to go all the way!

Hand 165

Blinds	My Position	My Hand	My Chip Stack
8K/16K/2K (6-handed)	1 off the button	A♠ T♠	1.147 million

Playing my third hand in a row since we moved upstairs, I open 1 off the button with A♠T♠. Emanuel Seal on the button calls my 51k raise, and the blinds fold. Flop comes:

Not exactly a dream flop, but if Emanuel does not have a King it might not be that bad. He doesn't figure to have a Two or a Three in his hand, so I could very easily still be ahead. It is of course not certain that I was ahead to begin with, but having played with Emanuel earlier in this tournament I thought he would have re-raised with a better Ace or a pair. I bet 66k into a 132k pot, exactly a 50% continuation bet, which is sufficient to win it. A pretty good start at my new table—winning the first three hands!

I now have about 1.2 million, which is very close to pole position with about twenty-four players left!

Hand 166

Blinds	My Position	My Hand	My Chip Stack
8K/16K/2K	2 off the button	A♦ 2♠	1.232 million
(6-handed)			

Going for four in a row, I look down at an Ace and start to grab my chips. On second thought, I don't want to arouse too much suspicion by raising every pot. If everybody at the table starts to catch on to the fact that I raise with less than mediocre hands, it could start an avalanche of re-raises, specifically aimed at me. That would be very unfortunate and would seriously damage my run for the top spot. I therefore take a peek at the other card, only to find an off-suit Deuce.

That's quite a bit lower than what I had hoped for, so I decide to sit this one out.

Hand 167

Blinds	My Position	My Hand	My Chip Stack
8K/16K/2K (6-handed)	1st	2♣ 4♣	1.230 million

Although I just gave a speech about laying low unless the starting requirements are in order, it is only for a little while. It's the fifth hand since we moved tables and I'm first to act. 2♣ 4♣ is the name of the game and I feel like raising. The big blind is very tight and people in general have a lot of respect for a first-position raise, so at least I have two good reasons for making it 48k to go. Everybody folds and I can add 34k to my stack from another successful steal attempt.

Hand 168

Blinds	My Position	My Hand	My Chip Stack
8K/16K/2K (6-handed)	BB	9♣ 4♠	1.264 million

Folding my big blind to Paul Wasicka's raise didn't take much persuasion as I was holding 9♣ 4♠. Considering how much I have been picking up, I don't need to defend my blind with such lousy holdings.

Hand 169

Blinds	My Position	My Hand	My Chip Stack
8K/16K/2K (6-handed)	SB	9♥ 8♦	1.246 million

Everybody folds to my small blind and again I decide to limp, this time with 9♥ 8♦. Emanuel checks behind in the big blind and the flop comes:

We both check, and the turn brings:

Emanuel didn't seem too excited about the flop, so it is time to take charge. I bet 24k into a 44k pot and Emanuel quickly folds.

A case could be made for betting the flop—trying to pick it up right there, without giving him a chance to hit something on the turn. By waiting you get a little info about where he stands and you can usually save a bet in case he hits. There are always pros and cons—this time betting the turn worked out all right.

Hand 170

Blinds	My Position	My Hand	My Chip Stack
8K/16K/2K (6-handed)	Button	K♦ Q♠	1.272 million

I have said it a lot, but I'll keep saying it if I have to: Everybody folds to me. I have K♦ Q♠ on the button and put in three times the big blind for a standard 48k raise. Both blinds fold, as I stack up another 34k. I now have approximately 1.3 million in chips.

Hand 171

Blinds	My Position	My Hand	My Chip Stack
8K/16K/2K (6-handed)	SB	5♣ 3♦	1.282 million

That was it for the hand by hand scenario, as I play extremely tight for the next four hands. I even fold my big blind for the second time in a row without a fight. Having won two out of two limping from the small blind I see no reason to change the pace. My 5♣ 3♦ is probably below the minimum requirement for a small blind limp, but I can't help noticing the extra "juice" lying out there. Without the 12k from the 6 X 2k ante I would fold in a heartbeat, but as it is I can't help myself. Emanuel taps the table behind me for the third time in a row, and the flop comes:

Bluffing is the only way to win this one! I bet 24k only to have Emanuel announce all-in instantly. No need to think about this one, as my hand hits the muck in a split second. I guess I should have followed the pattern from last time! Checking the flop would have saved me 24k, or if he checked behind me, at least given me more confidence to bluff on the turn.

Hand 172

Blinds	My Position	My Hand	My Chip Stack
8K/16K/2K (6-handed)	1st	Q♠ 6♠	1.234 million

I opt for something different, as I limp in first position with Q♠ 6♠. Sometimes it is good to throw a curve ball. The small and the big blind limp along. The flop comes:

Check, check, check.

Turn:

Check, check, check.
River:

Check, check, check.

Small blind Paul Wasicka wins the pot with A♥ T♥. Big blind Hans Martin Vogel folded A♦ 6♣.

Very uncharacteristic—nine checks in a row! I guess nobody really wanted to win this one. So why didn't I take charge? Let's see what happened on the different streets.

The Flop: They both check, and I think betting is the best play. A small attempt to win it right here! After all, there is 60k in the pot, and neither blinds took a stab at it. Of course that doesn't necessarily mean that they have nothing, but getting 2.5 to 1 on a 24k bet feels like the right idea.

The Turn: Both blinds check. I now have an up-and-down straight-draw on a total rainbow board. I could have chosen to bet, but this time it is a little bit more treacherous. On the flop a check-raise from either opponent would have resulted in an easy fold on my part, as I would be looking at Q-high no draw. This time around a check-raise would again result in a fold on my part, but at a much higher cost. Now I have some real potential to actually make a hand, and a bet right here could prove costly in more than one way. Not only would I lose the bet, but I would also lose a chance to realize the potential my hand possessed. Checking seems fine.

The River: After they both check, I'm in no hurry to get any money in the pot. The King is a terrible bluffing card. It couldn't have improved my hand unless I already had something, and my two previous checks indicated otherwise. What hands would I be bluffing anyway? The Jack-high and the Ten-high! Or to put it another way, hands that I could beat. There is no way Paul Wasicka was folding his AT. As a matter of fact I think he would welcome a bet from me—playing the hand for a check-call. Checking is obvious!

All in all, two good checks and a bad one! I could have pulled out the big machinery and bluffed my way through this pot, but even though I would like to, I am not trying to win each and every pot.

Hand 173

Blinds	My Position	My Hand	My Chip Stack
8K/16K/2K (6-handed)	BB	J♦ 5♥	1.216 million

A walk. Everybody folds to my big blind. Nice way to pick up 18k with a double-suited J5. It pays to have a reputation as a vicious big-blind defender.

Hand 174

Blinds	My Position	My Hand	My Chip Stack
8K/16K/2K	BB	A♥ 3♦	1.216 million
(6-handed)			

Hans Martin Vogl raises from the small blind to 50k. So far Hans had been very conservative with his hand selection. A raise out of the small blind should therefore be treated with the utmost respect.

For a heads-up confrontation A♥ 3♦ is very reasonable—especially in position. I expect a fair amount of checks from Hans if he misses the flop, and I can therefore use my positional advantage to pick up some uncontested pots.

The flop comes:

Hans checks. Positional advantage or not, it just looks like I have the best hand with a pair of Threes. Betting is a must as any card not pairing the board could potentially ruin my party. I will not allow him to do that for free!

I bet 66,000 into a 122,000 pot and "Der Vogl" quickly folds.

Hand 175

Blinds	My Position	My Hand	My Chip Stack
8K/16K/2K	2nd	J♠J♥	1.260 million
(6-handed)			

Hans Martin Vogl to my right opens in first position for 45k. I look down at J♠J♣ and have to decide what to do. Although Hans Martin is the only other big-stack at the table and therefore the one opponent I have to be extra careful against, reraising seems to be the clearly superior play. I want to win the hand right here and now, or if not, at least have a little more info about his hand going into the flop. Re-raising fulfills both criteria, so I make it a total of 145k.

After five quick folds, I add 79k to my stack.

Hand 176

Blinds	My Position	My Hand	My Chip Stack
8K/16K/2K (6-handed)	1st	Q♦J♣	1.339 million

Very next hand I'm in first position looking down at yet another two picture cards. No pair this time though, as I have to settle for Q♦J♣. Still I find it good enough for a six-handed challenge. I make it 48k to go, everybody folds, and once again I'm happy to win 34k right there.

Hand 177

Blinds	My Position	My Hand	My Chip Stack
8K/16K/2K (6-handed)	BB	A♠5♦	1.373 million

Everybody folds to Hans in the SB, who limps for 8k more. I check my A♠5♦ behind. Under normal circumstances my hand is definitely worth a raise but I guess I wanted to change the pace a little bit. Hans Martin could also very well be limping with a better hand than mine as I was quite certain that he would fold any mediocre to unplayable hand.

Flop:

Hans leads out 20k into a 44k pot. I have bottom pair, top kicker but before I get too excited I should consider the circumstances. Hans Martin definitely didn't bet with total air and it is therefore very likely that I am behind. Getting more than 3:1, or 64k:20k to be exact, is too good to pass up though, and I therefore elect to call. Turn:

Hans checks and I quickly bet 45k. Hans calls and the river comes:

Hans checks, and it is time to cut my losses. At this point there is just about 0% chance of me having the best hand. My chance of pulling off a successful bluff also seems very limited and a check is the only reasonable course of action.

Hans turns over J♠ T♣ for the win, and I can only regret that I played the hand a little too quickly. My call on the flop and my check on the river were fine, but my turn-bet wasn't especially genius. I guess there was a chance I could knock out drawing hands like T8, 98, flush-draws, etc., but I just don't think those were the type of hands Hans would lead out with.

Most of the time I was just beat, so I should have checked and taken the free card.

I guess I should have listened more carefully to the words of my friend, one of the all-time poker greats, Chip Reese: "Keep your losses at a minimum!"

Hand 178

Blinds	My Position	My Hand	My Chip Stack
8K/16K/2K (6-handed)	SB	J♠ 2♠	1.293 million

I have limped a couple of times from the small blind with pretty good results, but I felt like changing the pace. I made it 50k with J♠ 2♠, indicating that I had a big hand. It worked! Emanuel Seal quickly folded and I took down the pot for a 26k profit.

Hand 179

Blinds	My Position	My Hand	My Chip Stack
8K/16K/2K (6-handed)	SB	K♥ T♦	1.293 million

My German friend opens on the button for 45,000. I call another 37,000 in the SB with K♥ T♦ and the big blind folds. The flop comes:

I check rather cautiously and quite frankly I have no idea why! Fortunately Hans Martin checks right behind me, and it is now plausible that my pair of Tens are in front. The turn card is:

Not really the card I was dreaming about. It is a close call whether an Eight or an Ace was the worst card. Still, if my two Tens was the best hand on the flop, the only way he has me beat is if he is holding a Queen or a Seven. I decide to bet 40k—a medium probe bet to try to win the pot right here. It doesn't take him long to muck his hand and for me to take down the pot.

Aftermath: I should have bet small on the flop and avoided any ugly turn cards! As it was, it didn't cost me, but it very well could have.

Hand 180

Blinds	My Position	My Hand	My Chip Stack
8K/16K/2K (6-handed)	1 off the button	8♠ 6♠	1.362 million

It seems like my ratio of four raises to one limp has worked flawlessly. *Flawlessly* is of course too big a word, but at least it has kept everybody off my back, and that is the way I want to keep it. I limp 1 off the button with 8♠ 6♠. The button gets out of the way, both blinds tag along, and we have one of our rare three-handed flops.

Not bad! I have the 1497th best hand, which might be just enough to squeak in a victory. If nobody has anything this pot has Mr. Hansen written all over it. Both blinds check and it looks like I can take it right here. I like to take one card off though, just to make sure nobody is sand-bagging. I check as well and the turn is:

Check, check. I feel I have the information I need to take a small well-timed stab at the pot—24k should be sufficient. Both blinds quickly fold to my 24k bet, and rather safely I take down the 60k pot.

Hand 181

CRUCIAL HAND 9: Folding A♣ K♣ vs. Hans Martin Vogl

Blinds	My Position	My Hand	My Chip Stack
10K/20K/3K	1st	A♣ K♣	1.401 million
(6-handed)			

We are now playing 10k–20k blinds with a 3k ante. I'm in first position looking down at A♣ K♣. I raise to 66k hoping that somebody will make a move. My hand should be strong enough to deal with most situations, as it is hard for me to find a scenario where folding my hand pre-flop would be the right play. Maybe a multi-way all-in could persuade me to dump it? Even then I might be getting the right price, barring that any opponent is holding Aces.

First opponent folds, second one, third, fourth—I guess I have to settle for a nice little ante and blind pickup of 45k. But wait, Hans Martin Vogl in the big blind starts grabbing some chips, it looks like I have a customer after all. I was soon to realize it was not the kind of customer I was looking for. The only guy at the table with a somewhat frightening chip stack had decided to move all-in for 875,000! Boom! Had he taken the standard route of making it 250k to go, I probably would have moved all-in on him. Instead he had completely turned the tables on me! Needless to say I didn't like it at all!

Well, there was nothing I could do about it except deal with the task at hand to the best of my abilities. I have to call 809k more to win 969k—it sounds like 45% exactly. Normally I wouldn't hesitate to take A♣ K♣ against some random kamikaze maneuver only needing a 45% winning chance. But this was hardly random and definitely not a kamikaze move. I was up against a quality hand, no doubt about it. All I need to figure out is how much quality. I could rule out Aces, but that was about it.

Over the table I put him on TT through KK and AK. It sounds like we are in the ball park of 45%. Before getting stuck too much on the math though, I have to consider what would happen to my table presence in case of defeat. It would be absolutely devastating, as I would be down to about 525k and lose my dominant table-captain image. The fact of the matter is that I have been able to control the pace, and maneuver at my convenience. There is just no way I'm going to risk losing that on some messed up coin flip. The more I think about it, the easier the fold becomes! I fold and Hans Martin drags down the pot.

Hand 182

Blinds	My Position	My Hand	My Chip Stack
10K/20K/3K	BB	9♣ 8♠	1.332 million
(6-handed)			

Paul Wasicka opens for 50k on the button and I call automatically in the BB holding 9♣ 8♠. I have noticed that Paul loves those small pre-flop raises, but I have to admit I have no idea why. My main objective, especially in these precious ante times, is to steal as much as possible. It seems to me that a 50k raise fails to deliver a forceful punch, as any poker player with regard for their own abilities will call 30k more in order to win 98k. Earlier in the tournament I did fold 72o getting 3 to 1 pre-flop but since I still have nightmares about it I'll never do it again. The flop comes:

Nice flop! A pair and a flush draw is a hard hand to domi-nate. I choose to lead out for 72k and all of a sudden Paul loses interest in continuing this battle. Even though my hand was arguably strong enough to check-raise, I wasn't really look-ing for that kind of action. I was aiming for small pick-ups rather than big shoot-outs. A statement easily proven by my humongous lay-down the previous hand. Nice to get right back on track with a small win after my AK hand, which is still lurk-ing in the back of my mind.

Hand 183

Blinds	My Position	My Hand	My Chip Stack
10K/20K/3K (6-handed)	2nd	A♣J♥	1.388 million

I open in second position for 65k with A♣J♥. Everybody folds and I pick up the blinds and antes for a 45k gain.

Hand 184

Blinds	My Position	My Hand	My Chip Stack
10K/20K/3K (6-handed)	BB	J♦5♥	1.430 million

Robert Goldfarb shoves his last 48,000 into the middle and I insta-call in the BB. My hand is of absolutely no importance, as I have no players behind me to worry about. I have to call 28,000 more to win 96,000, which means I only need 23 % winning chance. Easy call!

I flip over J5o and he shows A♦8♣. The board comes:

Robert hits a straight and stays alive in the tournament.

Hand 185

Blinds	My Position	My Hand	My Chip Stack
10K/20K/3K	1 off the button	Q♦J♠	1.363 million
(6-handed)			

Paul Wasicka opens in first position for 60,000 and I call with Q♦ J♠, 1 off the button. The flop comes:

The nut straight—unfortunately there are also three hearts on the board. Paul checks and once again I move too fast. I bet 76k and Paul shows off some acting talent before folding. It didn't look like a serious consideration and it seems like I made a bad bet. In case Paul had a heart in his hand I wouldn't be a big favorite and I wouldn't be able to get rid of him. On the other hand if he did not have a heart he would most likely be drawing dead and quickly lose interest. By betting I achieved the complete opposite. I wanted to keep weak holdings interested and against heart-draws I wouldn't mind keeping the pot small anyway.

As it was I lost Paul on the flop with an ill-timed bet. Who knows how much more I could have won had I played my cards properly?

Hand 186

Crucial Hand 10: Big Score—Calling
Two All-ins with J♣ J♠

Blinds	My Position	My Hand	My Chip Stack
10K/20K/3K	2nd	J♣J♠	1.468 million
(6-handed)			

I open for 66,000 in second position with two Jacks. My short-stacked opponent Kevin Atkins in seat three moves all-in for a total 192,000 and I get ready to call in a flash. Before it gets back to me my full-tilt colleague Robert Goldfarb decides to join the party. He pushes his entire stack of 333,000 toward the middle and suddenly I'm facing not one but two all-in moves with my two Jacks.

My first instinct is to call, but since we are looking at a rather substantial investment and even more substantial pot, I felt it was best to take my time to try to figure it all out.

Kevin Atkins could have many hands for his re-raise, but Robert had to have a premium holding to justify his actions. After all he moved all-in on top of an all-in re-raise—he did *not* have two fives! The other part of the equation looks a little more appealing. I have to call 267k to win 619k—I need an approximately 30% winning chance. I'm far from 30% if Goldfarb turns over one of the three big pairs, but there are also some very rosy scenarios where I would have more than a 50% winning chance. After contemplating for a while I come to the conclusion that this is just one of those must-call situations. Too many times you will be up against counterfeit high cards or a pair of Nines and folding in those spots is just too costly an error. I call!

We have ourselves two juicy pots: the 604k main pot and a 282k side pot between me and Goldfarb—886k all together.

Show-time: Kevin reveals a feisty little Q♥ T♥, Robert "Full Tilt" Goldfarb turns over A♠ K♠ and I still have my J♣ J♠. I have seen worse, after all, it is relatively close! Robert is in the lead with 40%, I'm next with 35%, and Kevin has 25%. As far as the side pot goes I'm a 53%–47% favorite. No more betting, no more moves, let's turn the cards!

The flop comes:

Good flop for me! I am now way ahead with 60%, 29% for Robert, and 11% for Kevin.

Turn:

Reasonable turn! Me 74%, Rob 14%, Kev 12%.

River:

Great river! I have knocked out two guys in one hand and at the same time I cross the 2 million mark for the first time.

Hand 187

Blinds	My Position	My Hand	My Chip Stack
10K/20K/3K (4-handed)	1st	T♠9♥	2.018 million

In one hand we go from short-handed to super short-handed. Two players left the building last hand, which leaves us with only four players at the table. Aggressive behavior will prevail and it only seems fitting that I throw the first punch. I raise to 66,000 from first position with T♠9♥.

Hans Martin calls 46k in the big blind and the flop comes:

A gut shot and two over cards! Hans Martin checks and I fire 88k with Ten high! He looks at me, at the pot, at his cards, at the flop, at the TV production team and at the cameraman as if to say, Do I ever hit a flop? Fortunately for me he hasn't hit too many today, and I have been the main beneficiary! He disgustedly tosses his hand in the muck and I pick up another small one.

Hand 188

Blinds	My Position	My Hand	My Chip Stack
10K/20K/3K (4-handed)	BB	5♠4♦	2.103 million

Aggressive poker has a lot of added benefits. I am notorious for my blind defending and during this tournament it has really paid dividends.

Fold + fold + fold = 42,000. Sometimes poker is a walk in the park!

Hand 189

Blinds	My Position	My Hand	My Chip Stack
10K/20K/3K (4-handed)	SB	8♥ 4♥	2.122 million

I limp for 10k more in the SB with 84 suited. The BB checks his option. The flop comes:

Middle pair! I bet 24,000 and the big blind folds. Another 29k profit.

Hand 190

Blinds	My Position	My Hand	My Chip Stack
10K/20K/3K (5-handed)	BB	3♠ 3♦	2.145 million

We have been joined by Emanuel Seal at the table, which means we are now playing five-handed. Let me give you a quick chip count from the table:

Gus Hansen	2,145,000
Hans Martin Vogl	700,000
Paul Wasicka	530,000
Patrick Fletcher	196,000
Emanuel Seal	630,000

Patrick Fletcher challenges my BB when he moves all-in for 196,000 from second position. Everybody folds and it is up to me in the big blind with two Treys. I have to call 176,000 to win 241,000, which means I need a 42% winning chance. Apart from the dream scenarios where Patrick moves all-in with A2, A3, or 22 it is either going to be 50–50 or 81–19 in his favor. I think it is fairly close, but calling comes out ahead! On top of the math pointing in that direction I also have a little agenda of my own. Remember yesterday when somebody got me off my game, and as a result I played some hands rather stupidly? Remember his name? Correct, Patrick Fletcher! If he was able to mess me up on a quiet Tuesday in Melbourne he might be able to do it again. Knocking him out, or at least trying to, seems like the right strategy: I call!

Patrick turns over A♠ T♥ and I am a tiny favorite in our coin-flip clash. The flop comes:

60–40 my way. Turn:

Bad card! 95–5 his way! I guess I won't get rid of Mr. Fletcher this time. River:

He wins! Patrick Fletcher is back in action with 417k.

Hand 191

Blinds	My Position	My Hand	My Chip Stack
10K/20K/3K	BB	K♦ 3♦	1.924 million
(5-handed)			

Final hand of day three. As always I remind everybody how unfortunate it would be to go broke on the last hand of the day. Apparently Paul Wasicka is not listening. He opens on the button for 60,000 and Hans Martin gets out of the way to start wrapping up his chips. I look down at K♦ 3♦. A great opportunity for a re-raise, just to emphasize that I meant what I said about going broke. Seriously, I think it would have more than a fair chance of working, but sadly enough I don't pull the trigger. I call and the flop comes:

Nothing with a nothing draw! I check and Paul bets 65,000. I muck my hand and Paul shows me A♠ 5♦. The day is over and I start racking up my chips!

End of Day 3

Recap, Day 3

Another solid day in Melbourne! I started with 562k and ended with 1.861 million. I had some good fortune in a couple of big hands against Lee Nelson, Paul Wasicka, and Robert Goldfarb. Nobody can survive a big field full of top players without a little bit of luck.

But that was not the only luck I encountered on day three. Once again I avoided the dominant big stacks that very well could have interfered with my plans. After my big hand against Lee Nelson I was the table captain throughout the day, which enabled me to be in charge both mentally and physically. There is another little luck factor that never gets any attention. I don't know if people fail to see the whole picture or if they are just too engulfed in their own misery, but the fact of the matter is: My opponents had bad hands! At least that is the way it seemed to me! People tell stories about their bad and unlucky hands, their opponents' great hitting percentage, somebody might even mention a couple big hands they won, but nobody ever talks about their opponents' misfortune. Most of my winnings today came from my opponents holding absolutely nothing! Don't get me wrong, it didn't just fall into my lap. I had to be alert and on top of the situation to take full advantage. Let me explain by showing you the four scenarios I am talking about:

Me good hand *vs*. You bad hand = I win
Me bad hand *vs*. You good hand = You win
Me good hand *vs*. You good hand = Big coin-flip
Me bad hand *vs*. You bad hand = Should be 50–50, but
   today I won them all.

For the most part I relied on controlled aggression and my big stack.

Three days are gone and I am up there with the overall chip

leaders. Equally important, we are down to only fourteen players. I am feeling great about the way I am playing and very much looking forward to day four.

The official chip count is as follows:

Jimmy Fricke	2,664,000
Gus Hansen	1,861,000
Andree Black	1,759,000
Patrik Antonius	1,637,000
Marc Karam	1,249,000
Julius Colman	1,018,000
Hans Vogl	849,000
Jonas Buskas	819,000
Kristy Gazes	713,000
Paul Wasicka	560,000
Jacob Glassl	464,000
Patrick Fletcher	462,000
Dennis Huntly	449,000
Emanuel Seal	434,000

CHAPTER 4

DAY 4

My Advice Before Today's Play

Keep the Pressure, but Avoid the Small-Stack All-in

It's a new day, things are looking good, you are in the money, you are playing the Aussie Millions and you are one of the chip-leaders sporting a healthy stack. You have a new table assignment and are looking forward to meeting your new combatants. You take a walk, find your table, look around, and with a grin on your face you say to yourself, "It looks good!" Not so much because of the unfamiliar faces, since at this point you have no idea what they will bring to the table, but because of the stack sizes surrounding you. You are the big stack at the table, and the only player you even have to worry about is conveniently placed to your right. It looks like a field day! You can pick on the short stacks at your convenience, taking advantage of their desire to survive that in turn will lead to reluctance to participate in the action. What could go wrong? Without taking any big risks you can slowly but surely add valuable blinds and antes to your stack by picking your spots and relentlessly attacking the poor, defenseless, innocent little chip stacks!

Or am I missing something? Well, there is one little thing I forgot to tell you: the small stacks are allowed to fight back! They usually only have one weapon at their disposal, but unfortunately for you it is a powerful one: the all-in move.

Let's change the scenery for a moment. One of the best ways to improve your game is to have long and healthy poker discussions with your peers. I have had those conversations many times with my good friend Howard Lederer. Needless to say one of our favorite topics is the ever-infatuating all-in! Howard is always eager to emphasize the importance of not giving your opponent the perfect all-in. I have to admit, once again I agree. All-ins are not easy to deal with, especially when they put you right on the spot, knowing you almost get the right price, but not quite. There's no chance even to make up for it with a solid value bet along the way, since your opponent is all-in. The best way to avoid it is to constantly keep an eye on surrounding stack sizes and deal with it to the best of your abilities.

I will give you some guidelines that I find appropriate when considering whether to call a pre-flop all-in. There are three components to take into account: your own cards, the pot odds, and the supposed strength of your opponent's hand. When mixing them all together you should be able to determine whether your winning chance exceeds your pot odds. If they do, calling is the right play. Of course, all three are very important if you want to compute an exact answer, but one of them constitutes a serious problem. You hear the words "I just knew what he had!" time and time again, when somebody makes a good read. But for some reason the same somebody keeps a very low profile when the read is way off the chart! Exact reads aren't easy to come by—especially not in pre-flop situations. Since it is impossible to know for sure what your opponent is holding, I believe it is better to exclude that parameter entirely from the equation. And then there were two! Given the uncertainty about your opponent's hand, your own hand becomes somewhat speculative. With little to no evidence about what you are up against, it is almost impossible to determine how good your T♠ 9♠ is. How the different hands match up are very key, since T♠ 9♠ is pretty sweet against 4♣ 4♦, but ugly against A♥ T♥. Let's exclude your own hand as well.

Down to one! The chart I will present to you is based solely on pot odds. The chart will show pot odds and the respective winning chance you need given those odds, and a brief comment about what to do about it. If you have a lot of trouble turning pot odds into approximate winning chances, you'd better put the book down, do yourself a favor, and study! One last important thing: This chart should only be used as a measure against small-stack all-ins that do not in any way threaten your survival.

WHEN TO CALL A SHORT STACK ALL-IN

Pot-Odds	Winning Chance You Need to Make the Call Profitable	My Opinion
4 to 1	20%+	I am not even gonna answer that one!
3 to 1	25%+	Must call!
2 to 1	33%+	If you are sure you are dominated fold, else call!
1x to 1	40%+	Grey area where your own judgment should be the deciding factor
1 to 1	50%+	You better have a good reason to call

Let's take an example: Blinds are 12k–24k with a 4k ante, you are in control with 1.4 million, and John Doe to your right has just over a million. He is irrelevant for the exercise at hand, as we are strictly talking small-stacked, pre-flop all-ins. The key opponents are the four short-stacked players to your left ranging from 150k to 300k. How should you proceed against each of them?

A standard raise or steal attempt at this level is normally in the 75k range. But there is nobody forcing you to stick with the norm if it doesn't float your boat. You want to manipulate the size of your bet so it fits your purposes and makes it uncomfortable for your opponents to proceed. Easier said than done! Let's do the best we can and take them case by case.

1. Against the "tiny" with 150k there is no middle ground. If you say A, B is coming along for the ride. Best play: Move all-in yourself and put your opponent to the test!

2. Against the "medium" with 225k you are allowed to fold. It might not be correct to fold, but it is at least a viable option. Raising it to 75k followed by a 225k all-in from the big blind leaves you with pot-odds of approximately 7 to 3. You need a 31% winning chance to call. According to the chart you have to convince yourself of a bad match-up to fold. You have basically put yourself in a position where you are "forced" to stick in the remaining 150k with whatever napkins you are holding. Not what you wanted to accomplish! A couple of years ago I put myself in that exact spot in the WPT finals at Bellagio. Within a couple of rounds I had managed to call three all-ins because I got the right price. What had actually happened was that I had wasted a lot of money with the second best hand, because I failed to see past the tip of my own nose. I could have miniraised to 50k, limped, or folded, all three being better options. *Best play:* Keep the aggressive touch, and try to manipulate the bet size so they fit into your agenda. Pairs and high cards go up in value whereas the speculative small suited connectors become exactly that—speculative.

3. Against "Biggie" with 300k, you can keep a more straightforward approach. Folding is okay if your holding is not up to the All-In task. Just remember that pushing the entire pile will be the preferred technique for even this stack size. Best play: Have the best hand when they move all-in!☺

To go back to the beginning, what is the best way to deal with small-stack all-ins? Here are four quick tips:

1. Keep the pot-odds in perspective and play accordingly.
2. Instead of raising aimlessly, analyze the situation and look a couple of moves ahead.
3. Be aware of what possible counter-measures might be available to your opponents.
4. Don't get stuck on standard raises, but use your imagination.

Back to the Table

Hand 192

Blinds	My Position	My Hand	My Chip Stack
12K/24K/4K	Button	T♣ 3♦	1.861 million

We are now starting day four. I am seated at a five-handed table with the guy I consider my toughest opponent, Patrik Antonius. Luckily for me he is seated to my right, which means I have the luxury of seeing what he is doing before I have to make a decision. The rest of the table consists of Jakob Glassl (Germany) with 460k in seat two, Dennis Huntly (Australia) with 450k in seat three, and Marc Karam (Canada) with 1.25 million in chips in seat four. There is a total of 5.66 million on the table. I am the chip leader with 1.86 million in chips, but Patrik in seat five is right behind me with 1.64 million.

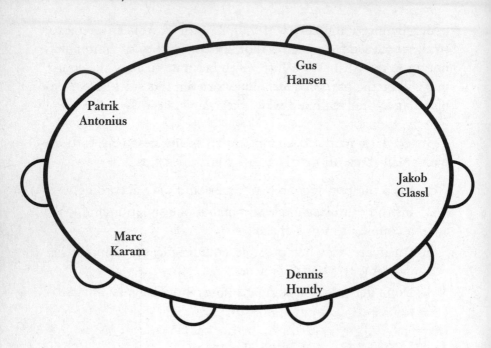

As mentioned above I have position on Patrik and the luxury of following his every move, but Jakob Glassl relied on a totally different kind of luxury—the Phil Hellmuth luxury—sleeping late. Showing up a couple of hours late is one of the many publicity stunts Hellmuth uses to create some attention when he finally enters the room. In his defense I will admit that the first level or two in a major championship is fairly insignificant in determining the final winner, so I am sure it is a well-calculated risk-reward maneuver that Mr. Hellmuth is pulling off. But showing up late for a five-handed table on day four is a totally different story. With a stack size of 460k, antes at 4k, and blinds at 12k–24k, Der Jakob better have an extremely good reason not to be here.

Bottom line: I'm not going to complain about it. It makes my job as an aggressive, premier blind- and ante-stealer a lot

easier. Every time the hand is folded to my button, I only have
to worry about Dennis Huntly in the big blind, since the small
blind is absent.

And that is the exact scenario for the first hand of the day:
Marc and Patrik fold and I'm left with the button against Mr.
Huntly. I am not going to let that opportunity slip away and I
quickly throw in 72k for a standard three-times-the-big-blind
raise. My actual holding is a lesser concern, since I have a feeling that Mr. Huntly would be very reluctant to leave the table
almost before he sat down, making him somewhat of a vulnerable target. In a specific scenario like this I rate my pickup vig
to be in the neighborhood of 75%, making my raise a positive
equity play right off the bat. On top of that I also win some of
the hands post-flop, adding even more potential to my hand.
All in all, a must-raise from the button!

Unfortunately Dennis calls and I have to go through the
well-known look-at-my-cards routine. My T♣ 3♦ is not what I
was looking for, but it has potential!

Flop comes:

I guess that was some of the potential I was talking about.

Dennis checks and I have to consider my options with my
beautiful top pair. There is a total of 176k in the pot and my
opponent has just about 380 left. There is a time for careful
play, good reads, and big laydowns, I just don't believe this is
one of them. Brute force seems to fit better into the equation.
Grabbing hold of the 176k in the middle is my main priority,
and I can't find a better way to do that than by pushing my
stack. I bet 500k, enough to put Dennis all-in, and he quickly

folds. A nice pick-up with a seemingly unplayable hand! Bear in mind though, that in this instance there were factors weighing much heavier than my actual holding. My post-flop decision was obviously made a lot easier by the extremely kind Ten-high board, but it is very likely I would have found a way to drag down the pot anyway—if Mr. Huntly missed, that is!

Hand 193

CRUCIAL HAND 11: My Toughest Opponent Gone— Busting Patrik Antonius

Blinds	My Position	My Hand	My Chip Stack
12K/24K/4K	BB	J♣J♠	1.953 million

After a couple of uneventful hands in which I wasn't involved, we are headed for a classic battle of the blinds. Everybody folds to Patrik in the small blind, who limps for another 12k. Even with the very significant ante, I don't think Patrik would limp with total garbage. As a matter of fact I think he has somewhat of a decent holding, since I know that Patrik is very reluctant to get involved in big-stack shoot-outs out of position. I look down at two Jacks and contemplate how much to raise.

I raise 72k more to a total of 96k, hoping to win the blinds and antes right here and now. Even with position I'm actually not too eager either to play a big all-in pot. I figure there are still targets out there more gullible than a guy who easily made my top-ten list of pretty, Finnish poker-players. Furthermore I'm not interested in facing any tough big-bet decisions later on in the hand when over cards hit the board. Especially not against a player of Patrik's caliber!

Patrik calls the 72k and there is now 212k in the middle. So, once again I would have preferred my opponent to fold pre-flop, but at least this time I enter the post-flop battle with a little more ammunition in hand.

Flop comes:

Middle set! What a beautiful flop. Of course the 9♥ could have been the 6♦, eliminating most straight- and flush-draws, but perfect set-ups are hard to find. I can just hope that if I get any action on this hand, that it is from a pair of Aces and not some straight-flush-draw. More often than not he will be drawing almost dead, in which case my biggest concern should be to extract as much money as possible from Patrik's stack.

Patrik checks, I bet 110k, just over half the pot, and Patrik quickly calls. I'm not quite sure what it means, since I thought Patrik was prone to check-raise with a lot of different hands. It feels like the check-calls is more of a mediocre holding. No aces, no flush-draw—bottom pair or a straight-draw seems more likely! With that in mind it is time for the turn.

Not really what I wanted to see! Completes two different straight-draws, and my hand is downgraded from the "nuts" to the "third-nuts"—Both KT and T8 have me beat. "Fifth-nuts" if you want to throw AA and QQ in the mix, but for obvious reasons I have discarded those.

Patrik checks, and even though the turn was a little bit of a scare-card I'm not about to check the hand down. I go into the tank, trying to figure out the best amount to bet. With 432k in the pot, and respectively 1.7 million and 1.5 million in front of me and Patrik there is a wide range of possibilities.

Even though the two straights worry me, I don't have to spend too much energy on those ugly scenarios, because if indeed he has made a straight all the money is going into the middle anyway and all I can do is to hope for a lucky river-card. No, I have to figure out the best way to deal with all the other possible holdings—the KQ, QJ, JT, T9, and I could go on! Although I kind of discarded the flush-draw and various ace-holdings because of the post-flop action, they are still lurking in the back of my mind, too.

So, what to do? Patrik will have somewhere in between 0–14 outs. Optimal strategy would therefore be to bet an amount that deals beautifully with all the different number of outs. Unfortunately that is absolutely impossible. What is possible is to take an average of his outs, and then make a bet that makes it unprofitable for him to draw. Even though seven outs seems to be the right number, I like to overestimate my opponent's chances when I make my calculations. Eight outs it is! Since I have a general tendency to over-bet, the math is going to be pretty accurate anyway.

So where does that leave me? Well, at this point I have narrowed it down to three bet-size categories:

1. *The small bet*: Betting between 200k and 250k doesn't put a lot of pressure on any kind of draw. Furthermore, it might give me a major headache when facing a large river-bet when an Eight, Ten, King, or heart hits the board. On a positive note it leaves a lot of room for Patrik to check-raise me and probably also keeps most of the drawing-dead hands in the loop. I'm not a big fan, but it has some merit.

2. *The pot-sized bet*: A bet in the 450k range builds a bigger pot, and doesn't give the eight-out drawing hands the proper pot-odds or even implied odds to call. The door is still open for an ingenious check-raise. Even though I might lose Patrik as a customer with this somewhat larger bet, I am not as interested in winning 250k more as I'm worried about a 1.5 million loss. I like this bet size.

3. *The all-in bet*: 1.7 million! Pulling the trigger is often-times my favorite play. No more nonsense, no more worrying about disgusting river bets, just the plain and simple

"Do you wanna dance?" puts on ultimate pressure! It doesn't allow anybody to draw out on you unless they are on some kind of suicide mission, and I am fairly certain that Patrik doesn't belong in that category. Last but not least, assuming a fold, taking 210k from my toughest competitor and thereby putting some distance between us is in itself a very satisfying result. On the other hand it fails to win more money against weaker hands as it will scare everything but the premium hands away. It doesn't allow Patrik to attempt any sneaky check-raise bluffs, either. I love the play, but here it seems to come up a tad bit short. My hand is probably too strong for that maneuver.

That is it for all the math, but there is still one factor to consider—Patrik's perception of the whole enchilada. Since Patrik started playing in the Big Game and I started playing online poker at Full Tilt, we have had plenty of chances to play together, giving both of us some insights of each other's strengths and weaknesses. I am certain that Patrik would attach serious strength to an all-in bet on my part—maybe even so much that he would lay down some very strong hands he would otherwise have chosen to check-raise with given the opportunity. Another indicator that the all-in bet isn't suitable for this specific situation!

I gave the pot-sized bet the notch, and decided to add 68k to spice it up a bit. I have to admit I don't know how long I spent going over the various scenarios, but I later found out that my time-consuming thought process played a significant role in Patrik's decision-making. As soon as I pushed 500k toward the middle, Patrik announced all-in, and just as quickly I called.

He turned over A♥ 8♥ for top pair nut-flush draw, and I showed J♣ J♠ for a set of Jacks.

Afterward he told me that when I deliberated for that long,

he thought it was whether to value-bet a weak Ace, try to bluff, or maybe just give up the pot, all of which would not only give him the best hand but also the best draw, making his all-in move a gimme!

As it turned out my careful considerations were merely to decide on the right bet size, and didn't indicate anything whatsoever about the strength of my hand. My initial read was a little bit off too, as I had misjudged Patrick's hand on the flop! He not only had an Ace, he had the flush-draw to boot.

Had Patrik played the hand straightforwardly and check-raised the flop, all the money would have been in the middle a long time ago. Instead he slow-played his hand, as I easily could have been the one drawing dead. Not an unreasonable assumption at all! I personally have a preference for the straightforward play, but all that doesn't matter now. All the money is in the middle and the river card is the only thing standing between Patrik, me, and the 3.5 million pot.

Against my set of Jacks, Patrik has eleven outs with one card to come, making mc a 3 to 1 favorite, or 75%–25% favorite if you prefer.

River:

What a big card! Patrik was out and I was in the lead! Whoever would have come up with the right end of the stick in this hand would be well prepared for a serious stab at the title. Strangely enough the hand started out with both of us taking a conservative approach, but ended up being the biggest pot in the tournament so far. That is what happens in a blind-versus-blind match-up where both players connect heavily with the flop—sparks are bound to fly. I could have tried to avoid a big clash by moving all-in on the turn, but given the opposition it was worth it to take the extra, well-calculated risk to try to deliver a striking blow. Luckily for me no heart showed up!

After all the commotion had settled, I counted my chips, which totaled a whopping 3.729 million. With twelve players left I had amassed more than 25% of all the chips in the tournament, and barring a series of unfortunate events I was on cruise control to the final table!

Hand 194

Blinds	My Position	My Hand	My Chip Stack
12K/24K/4K	1 off the button	Q♦J♣	3.709 million

After Patrik was eliminated two new players were assigned to our table.

Julius Colman in seat five, Jonas Buskas in seat six. Jakob Glassl, Dennis Huntly, and Marc Karam were still to my left in that order. Jonas Buskas didn't stay with us long as he and Julius Colman got entangled in an AQ vs. AK battle, and Julius's AK held up. Back to five-handed it is! With a total of 6.9 million on the table and me holding the largest share, 3.7 million to be exact, I was planning to dominate the table. If anybody showed any kind of fear of getting knocked out, I was going to be right up in their face, raising their blinds with meticulous persistence.

I open 1 off the button with Q♦J♣ for 72k. Jakob Glassl, on the button, who is still in the midst of stacking his chips from the previous hand, looks quickly at his cards and moves all-in! The blinds fold, and action is back to me. There is now 642k in the pot and I have to put in 442k to call. I need slightly more than 40% winning chances to make this a profitable call. Against the small pairs I'm okay, but that is about it!

The big pairs, the AJ, the KQ are not nice to think about, tipping the scale in favor of a fold. Although the math is important, it becomes somewhat obsolete compared to the "obvious" read I have!

Ten players left in a major championship spread out on two five-handed tables. It is Jakob Glassl's first top-ten appearance and he just won a decent-sized pot. The chip leader to his right opens the pot for a raise and he barely glances at his cards before announcing all-in. Is he making a move or is it the real deal? I for one have no doubts that the all-in move represents genuine strength. Just about nobody I know pulls a move like that!

Jakob Glassl had been short stacked for a while but had gained some momentum winning a pot from Dennis Huntly—one of the other short stacks at the table. I don't think he wanted to throw it all away the very next hand on some crazy bluff against me! Adding it all together, my QJ was starting to look very bleak!

I folded and Jakob took down the second pot in a row.

Hand 195

Blinds	My Position	My Hand	My Chip Stack
12K/24K/4K	1 off the button	A♠ Q♥	3.581 million

Julius Colman opens in first position for 70k. I am next to act and look down at A♠ Q♥. I re-raise to 222,000 and the button and the blinds fold. A little bit to my surprise, Julius Colman calls. At this point I have no specific read on Mr. Colman, but it is obvious he is not holding two napkins. I still figure to be ahead, but could be behind as AK TT are in the realm of possible holdings.

The flop comes:

Julius checks and it is time to find out whether I do have the best hand or not. I figure a small stab should be enough to find out. I bet 300k into a 500k pot and fortunately Julius quickly folds.

Even though the result was very satisfying, I made a minor mistake on the flop. Choosing the right bet size can save you tons of chips at the end of the day.

With no significant draws on the flop, a "tiny" bet of more than 200k would have been sufficient to knock out hands like JT of clubs. If I was behind, neither 200k nor 300k would win me the pot. It is not only about winning and losing pots. It is just as important to win the maximum and lose the minimum!

Hand 196

Blinds	My Position	My Hand	My Chip Stack
12K/24K/4K	1 off the button	J♣ 8♣	3.803 million

I open 1 off the button for 72k with J♣ 8♣ only to have Marc Karam in the big blind re-raise to 300k. I'm not very eager to put in another 228k with Jack high, especially since Marc Karam had kept a fairly low profile until now. I have a tendency to give people a lot of credit the first time around. If the pressure continues and they start to re-raise a lot, I am of course forced to change course! Until then, I can afford to let this one go. I fold and Marc Karam picks up the pot.

Hand 197

Blinds	My Position	My Hand	My Chip Stack
12K/24K/4K	1st	A♠ 6♥	3.727 million

Next hand I open for 71k in first position with A♠ 6♥. We are still playing five-handed, so A6o is a reasonable holding. It is folded to the big blind, who calls another 47k. Julius Colman is second in chips at the table, so he is the only one who can really put a dent in my stack. The flop comes:

Not a great flop, but that really hasn't slowed me down so far, so I see no reason to change gears now. Julius checks and I fire a classic 53% bullet—93k into a 174k pot. Julius folds without hesitation. Once again the continuation bet has proven itself to be a very important tool in successful No Limit Hold'em tournament strategy!

Hand 198

Blinds	My Position	My Hand	My Chip Stack
12K/24K/4K	BB	J♠ 7♠	3.826 million

Marc Karam opens on the button for 65k. An unusually small amount considering it is me in the big blind and defending against such a tiny raise is a must. I am holding J♠ 7♠ and looking forward to seeing a lot of spades on the flop. No such luck.

Flop:

Middle pair instead. I lead out for 103k, Marc doesn't want to tag along and I pick the 162k in the middle. In my opinion, it is a lot better to lead out and send the message right away instead of leaving the initiative in the hands of the raiser—especially with hands of vulnerable middle pair nature.

Hand 199

Blinds	My Position	My Hand	My Chip Stack
15K/30K/5K	SB	4♥ 7♠	3.919 million

We are now at a new level and chip counts are as follows: myself: 3.9 million, Jakob Glassl: 634k, Dennis Huntly: 223k, Marc Karam: 1.148 million, Julius Colman: 1.099 million.

With a 5k ante and blinds of 15k–30k the playing-it-safe days are over! This is a level for brute force, meticulous violence, and bad behavior—although I will have to admit for some, more than others. It costs 70k a round to play at this table and apart from me nobody has enough money to sit back, relax, and enjoy the movie. Picking up pots has become not only crucial for survival, but an utmost necessity for accumulating chips. I for one am a big believer in accumulating chips as it is the only way you will be in a commanding position once the final table comes around!

Let's take a minute or two going over the mathematical aspect of the situation.

The urgency with which you should proceed depends largely

on your chip stack compared to the blinds and antes. Your opponents' chip stacks are of course relevant too as they give you an indication of how desperate they are.

A very helpful tool in determining the appropriate measures is "M." M is a concept introduced a couple of years back by my good friend, backgammon guru Paul Magriel. It basically tells you how long you can survive without playing a hand before going bust. M is always measured in number of rounds you can afford with your current chip stack. Using Mr. Huntly as an example the two relevant numbers are 223k, his chip stack, and 70k, the cost of living per round. Dividing 223 by 70 you get approximately 3.2 rounds. I am not going to cover all the specific details about M, but just inform you of some quick guidelines used by a lot of pros:

M>20—deep-stacked, flying high as an eagle
20>M>7—medium-stacked, cruising at a somewhat
    comfortable altitude, since this is where you will spend
    most of your adult tournament life
7>M>3—short-stacked, prepare for crash-landing
M<3—good-bye

As you can see Mr. Huntley had better start making a move or else he will very soon be saying *"arriverderci."* Once he's reached an M of 3.2 due to the increase in blinds and antes, desperate measures should prevail. Waiting just a couple more hands before he announces the famous all-in words could be devastating. By doubling up right away he will get back to an M of about 7, giving him a little breathing room. If he lets his stack drizzle down before he attempts to double up, he will just get back to his starting point of approximately 3.2—if he wins the hand, that is! He will have risked everything and accomplished nothing. Mr. Huntly should pull out his trigger finger right now if he wants to make an impact on the final table.

For you sitting at home my sound advice will be to never ever enter the M<3 area! Of course it could happen due to unfortunate circumstances, but chances are that if you ever allow yourself to get there, you will have made some serious errors along the way. Not taking the blind and ante structure seriously is simply a recipe for disaster.

Back to the action! Dennis didn't take my "kamikaze advice" as he folded in first position. Admittedly a little caution should be exercised, as one of the sickest all-in callers of all time is in the small blind. Marc and Julius fold and it is up to me in the small blind. Jakob Glassl in the big blind has 634k left and an M of 9. Normally I consider it a must-raise situation facing a single opponent in a medium-low M environment. For some reason this time I just decided otherwise. I folded my 7♠4♥ and Jakob got a very unusual walk in the big blind. Maybe it was for advertising purposes—I of course made sure that every-body around the table was aware of my "tight" fold in the small blind. Maybe it was because of my poor holding—Even I think 74 off is a sub-par holding. And maybe I just didn't like the size of Jakob's chip stack. There wasn't enough money to scare him away from any decent holding, and too much to tango without some precautions. It was obviously a mixture of them all.

Funny how you sometimes spend the break trying to figure out the optimal strategy for the five different players around the table. You come to the conclusion that at least four of them should be pushing the envelope because of the high structure and low Ms—only to sit down and witness a most peculiar walk. Maybe it is just time for me to reconsider my strategy!

Hand 200

CRUCIAL HAND 12: Folding A♣ K♦ vs. Jimmy Fricke

Blinds	My Position	My Hand	My Chip Stack
15K/30K/5K	1st	A♣ K♦	3.84 million

It didn't take long before I had to reconsider anyway! Our five-handed table had vanished, which meant that the situation at hand had changed severely. Dennis Huntly played correctly and took a stab at it, only to see his hopes of victory dwindle away as he lost the hand to a full house. With eight players left it was decided to combine the two four-handed tables into one eight-handed preliminary final table. Day five, Friday, was going to be the real final table with only seven players, so one more player has to get knocked out before the day was over. That of course brings the well-known Bubble/TV factor into play. Over the years I have seen plenty of suspicious plays made because a TV appearance was of utmost importance to some players. Hopefully I can increase my chip stack by picking on those vain souls among us!

The line-up is as follows: Seat 1: Hans Martin Vogl, 785k; seat 2: Gus Hansen, 3.84 million; seat 3: Marc Karam, 1.47 million; seat 4: Julius Colman, 1.17 million; seat 5: Jimmy Fricke, 3.97 million; seat 6: Andy Black, 1.797 million; seat 7: Jakob Glassl, 535k; seat 8: Kristy Gazes, 1.385 million.

I will from now on try to give more precise chip counts, not only for myself but also the other players. Knowing the size of your opponent's chip stack has become increasingly more important with the ladder principle lurking around and some serious prize money on the line.

Blinds are still 15k–30k with a 5k ante, so with eight people around the table you can pick up a whopping 85k on a successful steal attempt. I open in first position for 100k with A♣ K♦, hoping that someone will make a move as I'm prepared to play a big pot. Oops, not that big!

The only guy who could make me step on the brakes has entered the building—Jimmy Fricke. Jimmy raises to 325k and it is another 225k for me to call. How I handle this situation is absolutely crucial, as Jimmy and I have more than half the chips in the tournament. Making the right or the wrong move could very well mean the difference between a solid chip lead and a place in obscurity. I take my time before coming up with the verdict. I want to make sure I consider every angle before committing to much money on Ace-high.

1. Folding! Seems to fit perfectly into a tournament-strategy scheme. Avoid the big shoot-out and cruise to third place before making a move! On the other hand it strikes me as a lay-down-and-die maneuver in which I shouldn't look at my hand for the next couple of hours—or at least till four more people are out of the tournament. My hand is way too good for that kind of bend-over tactic. I have never played that way, and I doubt I ever will! Discarded!

2. Calling! Keeps the pot at a manageable size. Delays the decision till after the flop, at which point I will have a lot more information about the strength of my hand—basically playing AK as a drawing hand. On the downside it fails to take charge with what is most likely the best starting hand and leaves the initiative in the hands of a young aggressive internet-player. Submissive, but keeps the all-important ladder-principle in perspective. Not great—still looking for better options.

3. Re-raising to 1 million with the intention of folding to an all-in move! Fights back instead of retaliating! This would force Jimmy to make a decision that could end up being his last. I don't think he is ready for that unless he is

holding a monster. I pick up 405k in profits if he obeys orders and folds all inferior Ace-holdings as well as medium-small pairs—a very likely and profitable scenario! Sends a message for future reference—don't re-raise me unless you are prepared to go all the way! Loses a cool million to AA and KK, and maybe QQ and AK if Jimmy decides to go berserk. Much more "in-your-face" type of poker. Looks like the winner!

4. Re-raising to 1 million with the intention of going all the way—all-in! The all-out strategy! Has the same upsides as the previous play, but takes it a step too far. The downside of leaving the table in eighth place, when Jimmy turns over two Aces, would be unbearable. I have much better use for my last 2.84 million in chips. Leaving all sound tournament strategy at home is simply too crazy for me given the circumstances. Discarded!

The "non-committed-re-raise" comes out clearly ahead in the polls, but for some reason I decide to just call. I can't explain the rationale behind it, but somehow I convinced myself to take the careful route.

The flop comes:

A solid miss! I follow my conservative pre-flop path and tap the table. Jimmy bets 400k and, a tad bit dejected, I decide to muck my cards. Jimmy takes down the 735k pot and puts a small but still significant gap between our chip stacks—I am down to 3.51 million and Jimmy crosses the 4M mark with 4.375 million.

I carefully analyzed my pre-flop options and came up with the wrong decision. Did I at least do a little better after the flop? Hard to say, but I will give you my best guesstimate.

Checking goes hand in hand with my pre-flop action of only calling Jimmy's re-raise. It follows the unwritten rule of checking to the raiser—the only problem is it's a bad rule! It leaves the initiative to the raiser, who can proceed at will. The only time you should be happy about checking to the raiser is when you have no pair, no draw, no nothing and check-folding is your only reasonable option. If there is the slightest bit of doubt in your mind as to whether you do have the best hand, leading out should be seriously considered. Of course I do have no pair, no draw, but my nothing is as good as it gets. It sounds like I'm about to beat myself up because of a horrible check, but actually I'm not. Both checking and leading out have some merits, but considering that I want to tread the waters carefully being up against the chip-leader, I believe checking to be the slightly superior play.

So, I check and Jimmy bets 400k—no surprise there! I have to call 400k more to win 1.135 million. I'm behind all pocket pairs and hands that connected with the flop, but I could also have a crushing lead against hands like AQ, KQ, and AJ. Judging from the updates I have received throughout the tournament, Jimmy is not one to back down. A continuation-bet on his part is to be expected, and therefore unfortunately doesn't really reveal anything about the strength of his hand. With Jimmy's holding being somewhere in between this and that, pot-odds of almost 3 to 1 seems to be more than adequate. I do have a couple of problems though.

1. The hand is not over if I call. I could be facing substantial action on turn and river, action that would surely eliminate me as a contestant for this pot, unless an Ace or King shows up.

2. Pot-size. The pot is already containing 1.135 million— 1.535 million if I call. When I first looked down at AK I was looking for a big showdown with one of the smaller stacks—not with the chip-leader. As the hand has progressed I am getting more and more gun-shy because of the devastating proportions the pot might reach.

3. Clarity. To this day I have no idea what Jimmy is holding, making my ensuing decisions ultimately much harder.

Playing big pots, in the dark, out of position, against the chip-leader, with nothing but Ace-high and a hunch is not very appetizing. All of the above points in the direction of a tight but solid fold! On the other hand I don't want to give Jimmy the impression that he can just walk all over me—bet at his leisure and have me fold at his command. Add in my "very realistic" chance of having the best hand—suddenly it looks like a clear-cut call!

There are obviously pros and cons no matter what I do. Given the circumstances I think it's a tight fit. As a poker player I lean toward the call as I'm not sure Jimmy would have the stomach to pull the trigger one more time with inferior holdings—allowing me to win the pot without further ado, if indeed I have the best hand. As a tournament player and ladder-climber I believe "the fold" has a big advantage. Folding is fine.

Check-raising was of course another "legal" option, but apart from seeing Paul Wasicka successfully pull off that stunt a couple of times, it's a little rich! You better be "damn" sure about your read before entering the world of "rock'n'roll"! I wasn't—so no go!

All in all I think I earned a better grade for my post-flop play than for my very mediocre pre-flop decision. It is of course very debatable how good a grade I can get for losing a hand of poker—especially if I could have won it taking a different route?

No matter what, I lost 325k being careful and playing what I would like to call protective poker. I maintained my second-place position, with a lot of room to spare down to Andy Black's 1.8 million. I'm not ecstatic about how it all played out, but all in all it is not the end of the world as I still have plenty of time to make a move!

Hand 201

Blinds	My Position	My Hand	My Chip Stack
15K/30K/5K	SB	A♥ 7♦	3.480 million

Kristy Gazes opens one off the button for a standard 100k raise. Button folds and I have A♥ 7♦ in the small blind. What is the correct course of action? Let me give you a little insight before I hand over the verdict.

Kristy is one of the best female players out there, and she definitely didn't get to 1.4 million by some random coincidence. She has been at it for four long and grueling days like the rest of us, and not surprisingly she has come out ahead!

To stay ahead she has to keep her focus and attack relentlessly—especially with the ever-increasing blinds and antes constantly eating away at her stack. She knows that blind and ante stealing is an inevitable part of late stage tournament success. All she needs to fight for the 85k in the middle is late position and a somewhat reasonable starting hand.

Adding it all up and consulting with the little red guy on my shoulder convinces me that we are talking about a pure steal-attempt! If I am correct in my assessment, all I have to do is put approximately 350k in the pot, and barring some accident in the big blind, I will pick up 175k in profit. Three hundred fifty thousand to win 175k or 2 to 1 is admittedly a big prize to lay, but this was just one of those instances where it all made sense!

I want to keep my expenses at a minimum, still upholding a high ratio of Kristy-folds. I therefore shave 20 off the 350 and raise to 330k. The big blind and Kristy quickly fold. Going with my read paid off. I was right this time, but bear in mind that I don't have to be wrong very often for this maneuver to prove unprofitable!

Hand 202

Blinds	My Position	My Hand	My Chip Stack
15K/30K/5000	Button	8♣ 6♣	3.655 million

Next hand I'm on the button with the 8♣ 6♣. Before it gets to me Hans Martin Vogl to my immediate right has opened for 110k. I could have followed my "re-raise the late-position raiser" tactics from the previous hand, but this time around I was facing a totally different situation!

1. Hans Martin has a tighter approach toward the game than Kristy. The quality of his starting hands is higher, and the success ratio for the re-steal is therefore lower.
2. I'm in position. Acting last on the flop hopefully allows me to get a better feel for Hans Martin's intentions.
3. Eight-high isn't exactly a powerhouse before the flop, and therefore better suited for post-flop action than a pre-flop shoot-out.

Three good reasons for stepping on the brake and just call. A case could be made for folding my hand, but after extensive discussions with my good friend Daniel Negreanu I'm not allowed to. Daniel has had tremendous success calling in position with small-suited connectors, so I see no reason not to follow his lead.

I call the 110k, but before I could reap the benefits of my

carefully planned "masterpiece," Marc Karam in the small blind re-raised to 400k. The big blind and Hans Martin fold, and it is right back to me—another 290k if I want to come along. This was definitely turning into a more expensive expedition than originally intended—maybe too expensive?

I am still in position, I still have a suited connector, but we are closing in on the pre-flop shoot-out I really wanted to avoid. Mr. Karam has about 1 million left in front of him, and the pot will reach almost 900k if I call—not the implied odds I want with this kind of hand! Given the size of his chip stack the correct action from Marc most of the time will be to move all-in on the flop, taking away most post-flop play. That's not the brute force action I am looking for with this kind of hand! Marc is representing a strong hand, and could very well be holding medium-big to big pairs—not the hands I want to face with this kind of hand! All in all it looks like I should stay away from this one.

The only incentive to call is the mouth-watering pot odds! 290k to win 690k—my fingers are itching just thinking about it. I go forth and back on this one, but end up deciding that the negative factors weigh too heavily in the wrong direction. Sorry Daniel—I fold!

Marc Karam chose to muck his hand face up: Two black Tens.

Folding my 8♣ 6♣ was correct against this specific hand. Unless I think I could pull off a genius bluff if a couple of over cards hit the board?

Hand 203

Blinds	My Position	My Hand	My Chip Stack
12K/24K/4K	BB	6♦ 5♥	3.53 million

Jimmy Fricke opens in third position for 90k and everybody folds to my big blind. I look down at 6♦ 5♥ and call another 60k. I think a lot of people out there disagree with some of my pre-flop decisions—this is probably one of them. Why would I butt heads with the chip leader, out of position with a hand like 56o? My response would be based solely on the very compelling pot odds! Sixty thousand to win 175k or just about 3 to 1 is, under normal circumstances, an extremely lucrative prize for any two cards on a heads-up pre-flop call. Unfortunately this was not normal circumstances! As we saw a couple of hands ago the dynamics change completely when the two big chip-leaders are up against each other. I did not need this one, and the proper play, even though I hate to admit it, would have been to let this one go.

Flop comes:

Never underestimate a gut shot! I check and Jimmy bets 100k. My second "meeting" with Jimmy and again I face a small continuation bet. I am very eager to find out whether the continuation bet is the extent of Jimmy's arsenal or if he also is capable of firing second and third bullets—knowledge that could prove helpful for future encounters. Right now I only have Six-high, but I do have a draw at the nuts and the pot size is also much more manageable than last time around. I am definitely skating on thin ice, but I think I can come up with just enough excuses to muster up a call.

Turn:

4♠ ♠

♥ ♥♧

The nuts! Hopefully I can reap some benefits from a very lucky turn-card. Best scenario would be Jimmy holding a big pocket pair, preferably Aces. Jimmy would then be drawing absolutely stone-cold dead, but would still have plenty of good reasons to put a lot more money in the pot. Dream scenarios are always nice to fantasize about, but here it actually isn't that far-fetched. There is of course also the nightmare version, a completed flush-draw on the river, which would put a serious dent in my Aussie Millions adventure. Fortunately that is much more of a long shot, as my quick calculations puts it in the 30 to 1 range. Enough daydreaming! I have to deal with the situation at hand. Going along with my post-flop approach, checking seems to be the right play, as it would give Jimmy a chance to fire again, with or without a hand.

I check but without much hesitation Jimmy checks behind me. No more money in the pot—at least for now. At the same time Jimmy's winning chances have dipped into obscurity.

I am fairly certain that Jimmy didn't check two pair or a set behind me, so even if the river should pair the board, I would still consider my straight as the nuts. As far as the flush-draw goes, it has a little more uncertainty attached to it, but it is my gut feeling that Jimmy would have bet a hand like K♣ Q♣ as kind of a semi-bluff. If I am correct in my assumption, Jimmy can only improve to the second best hand, and I have therefore theoretically already won the pot! Without getting too far ahead of myself I now turn my attention to the only interesting remaining question: "How much money can I extract from Jimmy?"

River:

Ugly card! There is not so much a fear of getting beat by a flush, but more the very realistic possibility of not getting paid off! I think the 4♣ really diminished my chances of winning more money. Basically all the draws got there. If I had anything in resemblance to the flop when I called Jimmy's bet, I would now at least have made something. Jimmy's continuation bet on the flop could very well have been a random A♦J♦. As it was, now all he could beat was a complete bluff or a busted spade back-door flush-draw.

I don't think Jimmy is going to pay me off whether I bet big or small, so I might as well aim high just in case I misinterpreted something along the way. No need to play small ball here—400k it is. I bet, and Jimmy, who seems to have lost all interest in this pot long ago, folds instantly. I pick up the 435k in the middle.

Unfortunately I didn't win any money on my disguised little straight. The bottom line is Jimmy didn't have anything to pay me off with, probably Ace-high at best. With that in mind, my post-flop call, although a bit far-fetched, wasn't totally ludicrous, as a Five or a Six also would have given me the best hand.

Hand 204

Blinds	My Position	My Hand	My Chip Stack
15K/30K/5K	2nd	Q♦ 8♦	3.73 million

It is dawning on me that this eight-handed table might represent some lucrative possibilities! I'm sensing some strong reluctance around the table to enter a pot. That just makes it more essential to open every pot, if I have anything resembling a starting hand. Q♦ 8♦ in second position more than qualifies. I open for 100k, and when everybody quickly folds, I can safely add another 80k to my hopefully ever-increasing stack!

Hand 205

Blinds	My Position	My Hand	My Chip Stack
15K/30K/5K	BB	Q♦ 7♦	3.81 million

I take a break for one hand, but I am quickly back in the saddle as I look down at Q♦ 7♦ in the big blind. My plan is to at least offer some resistance if anybody should be crazy enough to try to steal my blind. I guess they all figured it out—attempting to steal my blind is just not a very lucrative business model. Unless you are prepared to go the extra mile, you will not be successful. At the moment nobody at the table seemed to possess that urge, so I can't even say I was surprised when everybody folded. With a little smile on my face, I go for another beautiful 50k walk in the park!

On a side note, I'm starting feel better about my AK decision against Jimmy Fricke from a round or two ago. Although it is possible I was too timid and folded the best hand, I kept proper tournament strategy in perspective and stayed away from the clash of the big stacks. Instead I have been able to pick up a lot of small pots with very little risk attached, thereby maintaining a strong foothold at the top of the leader board. A pretty good trade!

Hand 206

Blinds	My Position	My Hand	My Chip Stack
15K/30K/5K	SB	Q♥ 2♣	3.87 million

The button moves, and I'm now in the small blind. Again everybody folds to me, and with my current success ratio in the ante-stealing department, I can't come up with any good reason not to continue the onslaught. Qh 2c might be considered by many to be a mighty fine reason, but I am in an any-two-card-will-do mode, so raising is inevitable. I make it 100k to go, planning to add another 80k to my stack. Marc Karam wants it otherwise. A re-raise would have put an end to my participation in this hand, but luckily for me he only calls.

Flop comes:

Top pair, bottom kicker—a rare combination, but nonetheless a pretty strong hand heads-up! I lead out for 120k, and Marc calls.

Turn:

I still like my hand, as Marc hasn't exactly projected a lot of strength so far with his two calls. On the other hand he has to have a little bit of something, so I decide to proceed with caution. I check and Marc bets 200k. There was 240k in the pot before the flop, 480k after, and adding Marc's 200k, there is now a total of 680k in the pot. I have to call 200k to win 680k. Getting 3.4 to 1 with top pair in this specific situation seems like a good deal. Marc could have the real deal but just as likely he has used the I-bet-because-he-checked maneuver! I really don't know which one it is, but I am not going to give up that easy. I call!

River:

Didn't change much! It is highly unlikely that anyone has a Nine in their hand, therefore it seems like a very safe river card for whoever was ahead on the turn. I leave it up to Marc to value-bet or bluff. I check and Marc bets 300k. Not a particularly big bet for an 880k pot, but maybe he really wants me to call. I do have some kicker problems, but on the other hand my pair is top-notch. Let us just say I'm not convinced! I push 300k toward the middle and Marc immediately taps the table. I win the 1.48 million pot for a nice 755k gain.

Some curious players around the table ask to see Marc's hand and I have to admit I am a little interested to see it myself. Marc turns over 7♣ 8♠ for an Eight-high gut shot bluff. Gutsy move in a precarious spot like this! Although if it wasn't for my atypical check with top pair and somewhat curious nature, his bluff could easily have succeeded!

Hand 207

Blinds	My Position	My Hand	My Chip Stack
15K/30K/5K	2 off the button	T♣8♣	4.62 million

I was just in the mood for another quickie during this round. With the exception of Jimmy everybody seems to be waiting for the final-table-bubble to burst. I open for 100k, 2 off the button with T♣8♣, and the rest of the pack folds. Nice and easy.

Hand 208

Blinds	My Position	My Hand	My Chip Stack
15K/30K/5K	2nd	K♦5♦	4.69 million

I limp in second position with K♦5♦. Jimmy Fricke limps, Andy Black limps, small blind Jakob Glassl joins us, and last but not least, Kristy Gazes taps the table in the big blind. What did I start? A five-handed flop—we haven't had one of those for a long, long time. Flop comes:

Not perfect! Jakob and Kristy check and suddenly I have the honor. Going by Phil Ivey standards this is an obvious bet. Nobody hit the flop, so I might as well give them the impression that I did! It's kind of like saying, "If they don't want it, I'll take it!" Whoever pulls the trigger first will most likely win it.

I bet 70k and one by one they all fold. Got to give Mr. Ivey some credit, he knows what he is talking about! I drag down a 190k pot for a sweet 155k King-high profit!

Minutes later Jakob Glassl was all-in with two Jacks against Jimmy Fricke's AT and with an Ace in the door, Jakob was in dire straits. No Jack showed up, Jakob was out in eighth place, and it was time to call it a day. With seven players remaining, six guys and Kristy Gazes would all be back tomorrow for the final table.

End of Day 4

Recap, Day 4

Another day well done! It had been a very short day compara-
tively speaking, but I don't think any of the players really
minded since we'd get the night off instead of playing another
six or seven grueling hours. I was going to meet up with the
family—my sister Tine, my brother-in-law Erik and their beautiful daughter, my niece Sally. Later on we were going to have
dinner with some good friends of ours. A perfect way for me to
recharge my batteries and get ready for tomorrow. As far as
the play went the hand against Patrik Antonius was of course
the big turning point, or should I say starting point. The day
started out as well as I could ever have imagined, with a complete cold deck and a huge double up knocking out one of the
most feared players on the circuit. From then on things were a
little bit easier. I was the overwhelming chip-leader and unless
disaster struck I had already secured a spot at the final table.
No need to use that as an excuse to lay low, though!

I stayed on target, kept my priorities straight and my ante-
stealing urges intact, aggressively aiming at my beloved antes.
Mind you, it is a lot easier to grab hold of a little extra when
the entire table is preoccupied with survival and outlasting
opponents. The only debacle was when Jimmy Fricke came to
town and messed me up with some big-stack pressure. I might
have crumbled with AK but I regained my composure and
stayed on course. All in all, I'm pretty happy with my overall
performance.

Going into tomorrow's seven-handed final table I have
4,845,000, surpassed only by Jimmy "Gobboboy" Fricke's
5,175,000. Altogether we have ⅔ of the chips with 34.6% and
32.4% respectively. A pretty good spot if you ask me. Time to
rest my leftover brain cells, good night.

CHAPTER 5

FINAL TABLE—FROM SEVEN TO THREE

My Advice Before Today's Play

Final Table Considerations

Let's take it from the beginning. The tournament started Sunday afternoon with 747 players, a $10,000 buy-in, and 20,000 in chips. Now 740 players are gone and your chip stack has increased considerably. When you sat down five days ago playing good solid poker was your only concern—or at least it should have been! A green table, ten players, two cards each—no exterior considerations, just trying to win more money than you lost. Making good decisions brought you from there to here, so why not continue down the same path? Is there any reason to change your game plan? Shouldn't you just stick to your guns? Let's take a brief look at the different layout!

The table-setting has changed from ten-handed to seven-handed, but we have covered the different aspects of medium short-handed considerations earlier on. The media attention has increased from nonexistent to cameras observing your every move, but all that is hype anyway and shouldn't influence your game plan. We are playing at some astronomical, ridiculously expensive level of poker with 15,000–30,000 blinds and a 5,000 ante. We're at a level so unfathomable that most folks would shake their heads in disbelief. Don't worry about it, it is

only tournament chips. All in all, shutting out all the publicity
and glitter, this should just be like your everyday, seven-handed
home game—a little quiet Friday afternoon tournament with
your friends. Well, not quite! I forgot to mention the prize
pool! The prize money has reached considerable heights and
plays a significant part in final table strategy. It is therefore of
utmost importance that you are aware of the payout structure!
Let's take a look:

1. 1.5M
2. 1.0M
3. 700K
4. 500K
5. 400K
6. 300K
7. 200K

To quote the all-time great bowling movie, *The Kingpin,* they
could have made it a five-million-dollar, winner-takes-all, final
table shoot-out. But as you can see they stayed with their conservative ways and made it a more flat payout structure. What
implication is it going to have for my game plan? Well, it certainly depends whether you are the leader of the pack or the
crummy little short-stack. The chip-leader has several options
going from one end of the spectrum to the other—from Table
Bully to the I'm-not-going-to-play-a-hand-until-we-are-down-
to-three-players strategy. The short-stack has a much clearer
path to follow, as it can only go one way and that is up. The
most interesting considerations are actually placed in the hands
of Malcolm in the middle. Malcolm can move up, down, side-
ways, pretty much in all kinds of directions, which makes his
decisions that much more important. Enough talk! What is the
right approach in the current situation?

As a general principle you want to play pots against stacks

shorter than your own. You want to avoid elimination, but at the same time be able to deliver a knockout punch yourself. You can't always pick your opponent, but by being conscious about the repercussions you can at least make more informed decisions.

Every time somebody gets knocked out you move up a spot and earn some extra pocket change. How much extra? Let's go back to the payout structure for a second. What is really important is how big the steps are in between the different spots. Going from seventh to sixth, sixth to fifth, or fifth to fourth increases your pay day by exactly the same amount— $100,000. The next steps become a little steeper and therefore more valuable. It is interesting to notice that going from second to first earns you more than going from seventh to fourth.

There is always a reward for waiting around while your opponents get knocked out, but in this specific case the reward is not as big as it would be with a steeper payout structure. Patience should be a significant part of your strategy, but you can't afford to let it remove your focus from the main issue at hand—winning the tournament! To take the ultimate step from second to first you have to get hold of some chips, and you only do that by playing some hands. Cautiously waiting for others to leave the building can mean the difference between seventh and fourth, whereas aggressively pursuing marginal edges can be the difference between second and first. It is all part of a sneaky risk-reward scenario that fortunately changes from tournament to tournament. Depending on the payout structure one or the other could be the right approach.

The above-mentioned risk–reward calculation has another name in the poker world: the *ladder principle*. Having a good understanding of the ladder principle and the implications it might have on final table play is the Alpha and Omega. Therefore my best advice is, always pay attention and see what steps *you* want to take!

Back to the Table

There are seven players at the final table:

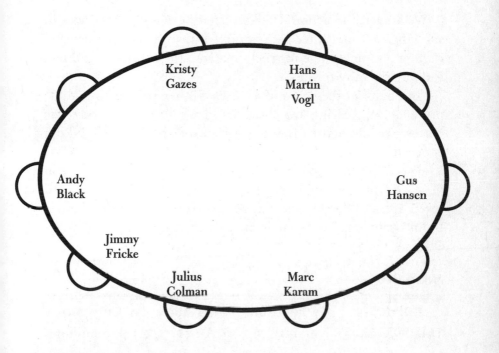

Seat one: Hans Martin Vogl—455,000
Seat two: Gus Hansen—4,845,000
Seat three: Marc Karam—530,000
Seat four: Julius Colman—780,000
Button: Jimmy Fricke—5,170,000
SB: Andy Black—2,095,000
BB: Kristy Gazes—1,045,000

Hand 209

Blinds	My Position	My Hand	My Chip Stack
15K/30K/5K	2nd	K♣ 7♣	4.845 million

We are back in action. Unlike yesterday everybody decides to show up on time. After getting miked up and getting the usual camera and final table instructions from the tournament director we are ready to play.

First hand of the day and as always I like to make my table presence felt. Firing from the get-go before everybody has gotten accustomed to the new situation always seems like a good choice. I open in second position for 90,000 with K♣ 7♣. Everybody folds. You are picking up 80,000 whenever you raise and they all fold. Thirty thousand BB, 15,000 SB, and seven antes of 5,000—it all adds up! Stealing blinds and antes should definitely be a significant part of your final stable strategy.

Hand 210

Blinds	My Position	My Hand	My Chip Stack
15K/30K/5K	1st	A♣ 2♣	4.935 million

I fold A♣ 2♣. This was a decent hand to try to pick up another set of blinds and antes. My main concern, and the reason I actually folded, is the fact that I don't want my ante-stealing strategy to be too obvious to the rest of the players. On top of that I was in first position and I very much dislike holding a deuce in my hand.

Andy raises on the button and Hans Martin Vogl moves all-in. Andy folds. This seems to be Hans Martin's favorite move.

I should probably watch out so that I don't give him too many perfect all-in moves before the flop. It is imperative to manipulate the size of my pre-flop raises so that Hans Martin either has to over-commit his chip stack for a small gain or else he will simply have to see a flop.

Hand 211

Blinds	My Position	My Hand	My Chip Stack
15K/30K/5K	BB	K♣ 6♥	4.93 million

Kristy makes it 90,000 on the button and I call 60,000 more with my K♣ 6♥. I will not give in to the people saying you shouldn't call with discombobulated hands out of position. I am calling 60,000 to win 170,000—almost 3:1—and I personally think that that warrants a call with any two cards against a button raise. The flop comes:

I check my King high no nothing, planning to give it up right here. Even though Kristy could be holding just about any two cards for raising on the button, I am not going to pursue this one. Due to the fact that I am in the big blind I actually give her a little credit. She knows that I will call with just about any two cards and I don't think she is particularly interested in butting heads with me when I am holding a big stack.

Kristy surprisingly checks behind me—a freebie.

The turn is:

No improvement and Kristy bets 250,000. I do have no pair top kicker, but I still see no reason to continue this confrontation. I fold and Kristy takes down the pot.

Hand 212

Blinds	My Position	My Hand	My Chip Stack
15K/30K/5K	SB	A♣9♥	4.845 million

Jimmy opens in second position for 90,000 and everybody folds to my small blind. I am holding A♣9♥ and decide to call 75,000 more. I am not a big fan of that hand and think my call is very marginal, the main reason being that it was the chip-leader raising. Against any other player at the final table my options would have been more open and against a late position raiser I could even have considered a re-raise. Jimmy was the only person who could really hurt me and it would therefore be stupid to get entangled in a big pot with a "dangerous" holding. In hindsight I think the fold would have been the better play.

Marc Karam folds his BB and the flop comes:

I check and Jimmy bets 150,000. Following my pre-flop advice this was an easy fold—a questionable holding followed by a miss on the flop. Unfortunately there was a little devil sitting on my shoulder whispering: "Raise, raise, raise!" And so I did, shoving 350,000 into the pot—kind of a mini-raise but it seemed suitable for the situation since I didn't want to get *too* involved.

The re-raise, although a little crazy, had a reasonable chance of working. It wasn't easy for Jimmy to connect either, and I did hold the master club.

Jimmy called the 200,000. Turn is:

Great card for me! Whatever Jimmy was holding there is a good chance he did not want to see a big club, making my next bet a high-percentage play! Let's take a quick look at some of Jimmy's possible holdings: J♦ T♦, A♥ Q♥, 8♠ 8♦. All three very reasonable for an early-position raise. Being in position, it was also reasonable for Jimmy to call my mini re-raise to see what develops.

Looking at the K♣ all those "reasonable" holdings wouldn't be worth much. I bet 465k, and Jimmy did not seem interested in coming along for the ride, and quickly folded.

I didn't need to get involved in this hand. Once I did, it was important that I stayed the course. Pulling the trigger for the second time—maybe with a little help from K♣—won me the pot. That's the beauty of poker! Sometimes a bad call, a crazy re-raise, and a scary turn-card are all you need to take down the pot!

Hand 213

Blinds	My Position	My Hand	My Chip Stack
15K/30K/5K	1 off the button	A♠J♥	5.335 million

I open for 110,000, 1 off the button with A♠ J♥.

There is a tendency in poker to follow the first raise. In the first hand of the final table I opened for 90,000. Since then, in hands two through five, everybody adopted that strategy. You want to find a reasonable amount that gives you a decent chance to pick up the blind without committing too much money. So why stray away from the standard? There is one obvious reason—the big stack is in the big blind.

I have a very reasonable holding, A♠ J♥. With only three remaining players it is very likely to be the best hand, so raising is obvious. Instead of butting heads with Jimmy my main objective is to pick up the 80,000 floating around in there.

Marc Karam follows orders and folds the button but Julius Colman has different ideas. Julius moves all-in for a total of 725,000 and before I can react, Jimmy has called. My initial reaction was that my hand was strong enough to call Julius's all-in move, but with Jimmy putting 695,000 in cold, my hand immediately loses all of its sex appeal. I wasn't interested in getting involved with Jimmy in this hand, and with this kind of action I definitely didn't want to—I fold.

I fold. Julius turns over A♣ Q♠ against Jimmy's T♥ T♣. The board shows four clubs and Julius wins with the nuts.

In a situation like this you normally always root for the biggest stack trying to get a player knocked out and take a step up the ladder. I am sure that the rest of the players around the table were rooting for Jimmy, but not me. I had the chip lead and was facing no immediate danger from any of the players except for Jimmy. I was actually happy to see

Jimmy's stack drop to the 4M mark, giving me a more commanding role.

Hand 214

Blinds	My Position	My Hand	My Chip Stack
15K/30K/5K	BB	T♥ 7♥	5.165 million

A little side note before the next hand: After a couple of raise-fold hands, it is getting more and more obvious that nobody except for me is really interested in defending their blinds. I can't really blame them since waiting around and watching other players getting knocked out could easily earn them a couple of valuable steps up the prize money ladder. But it does seem to me that everybody is taking that strategy a little bit too far. Not me!

Julius opens in second position for 100,000. Everybody folds to my BB. I am holding the T♥ 7♥ and decide to call. I am afraid this is one of those situations where I often get myself in trouble.

Consider the situation: I am at a final table with seven players and at least a couple of them, if not five, are in waiting-around mode. All of a sudden Julius, who has been playing fairly tight throughout the tournament, opens for 100,000 in early position. It is a close call, but I really don't need to fight City Hall with a suited double-gapper!

The flop comes:

A low straighty flop that doesn't figure to be in Julius' range! I have a straight draw, a back door flush draw, and two over cards, a lot more than I usually need to lead out. I lead out for 130,000 and Julius doesn't waste a lot of time before pushing all-in for a total of 1.5M. Needless to say, I fold.

Post hand analysis: The pre-flop call was questionable, but I like my lead-out. I think I was a favorite to win the hand right there since I couldn't see Julius calling while holding two random big cards like AJ or KQs. As it was his all-in raise indicated that he was holding a big pair, making it an easy fold for me.

Hand 215

CRUCIAL HAND 13: Busting Full Tilt's
Kristy Gazes—9♣ 9♥ vs. AQ

Blinds	My Position	My Hand	My Chip Stack
15K/30K/5K	Button	9♣ 9♥	4.91 million

Kristy opens 2 off the button for 100,000. I am on the button with 99 and I have to decide in which direction I want to take this.

Fold—never going to happen.
Call—seems stupid. My hand plays better pre-flop than
  when facing over cards on the flop.
Re-raise to 350,000—a bit silly, since I will then be pot-
  committed against Kristy's 1.07 million.
All-in—much better! Puts Kristy to the test and I am pot-
  committed anyway.

I make it a total of 380,000. The blinds fold and after a quick study Kristy goes all-in. I take a couple of seconds just for the heck of it and call the remaining 720,000. Kristy turns over A♥ Q♥ and my 9♣ 9♥ is a 53–47% favorite. The board comes:

Showdown

My Hand						Kristy's Hand

Kristy is out in seventh place and I move into the six millions. So why did I make the second-best play instead of just moving all-in? Well, in this case there was a third horse in play—Julius Colman with 1.815M in the big blind. I was ready to play a 2.2M pot against Kristy's original raise but if Julius showed any sign of interest in re-re-raising I was prepared to fold my 99. This made the intermediate raise my preferred play.

Hand 216

Blinds	My Position	My Hand	My Chip Stack
15K/30K/5K	1 off the button	K♥ 8♦	6.055 million

I open 1 off the button for 105,000 with K♥ 8♦. When Jimmy is in the BB I just want to pick up the blinds and antes, not get entangled in some big showdown. That's why I make it 105,000 instead of the standard 90,000.

Marc and Julius folds but alas—Jimmy calls. The flop comes:

Jimmy checks and I make my usual continuation bet . . . *nope,* not this time. Damage control! Even though I flopped top pair I am not at all interested in facing a check-raise, making it a potential 8M pot. Playing it small against the second chip-leader seems to be a good choice.

There are three upsides when checking the flop:

1. Pot size control
2. Picking up bluffs
3. Creating an opportunity for a decent-size value bet on the river.

Downside:

1. Giving free cards—getting beat by a hand that couldn't call a bet on the flop.

Giving a free card in this spot is not too dangerous since there is only one over card left—the Ace.

The turn card is the:

Jimmy bets 150,000 into a 255,000 pot and even though I am looking to play it small I have no plans to ever fold this hand. I call.

The river is:

Jimmy bets 350,000 and I call. Jimmy turns over K♣ 8♣ and we split the 1.25M pot.

When checking a top pair of Kings you have to make it clear to yourself that you can never fold this hand to two standard bets. And on top of it all, what did I really know about Jimmy's hand?

My check on the flop indicated weakness, which means he could be taking a stab at the pot on the turn with just about any two cards. His river bet could easily be a value bet with a random King or even a good Queen—not to mention all the possible bluffs lurking out there. Everything added up to a fairly easy call on my part!

Hand 217

CRUCIAL HAND 14: Getting Called Holding 5th Pair

Blinds	My Position	My Hand	My Chip Stack
15K/30K/5K	1st	2♠ 3♠	6.065 million

I open for 105,000 in first position with 2♠ 3♠, not so much because of my powerful Three high but more because Hans Martin Vogl had so far seemed very reluctant to defend his BB. Jimmy calls on the button and both blinds fold. At this point I am not sure what kind of hand to put Jimmy on.

The flop comes:

A hit! No reason to slow-play my pair of Treys and no reason to give a free card either. My pair has a good chance of being in front and therefore I bet. Jimmy calls my 140,000 bet and we see the turn:

I still have reasons to believe that I might have the best hand and although I am a little bit in the dark I elect to fire another bullet. Three hundred thirty thousand with fourth pair seems reasonable for a *madman*. Jimmy calls again and I have to admit there is a chance my pair of Treys is in trouble. The river brings:

I bet 770,000 into a 1.2M pot on a stone-cold I-don't-know-what! Different thoughts were going through my mind, and one of the thoughts convinced the others to bet 770,000. Jimmy gave a little "spiel" for the audience and called. His A♦ J♣ easily overpowered my 2♠ 3♠. Jimmy took down the biggest pot at the final table so far and regained the chip lead.

Let's take it step by step.

Pre-flop: I don't mind my initial raise trying to pick up the blinds. Jimmy's call is very optional as both folding and re-raising are viable options.

On the flop: Leading out when connecting on the flop is a standard play. Jimmy's call is somewhat questionable. He has position and what could still be the best hand, but it is a little bit of a stretch.

Turn: I am not quite sure what is going on here. I know I'm out on a limb still betting my fourth pair, but why would Jimmy have a Queen?

Jimmy's call is probably somewhere in between sick and very sick.

1. He has Ace high with four random unpaired cards on the board—not very good!
2. He is up against a first-position raiser—I know it is me but . . . not very good!
3. He is up against the chip leader, who is the only one who can really hurt him—not very good!

4. He is second in chips with no immediate danger of being caught by any of the other four players, unless he loses a big pot to me—not very good!

5. He is facing not only one but *two* bullets with maybe a third to come—not very good!

6. There is a Queen on the board making his Jack look very so-so—not very good!

All adding up to a more or less insane call!

River: My river bet probably deserves the same label—not very good!

I think a check-call on my part would have been a better route to take. Some people out there would probably prefer the check-fold. The reason that I didn't particularly like the check-fold was the fact that I thought Jimmy was crazy enough to call the turn with a weak hand and then try to take it away from me if I checked the river. I wanted to take it away first. It should be clear by now that I didn't put Jimmy on a very good hand.

I will admit that I was a bit shocked when Jimmy turned over the AJ. This leads me to believe that Jimmy might have called with Ace high had it been a blank on the river, giving my 770,000 bet some merit. I know the last theory is far-fetched, but it lets me sleep at night, so . . .

Hand 218

Blinds	My Position	My Hand	My Chip Stack
15K/30K/5K	BB	K♥ T♦	4.715 million

Marc Karam opens in first position for 90,000 and everybody folds to my BB. I call with K♥ T♦.

The flop comes:

I check and Marc bets 125,000 into a 225,000 pot. No pair, no draw, no nothing—easy fold!

Hand 219

Blinds	My Position	My Hand	My Chip Stack
15K/30K/5K	SB	A♥ 2♥	4.62 million

Jimmy raises to 90,000 in second position and as always your faithful soldier calls from the SB with A♥ 2♥. The flop comes:

A little too "clubby" for my taste! I check and Jimmy's 150,000 bet takes down the pot.

Hand 220

Blinds	My Position	My Hand	My Chip Stack
20K/40K/5K	1st	K♠ 5♠	4.51 million

Blinds have gone up to 20,000/40,000 which definitely puts our two short stacks, Marc Karam and Hans Martin Vogl, under a little more pressure. I guess they haven't noticed because they seem very reluctant to enter a pot. Maybe they are each trying to outlast the other!

I open for 120,000 with K♠ 5♠ in first position. According to my observations Hans Martin Vogl's BB should be an obvious target. This time I was wrong!

Everybody folds except for Hans Martin, who moves all-in for 385,000. I have to call 265,000 to win 555,000—a classic 2:1 match-up. Even though I know I am up against a stronger holding I am a sucker for 2:1s.

In this situation I think it is very borderline whether to call or not. I need 32% to call, and against the various holdings such as AK, AQ, 88 I am right in the neighborhood. As it turned out he had J♠ J♥, giving me exactly 31.5% winning chance.

Showdown

My Hand   **Hans Martin's Hand**

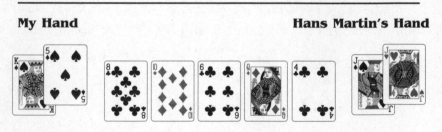

No help for me, and Hans Martin doubles up to 820,000.

Hand 221

Blinds	My Position	My Hand	My Chip Stack
20K/40K/5K	BB	A♣ 9♠	4.08 million

Marc Karam opens for a standard raise of 535,000. Well, not quite the standard. Marc realizes that a standard raise of 120,000 would put him in a more or less pot-committed spot and therefore chooses the more aggressive all-in move.

Everybody folds to my BB and as we know I am not easy to

get by. I am holding A♣ 9♠ and I am looking at yet another borderline decision. After losing the last hand to Hans Martin I am starting to feel Andy Black breathing down my neck. My position as the second chip leader is slowly deteriorating and I should therefore proceed a little bit more carefully. But then again, that has never been my style—so I call! Is A9o really good enough to call a 495,000 raise? Four hundred ninety-five thousand to win 625,000, or close to 5:4, translates into about a 44% winning chance.

Well, Marc obviously doesn't have AA! KK and QQ are pretty unlikely too! Taking these three hands out of the equation, my A9 is starting to look better.

The bottom line is that people play a little too backward for my taste in some of these short-stacked all-in situations. They move all-in with hands like AT, 77, and KQ but not with the really big hands. In my mind it totally defies logic since one of the basic poker rules is to put as much money in the pot when you have the best hand. On top of it all you have a "crazy" guy like me in the BB who is bound to call you with a silly A9o, making the backward plays even worse.

Marc turns over K♣ J♦, giving me a nice 58–42 edge.

Showdown

| **My Hand** | | | **Marc Karam's Hand** |

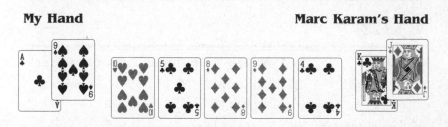

Marc Karam is gone, we are down to five players, and my second spot is a little bit more secure.

Hand 222

Blinds	My Position	My Hand	My Chip Stack
20K/40K/5K	1 off the button	T♦8♦	4.68 million

I open for 120,000 with T♦8♦. Andy re-raises to 620,000 and I see no need to fight an uphill battle. I fold.

Hand 223

Blinds	My Position	My Hand	My Chip Stack
20K/40K/5K	Button	K♣4♣	4.48 million

I open for 120,000 with K♣4♣ in third position. Wait a minute, I'm on the button. Mind you, it is a little bit ludicrous talking about first, second, or third position in a five-handed game! It is a short-handed game and you should be careful about giving anybody credit for a big hand, no matter what position they raise from. Blinds and antes are increasing fairly quickly, putting everybody under a little bit of pressure.

Nobody wants to play with me and I pick up 80,000 from the blinds and antes.

Hand 224

Blinds	My Position	My Hand	My Chip Stack
20K/40K/5K	1 off the button	4♣4♦	4.56 million

I open for 120,000, 1 off the button with 44 and everybody folds. This has been going on for quite a while. Someone raises—everybody folds. No flops, no "real" poker, but I'm not complaining since I have taken down just above my fair share of blinds and antes. For all I care we can continue this nip-and-tuck way of playing since I feel pretty confident I can hold my own.

Hand 225

Blinds	My Position	My Hand	My Chip Stack
20K/40K/5K	BB	Q♣4♣	4.635 million

First flop in ages, as somebody finally decides to defend their blind. Strangely enough, that somebody was me. Jimmy opens for 120,000 and I call in my BB with the suited eight-gapper Q♣4♣. The flop comes:

I check, Jimmy bets 200,000. No contest—bad defense—I fold.

Hand 226

Blinds	My Position	My Hand	My Chip Stack
20K/40K/5K	SB	Q♥T♥	4.49 million

Andy raises 110,000, 1 off the button and I call in my small blind with Q♥T♥.

The flop comes:

This hand can be played many different ways. Check-call, check-raise, and leading out are all viable options, whereas the check-fold is discarded. The check-call is not my kind of play as it fails to define the hand, and leaves Andy in control. The check-raise option is not as tasty either since I have noticed that Andy is a little bit conservative on his continuation bets.

I personally prefer the lead-out because of the big potential of picking up the pot right here. Leading out also has the advantage that if Andy should choose to raise I can put him to the ultimate test by moving all-in. Andy would be hard pressed to call an all-in move from either me or Jimmy considering the two short stacks. Even if he does call an all-in move with a monster hand, my hand still has a lot of drawing potential.

Lead-out it is! I bet 140,000 and Black calls. The turn comes:

What an ugly card. I decided to take another 330,000 jab. Unfortunately Andy's guard was up as he quickly called. The river card is:

Time to throw in the towel! I check and Andy delivers the 1M knockout punch.

POST-FIGHT COMMENTARY

The flop: I am a big fan of lead-out bets, and given the choice I would do it again.

The turn: Sensing that Andy was probably stronger than his call on the flop indicated, I think the check-call would have been more appropriate. Of course that's a lot easier to say after the fact!

The river: What is there to say? I had Queen high.

Hand 227

Blinds	My Position	My Hand	My Chip Stack
20K/40K/5K	Button	A♠ 3♠	3.925 million

Andy opens for 120,000, I call on the button, and Jimmy calls in the BB. My A♠ 3♠ is in the questionable department but then again I have played many worse hands.

The flop comes:

My two opponents both check, leaving the door open for me. If anyone had so much as attempted to sniff at the pot I would have folded instantly! With both of them showing a lack of interest in the hand it was time for me to take charge. There's 405,000 floating around out there waiting for someone to claim ownership! I was going to make that claim. One hundred seventy-five thousand seemed like a reasonable investment for a 405,000 return. I bet and they both quickly folded.

I guess my A♠ 3♠ was not that bad after all!

Hand 228

Blinds	My Position	My Hand	My Chip Stack
20K/40K/5K	1st	6♣ 6♦	4.2 million

I open for 120,000 in first position with the 6♣ 6♦ and it is folded to the big blind. Hans Martin re-raises and I am contemplating whether I can call 685,000 more with medium-small pair. Much to my surprise Hans Martin decided to stray away from his all-in signature move and instead made it 475,000. What was that all about? He was leaving himself with 330,000 looking at a 1 million pot—if I called, that is. He was obviously pot-committed and unless it was some kind of funky move he was trying to rope me in. I couldn't really make sense of it all. When that happens, I usually like to bail out as quickly and cheaply as possible. I fold and Vogl takes down the pot.

I'd made a surprisingly tight fold on my part with what could easily be the best hand, but I just didn't like the vibe. Had Hans Martin moved all-in, there is a very realistic chance that I could be up against a small pair like 44 and 55, with the in-between raise I think it is safe to discard those holdings. It was either 50% / 50% or 18% / 82% the wrong way, making the conservative fold more reasonable.

Hand 229

Blinds	My Position	My Hand	My Chip Stack
20K/40K/5K	BB	K♦ 2♥	4.075 million

I added another notch to my belt, going from 722 to 723 walks in major tournaments. I am probably the all-time leader in that department because of my crazy image. People don't like to mess around with my BB without having some kind of hand. Not that I can blame them. I know that I think twice before raising big blinds belonging to Mr. Ivey, The Grinder, or The Mad Hatter.

Hand 230

Blinds	My Position	My Hand	My Chip Stack
20K/40K/5K	1st	A♥ 6♣	4.08 million

I make it 120,000 and Hans Martin calls in the BB. The flop comes:

Hans Martin checks and I make a standard continuation bet of 140,000. No need to give a free card when my Ace high is probably the best hand. Hans Martin folds.

Hand 231

Blinds	My Position	My Hand	My Chip Stack
20K/40K/5K	BB	5♠ 5♣	4.24 million

Jimmy raises to 120,000, 1 off the button and I call in the BB with 55. I know some people like to re-raise in that spot since the 55 is very likely the best hand right now. I don't. Not that I would never do it, but this would certainly be the wrong time. Re-raising with small pairs works a lot better when it is an actual all-in move taking the play out of the hand. Here I would just build a bigger pot for Jimmy to bluff me out of, not to mention the fact that I could never call a re-re-raise facing the chip leader. Calling definitely seems like the best option.

The flop comes:

Great—Five ugly hearts! I check, Jimmy bets 175,000, I check-raise to 500,000, Jimmy folds.

To re-cap: Checking the flop is very optional against a random opponent. Against aggressive opposition you've got to give them some room to bluff. Checking is therefore my preferred play. After Jimmy's bet I can call or raise.

Calling has some big flaws:

1. I would still have absolutely no idea of what he is holding.
2. A heart could ruin my action, create unwanted action, or at worst, have Jimmy bluff me out of the hand.

Check-raising on the other hand has some lucrative upsides:

1. Creating a bigger pot against various Ace-holdings.
2. Having Jimmy fold a medium heart with no pair.

On a not so lucrative note the check-raise might also create some all-in scenarios:

1. If Jimmy is holding an Ace or a King with a big heart—69–31% favorite.
2. If Jimmy is holding two hearts—34–66% underdog.

Having already committed 620,000 in the pot I would be forced to call Jimmy's all-in although I wouldn't be very happy about it. With five players left at the table and two of them being short-stacked I am definitely not looking for any all-in scenarios against the chip leader.

Note that the ladder principle is very much in play here. Risking your entire stack as second chip-leader in a clash with the "big fella" is not recommended. But flopping a set sometimes forces your hand.

Since Jimmy folded, my entire thought process was in vain, but being aware of all the different consequences will ultimately help you make better decisions at the poker table.

Hand 232

Blinds	My Position	My Hand	My Chip Stack
30K/60K/5K	SB	K♦ T♦	4.58 million

The blinds have gone up to 30,000/60,000, and everybody folds to my SB. I look down at K♦ T♦— a very strong starting hand for a heads-up confrontation. Raising is inevitable. I count down Julius Colman's stack and convince myself that the best approach is to move all-in. I push 600,000 toward the middle easily enough to cover Julius, then I lean back in my chair. The rest is up to him and in case he calls to the flop, turn, and river. He complains that I robbed him of the chance to say all-in and quickly calls. He turns over A♥ 3♥.

Showdown

My Hand	Julius Colman's Hand

I'm way in front, as Julius will need an Ace or running hearts to stay alive. The turn:

No heart, no Ace, but instead some split-pot scenarios. River:

Straight on the board and we split the pot.

I think we both made the right play and a split pot was a fair settlement.

Hand 233

Blinds	My Position	My Hand	My Chip Stack
30K/60K/5K	Button	7♦ 8♠	4.618 million

Mr. Vogl opens for 210,000, 1 off the button, and this time it is Jimmy who takes a stand. He makes it 1M to go, and the German is all-in again. A♠ 9♣ for Hans Martin and K♣ J♦ for Jimmy, another slight advantage for the high-card Ace being about a 57–43% favorite. Pretty much the same as in the previous hand!

The board comes:

And then there were four! A river-hit for Jimmy leaves Hans Martin stranded in fifth place, and unfortunately, Jimmy is starting to pull away.

Hand 234

Blinds	My Position	My Hand	My Chip Stack
30K/60K/5K	1st	J♣ 6♥	4.613 million

We are down to four players, and unless Julius Colman starts to do some serious damage we are going to be three pretty soon! With only 465,000 left and a starting pot of 110,000 (90,000 in blinds + 20,000 in antes) Julius should be considering moving all-in without even looking at his hand. I guess he did look and must have found absolutely nothing because he folded on the button.

In a fairly uneventful hand Andy wins a small pot from Jimmy.

On a mental note: On the river Jimmy bets 90,000 into a 260,000 pot, about ⅓, on a stone-cold bluff.

On a side note: Julius would have picked up the blinds and antes as Jimmy showed 8♥ 2♥ and Andy 7♥ 9♦.

Hand 235

Blinds	My Position	My Hand	My Chip Stack
30K/60K/5K	SB	8♣ 5♦	4.543 million

Andy Black opens for 200,000 on the button. Julius Colman, who at this point is on some serious life support, decides to have a go at it with his A♠ 6♣. Not a good match up against Andy's two Queens. Looking at an Ace in the door it seemed like Julius might be back in the game, but . . .

The flop comes:

A devastating Queen, but the two Aces gives Julius some hope. The turn and river come:

And then there were three.

CHAPTER 6

FINAL TABLE—THREE-HANDED

My Advice Before Today's Play

Waiting for Second or Go for the Gold?

Let's take a homemade but very realistic scenario. Jimmy has 6 million left and Andy and I have 3 million each. Prize money is as follows: first place gets 1.5 million, second place gets 1 million, and third place gets 700,000, so the total pool is 3.2 million. Let's for simplicity's sake assume equal play/standards/skill levels, so that no one has an edge over the others. Without going into some long complicated calculations I think it is fair to say that Jimmy wins 50% of the time, takes second 30%, and finishes third 20%. Andy and I split the rest with 25% wins each. My expected value is $(25\% \times 1.5) + (35\% \times 1.0) + (40\% \times 0.7) = 375,000 + 350,000 + 280,000 = 1.005$ million. Andy's expected value is obviously the same as mine, 1.005 million, and Jimmy's expected value is: $(50\% \times 1.5) + (30\% \times 1.0) + (20\% \times 0.7) = 750,000 + 300,000 + 140,000 = 1.190$ million. If I played a fifty-fifty, coin-flip, all-in pot against Jimmy I will be out in third place half of the time, and the other half Jimmy and I will swap places. My expected value would instead look like this: $(50\% \times 0.7) + (50\% \times 1.190) = 350,000 + 595,000 = 945K$. Jimmy's expected value will be at: $(50\% \times 1.005) + (37.5\% \times 1.5) + (12.5\% \times 1.0) = 503k + 562k + 125,000 = 1.190$ million.

I lost 65,000 and Jimmy didn't make a penny. Where did the

money go? Well, obviously the third party took care of the left-overs. Without lifting a finger Andy made 65,000, not bad for mucking a hand! What about the other scenario, with me and Andy playing an all-in pot and Jimmy on the sideline? Is the bystander again the sole beneficiary? I'll spare you the details and just give you the result. Jimmy will gain 60,000 on that exchange and I won't bother to tell you who the losers are. As you can see the waiting game has a lot of merit! Whoever sits out, watching a big shoot-out amongst the two other combatants, will inevitably gain! Given the circumstances it sounds like patience is the premier virtue in our little three-handed charade, but unfortunately the example has a couple of flaws. The above examples are based on a completely dry pot to start with, and as we all know that is not the case. There are substantial blinds and antes added every hand that change the equation somewhat in favor of aggression.

There is another hurdle. The expected value you gain from sitting still stems solely from opponents getting knocked out, and you taking a step up the ladder. There is no way to guarantee a big, all-in pot just because you sit out a hand. If your opponents only play a small pot you have lost your blind and ante and gained nothing.

Adding it all up, we have one argument for waiting and two for playing. Is one compelling enough to overturn the jury? I don't think so! Even though I'm aware of specific situations where doing nothing is absolutely the best play, this is just not one of them. The relatively big blinds combined with the high ante-structure create an aggressive environment, and no ladder principle is going to change that. You should of course be aware of the implications all-in pots can have on your overall expected value, but you can't afford to go into a shell. My advice: be aggressive but careful.

Back to the Table

Hand 236

Blinds	My Position	My Hand	My Chip Stack	JF	AB
30K/60K/5K	Button	A♠T♠	4.8M	6.3M	4.14M

As always when there is a change in scenery I like to swing at the first opportunity. Of course it doesn't hurt to have A♠T♠. I make it 200,000 in the button and Jimmy folds his lonely BB. Julius should have been the SB but decided to leave the party early.

Hand 237

CRUCIAL HAND 15: Misplaying a Big Pot— In Trouble with K♥ Q♦

Blinds	My Position	My Hand	My Chip Stack	JF	AB
30K/60K/5K	BB	K♥ Q♦	4.865M	6.385M	4M

Jimmy opens for 175,000 on the button, Andy folds, and I re-raise to 675,000 with KQ from the BB. Here are some reasons:

1. In a three-handed game KQ is usually the best hand.
2. I want to send Jimmy a message not to mess with my BB.
3. I love to re-raise with KQ!

Gobboboy calls, which I have to admit was not part of the plan. The flop comes:

Not really part of the plan either. My nice-looking hand has turned very mediocre as I am still looking at King high.

There are a couple of different routes to take on the flop:

The conservative route: checking and folding to any meaningful bet on Jimmy's part. If Jimmy checks behind, see the turn card for free and proceed with caution.

The continuation bet: leading out for about 50–70% of the pot—in this case in the 800,000 range. If called or raised, give up except in the case of a hit on the turn.

The sneaky check-raise: check, planning to click-raise whatever bet Jimmy might come up with, implying that I am holding an Ace. By *click-raising* I mean doubling his bet. If he bets 700,000 I make it 1.4M.

The insane route: in some way, shape, or form shooting 4.2M into the pot giving me the best chance of claiming the 1.4M in there.

They all have some merit but leading out for 800,000 gives me an immediate chance of picking up the 1.4M, and I love to pick up pots.

I bet 800,000 only to see Jimmy click-raise me instead. This pot was getting too big for comfort. My 800,000 bet was meant as an investment with a probable return of 1.4M but obviously Jimmy had a different opinion. He had turned the tables and now it was me facing an 800,000 bet. The sneaky check-raise and the conservative route had been eliminated by my lead-out bet but I still had two ways to go.

The insane route would practically demand an all-in move on my part right here and now. I am not sure I am ready for it. The continuation-bet route had come to a sudden stop. My 800,000 bet had been foiled by Jimmy's re-raise and it was time to face the facts. I only had King high and if Jimmy had the Ace he was representing I was down to four outs. Adding it all together, folding seems like the more reasonable choice. So I did.

One point five million is enough to lose with KQ, when you don't connect on the flop!

In retrospect I would have liked to save the 800,000, but then again, I like the continuation bet, but I think my facial expression might have given me away. Jimmy could very well have picked up on the fact that I really didn't like the flop and used that information to his advantage. Whatever he had, he got the best of me and for the first time I relinquished my second spot and was now the small stack.

Hand 238

Blinds	My Position	My Hand	My Chip Stack	JF	AB
30K/60K/5K	BB	K♦ 8♠	3.345M	7.905M	4M

A fairly conservative start, as we have all received a free one in the big blind. This time it is my turn. I get a walk. At least we are all walking together.

Hand 239

Blinds	My Position	My Hand	My Chip Stack	JF	AB
30K/60K/5K	SB	T♣ 8♥	3.385M	7.9M	3.965M

Not wanting to give Jimmy another freebie, I limp from the small blind with T♣ 8♥. It wasn't a very successful strategy! Jimmy raised to 210,000 and I folded.

Hand 240

CRUCIAL HAND 16: All-in Pre-Flop for
3.2 Million Holding 7♠7♦

Blinds	My Position	My Hand	My Chip Stack	JF	AB
30K/60K/5K	BB	7♠7♦	3.21M	8.685M	3.35M

After losing my second spot to Andy I have been folding five or six consecutive hands. I wasn't going to fold this one. Jimmy raises on the button to 200,000 and Andy folds. Now it's up to me and my 77.

Holding medium to small pairs is a very delicate matter. The best way to play them depends very much on the two stack sizes involved. You should therefore try to manipulate the size of the pot so it plays into the strength of your hand. When both players are very deep stacked your best option is usually to keep the pre-flop pot as small as possible, hoping to flop a set and then reap the benefits. When you are medium-to-short-stacked your best bet is usually to move all-in hoping your opponent will fold, and if called, that he/she doesn't have an over pair.

So which category do I fit into? Blinds and antes cost 105,000 a round, giving me about 31 rounds to play at this level. We will soon be moving up to the 40,000/80,000 level with 10,000 antes, giving me only 21 rounds to play. According-ing to various charts in different poker books both numbers indicate deep-stack scenarios. That is of course only half the truth. In my book the most significant number is that we are only three-handed. Dividing the number of rounds by 3, the number of players, gives a more accurate figure of 7–10 rounds to play, clearly a more short-stacked situation! Add in the pleasure of saying, "I am all-in," and the choice should be pretty clear.

I move all-in and Jimmy quickly folds.

Hand 241

Blinds	My Position	My Hand	My Chip Stack	JF	AB
30K/60K/5K	SB	9♣ 6♥	3.45M	8.48M	3.32M

Andy limps, I limp along, and Jimmy checks his BB. Three-way it is. The flop comes:

Over the years I have had very good success leading out on paired boards. It is very hard for anybody to connect, and a lot of times whoever makes the first move wins the pot. I like to take the first stab, especially in a tournament situation, where people in general are a little bit more careful with their chips. The seat assignments also help a little. Jimmy is not going to call without a decent hand with Andy lurking behind him. Andy is probably not going to play without a decent hand period! Had the seats been reversed, it would instead have been Andy caught in the middle. With Jimmy being last to act and holding a big chip lead, he would be a lot more prone to mess around with an inferior holding!

I bet 90,000 trying to pick up the 195,000 in the center. Jimmy plays along and folds, but Andy had different plans. He calls. For all I care he could be holding a Q, 2, or some clubs. On a scarier note, he could also be picking up on the fact that

I like to bluff in these situations, and using his positional advantage to see my next move. No matter what, I predict that my Nine-high has a very bleak future. I decided that this was not the time to fire second or third bullets, basically sealing my fate in this hand. A classic well-timed give-up play! Even if a Six or a Nine should happen to show up on the turn, I might still be in the check-folding mode!

The turn is a very uneventful:

I check and Andy bets 90,000. Betting 90,000 into a 375,000 pot seems very weak, and it indicates that he is not that strong either! Is it enough to go by to change my plans and try for a check-raise? I'm not sure. I definitely would like to with a bigger chip stack, but not this time!

I fold and Andy drags the pot.

All in all I think my lead-out bet was a profitable play, with maybe as much as a 50% chance of working. This time it didn't work, but that is not going to stop me from doing it again and again.

Hand 242

Blinds	My Position	My Hand	My Chip Stack	JF	AB
30K/60K/5K	Button	A♠6♥	3.295M	8.415M	3.54M

I open on the button for 200,000 with A6o. Jimmy calls in the SB, Andy folds.

The flop comes:

Jimmy checks and even though I totally missed the flop I decided to bet out anyway. This is a standard continuation-bet type of play, trying to take advantage of the fact that your opponent is only holding two cards, which makes him more likely than not to miss the flop. Add in the fact that my Ace high could easily still be the best hand, making it a cardinal sin to give a free card to a hand like T♠7♠.

I bet 220,000 into a 475,000 pot and Jimmy folds.

Hand 243

Blinds	My Position	My Hand	My Chip Stack	JF	AB
30K/60K/5K	SB	T♣8♣	3.5M	8.31M	3.44M

I have folded more blinds than I'm used to and it is definitely not to my liking. I really want to change gears, but my aggressive opponents and my somewhat mediocre holdings have kept me quiet. A medium-suited connector like T♣8♣ is enough to raise my voice and get back into raising mode. I raise in the SB to 200,000 and Jimmy folds.

Hand 244

Blinds	My Position	My Hand	My Chip Stack	JF	AB
30K/60K/5K	BB	K♠6♥	3.565M	8.21M	3.475M

Jimmy makes it 200,000, Andy gets out of the way, and I call in the BB with K6o. The flop comes:

I missed the flop completely and had no intention of getting fancy so I check. Jimmy bets 300,000 and I fold.

Remember that outlasting Andy Black still has a very high priority with this pay-off structure, which is one of the reasons why I am not playing as aggressively as I normally do.

Hand 245

Blinds	My Position	My Hand	My Chip Stack	JF	AB
30K/60K/5K	SB	7♣ 6♥	3.36M	8.45M	3.44M

Andy folds and I call with 7♣ 6♥, trying the limp one more time. Jimmy checks his BB—at least this time I got to the flop!

But not any further! My Seven-high is aimed right at the muck, so once again I go for the check-fold. Jimmy bets 75,000 and wins the pot.

Hand 246

	My	My	My Chip		
Blinds	Position	Hand	Stack	JF	AB
30K/60K/5K	Button	A♠ 6♦	3.295M	8.52M	3.435M

I open for 200,000 on the button with A♠ 6♦ and take away the blinds and antes.

Hand 247

	My	My	My Chip		
Blinds	Position	Hand	Stack	JF	AB
30K/60K/5K	BB	8♣ 3♦	3.395M	8.485M	3.37M

Jimmy raises to 200,000, Andy calls, and I fold my BB! It is not very often that you see me throw away a hand getting 3.5:1. I only need to win this hand about 22% of the time, which basically makes every hand playable. Had I had any straighty, flushy, or high-card possibilities I would have called the extra 140,000. The 8♣ 3♦ offers none of the above and I therefore elect to fold.

Flop is:

Andy checks, Jimmy bets 300,000, and Andy folds.

Hand 248

Blinds	My Position	My Hand	My Chip Stack	JF	AB
30K/60K/5K	Button	Q♦8♥	3.295M	9.015M	2.94M

Another button raise and another 100,000 pickup! I'm trying to stay afloat while Jimmy is making progress. Andy's stack has been dwindling, maybe due to slightly conservative starting requirements. Whatever it is, it seems like Jimmy is taking control, building his stack to over 9 million with me and Andy fighting for the scrubs. For now I'll try to be second scrub and not third!

Hand 249

Blinds	My Position	My Hand	My Chip Stack	JF	AB
30K/60K/5K	BB	J♠6♥	3.395M	8.98M	2.875M

Jimmy raises to 200,000, Andy folds, and I call in the BB with J6o. Another questionable call on my part! Don't get me wrong—calling 140,000 from a button raise to win 305,000 is something I will do day in and day out. All I need to make that call is basically two cards in my hand.

But is it really necessary for me to get involved in a pot, out of position, with a mediocre holding against the massive chipleader? I don't think so—the main reason being that Andy and I are pretty much tied for second. Each of us is trying to outlast the other and I probably shouldn't waste valuable chips in marginal situations.

The flop comes:

Not a great flop but I do have a gut-shot straight draw, a back-door flush draw, and an over card. You have to stay positive!

I check and Jimmy checks behind me. The turn card is the:

A very good card for me! The 3♠ is very unlikely to have helped Jimmy in any way, whereas my hand suddenly has a big drawing potential.

My J-high has just about no chance of being the best hand right now but since Jimmy's check indicated weakness, betting here is a must. Leading out as a semi-bluff is the obvious play.

I bet 260,000 and Jimmy folds. I win the 445,000 pot.

Hand 250

	My	My	My Chip		
Blinds	**Position**	**Hand**	**Stack**	**JF**	**AB**
30K/60K/5K	SB	5♥ 4♥	3.635M	8.775M	2.84M

Andy folds and I limp in with 4♥ 5♥. No reason to jack up the stakes pre-flop with that kind of holding. If the flop comes high I'll go for the check-fold, losing the minimum, but if it comes down in my range I might try to play a big pot. Jimmy checks his BB.

The flop comes:

Definitely in my neighborhood! Leading out with second pair is trivial. I bet 60,000 and Jimmy calls, indicating that he has some kind of hand. Then again what is some kind of hand on a 2–5–8 rainbow flop? More or less any two cards will qualify. 34 is an up-and-down, 69 is a gut shot with an over card, and a JT are two over cards. The way Jimmy has been playing so far all of those three hands are in play as well as many, many others. I do think though that Jimmy would have raised with an Eight in his hand, leading me to believe that my pair of Fives is right now the best hand.

The turn is:

Adding a flush draw to my hand gives me little more courage to pull off the play I had intended. Still believing that I have the best hand, and convinced that Jimmy is going to bet if I check, my plan is to check-raise. And so it goes. I check, Jimmy bets 150,000, and I check-raise to 500,000.

Fairly certain that my check-raise was going to be the last play of the hand, I must admit that I felt a little bit uneasy when Jimmy put another 350,000 into the pot. Oops! I hadn't planned that far ahead. Not really sure how much more money I would be willing to put in the pot with my two Fives, we were off to the river.

The river comes:

Salvation! One of my fourteen outs! I don't know whether I needed to hit but it sure was nice to do so. Still in a fog as to what Jimmy was holding, I opted for the straightforward value-bet. Seven hundred thousand into a 1,255,000 pot is in the very low range of my value-betting chart. On the other hand I thought Jimmy was much more likely to call a medium-sized bet than my more standard pot-sized bets.

I bet 700,000 and Jimmy folds.

Post-hand comments:

Pre-flop: keeping the pot small with low-suited connectors—good

Flop: leading out when connecting with the board—no-brainer

Turn: check-raising with third pair and a flush draw—tricky

River: value-betting when hitting your draw—usually recommended but maybe not this time.

There is a good chance I could have induced a bluff from Jimmy by checking the river. If Jimmy had a Jack he would for sure call a value-bet on my part. But he would also value-bet a Jack himself if I checked, making it somewhat a matter of indifference what I do. If Jimmy was on a draw my only chance to pick up extra money would be to check. From that perspective checking the river seems superior. On the other hand I have to give a couple of style points for testing Jimmy's seemingly curious nature! There are definitely a lot of hands out there that

Jimmy would call with, but not value-bet himself. Some pros, some cons—personally I think it all ends up in a great big tie!

Bottom line: I took home the 1,255,000 pot for a 625,000 gain, putting some much-needed distance between myself and Andy!

Hand 251

Blinds	My Position	My Hand	My Chip Stack	JF	AB
30K/60K/5K	Button	J♥ T♣	4.265M	8.15M	2.835M

I raise to 200,000 on the button with JTo and Andy calls in the BB. The flop comes:

Andy checks and once again the continuation bet is effective. I bet 220,000 with my J-high, no draw, hoping that Andy has the same kind of hand. I don't know if he did, but he surely missed the flop and quickly mucked his hand.

Hand 252

Blinds	My Position	My Hand	My Chip Stack	JF	AB
30K/60K/5K	BB	6♣ 7♣	4.505M	8.115M	2.63M

Jimmy folds, Black limps, and I check my BB with 6♣ 7♣. Compared to my 4♥ 5♥ two hands ago there is one major difference: position. I don't think it is quite enough to raise as

Andy has been playing fairly tight the entire way and obviously has me high-carded.

The flop comes:

Although I still have Seven-high this should be considered a very good flop. Having the high end of open-ended straight-draw is significantly stronger than the sucker end. Right now I am very happy about my hand and prepared to play it strong.

Let us look at the sucker end for a second. Same hand, 6♣ 7♣, but this time the flop is 8♣ 9♦ K♥. This time I am hoping to see the turn as cheaply as possible and if nothing materializes to be in a folding mode! Be careful about the sucker end!

Back to the action. Andy checks and I bet 60,000. Andy calls. The turn brings:

Not my kind of card, but since Andy checks again I decide to take another stab at it. With 240,000 in the pot I bet 160,000 and luckily Andy surrendered.

I am usually very careful about firing second bullets, especially against Andy. I know he is prone to check a big hand twice, thereby making it a little more treacherous for me to make a move. On the other hand Andy did not seem over-whelmed with joy when the second Five appeared, so betting was definitely in order.

Hand 253

Blinds	My Position	My Hand	My Chip Stack	JF	AB
40K/80K/10K	SB	9♠ 6♠	4.53M	7.795M	2.62M

We are picking up speed. The blinds have increased to 40,000/80,000 and the ante has moved up to a very significant 10,000. There is 150,000 up for grabs each hand which means that Andy and I can't afford to let Jimmy run over the table.

After receiving a very welcome walk in the big blind the previous hand, I'm now in the small blind.

I have been advocating keeping the pots small pre-flop with low-suited connectors and my 6♠9♠ is no exception, although I will say that it has been a while since I raised in my and Jimmy's blind vs. blind confrontation. So for the sake of randomness—and 150,000—I decide to raise! I make it 260,000 and Jimmy folds.

Hand 254

Blinds	My Position	My Hand	My Chip Stack	JF	AB
40K/80K/10K	Button	K♠ 6♥	4.63M	7.705M	2.61M

I fold K6o on the button which is a little too conservative for my style with this high-ante structure. I didn't feel like playing the hand and sometimes you just have to follow your instincts.

Jimmy felt the same way and Andy gets a walk.

Hand 255

Blinds	My Position	My Hand	My Chip Stack	JF	AB
40K/80K/10K	BB	A♣9♣	4.62M	7.65M	2.67M

Jimmy opens for 250,000, Black folds, and I opt to call with my A♣9♣. A rather unusual call! A9 suited is, if not a power-house, at least a very strong holding in a three-handed game. Jimmy had been playing very aggressively on the button so there was really no reason to let him get away with another raise. Re-raising is simply the best play!

So what happened? To be honest I can't exactly put my finger on it. This was the best holding I had had for a good twenty hands and only calling didn't quite do it justice. I will say that I was contemplating to check-raise the flop no matter what showed up. So for now let us just call it a slow play.

The flop comes:

Triple X! Not at all what I wanted to see out there! Even though a paired board makes it more likely that my Ace high is still the best hand, I would have much preferred a 4–4–5 flop.

I decided to follow the first leg of my check-raising-the-flop plan. I checked. Jimmy bets 350,000 and suddenly I got a bad taste in my mouth. Just calling before the flop followed by a check-fold is the kind of weak-tight play that I love to hate. I shouldn't even be allowed to do it! Nevertheless, for the second hand in a row I went with my instincts and folded.

Playing like this in a three-handed game with a high ante-

and blind structure is a sure recipe for disaster. Maybe I will watch it on TV and pat myself on the back because of my "good read," but most likely I will ask myself what the hell I was doing!

Hand 256

Blinds	My Position	My Hand	My Chip Stack	JF	AB
40K/80K/10K	BB	Q♣5♥	4.3M	8.125M	2.52M

Jimmy folds, Andy limps, and I check my Q♣5♥ in the BB. The flop comes:

Andy checks and instead of my usual stab I decide to let this one go. I check as well. The turn brings:

Andy checks and so do I, once again straying away from my normal betting procedure. The river is:

Again we both check and my Queen-high prevails. Happy to win it, but I still think it is safe to say that we both could have been more active in this hand. I should have taken a stab on the flop, on the turn, or both trying to pick up the 190,000 lying out there. It didn't cost me the pot this time, but if Andy hit one of his cards or decided to bluff me it would have!

Hand 257

Blinds	My Position	My Hand	My Chip Stack	JF	AB
40K/80K/10K	SB	K♠ 8♥	4.4M	8.115M	2.43M

Andy Black limps for 80,000 on the button and I felt it was time to make a little move. I raised to a total of 320,000. Raising in an already limped pot usually indicates more strength than an opening raise in an uncontested pot. I was hoping that Jimmy and Andy would see it the same way. The strength of my K8*o* didn't warrant a raise but I thought I was a decent favorite to pick up the 240,000 pot right there. I was wrong! Jimmy immediately comes over the top, making it a total of 1.1M. Andy quickly gets out of the way and I am stuck in a situation I definitely didn't want. I could call another 780,000 trying to win the 1.5M pot, but do I really want to? I am a sucker for 2 to 1 but staying away from this one clearly seems to be the right choice. This was not a good time to get involved with the chip-leader. My game plan is still to get Andy out of the way before getting entangled too deeply.

I fold and Jimmy picks up the pot and a nice 420,000 profit.

Hand 258

Blinds	My Position	My Hand	My Chip Stack	JF	AB
40K/80K/10K	BB	T♣ 6♠	4.06M	8.635M	2.25M

Jimmy folds his button and Andy limps in the SB. I look down at T6o and the standard play would be to just check behind and see a flop. Just two hands ago I made an unsuccessful attempt to raise after Andy had limped. That failure wasn't going to stop me from trying again. If one unsuccessful bluff is going to stop you from ever bluffing again, poker is not the right game for you!

The second attempt worked a lot better as Andy folded to my 240,000 raise.

Hand 259

Blinds	My Position	My Hand	My Chip Stack	JF	AB
40K/80K/10K	SB	A♣Q♠	4.16M	8.625M	2.16M

Andy opens for 250,000 and I am very happy to find AQo in the SB. It doesn't take a lot of consideration on my part to re-raise. The only question is how much?

I am not really interested in playing a big hand post-flop, out of position, so I am going to put a lot of effort into winning it right now. This translates into a big re-raise. I raise 790,000 more, making it a total of 1.04M.

Jimmy and Andy both fold.

Hand 260

Blinds	My Position	My Hand	My Chip Stack	JF	AB
40K/80K/10K	BB	6♣5♣	4.5M	8.635M	1.81M

Jimmy folds, Andy limps, and I check behind with my 6♣5♣.

The flop comes:

A lot of hearts! Andy bets 175,000 and I call. I am not espe-cially happy about Andy's sudden interest in the pot, or the size of his bet. Even though it is a pot-sized bet I feel that being in position with second pair is good enough to merit a call.

The turn is:

Andy checks and all the alarm bells go off in the studio! I smell a rat; something just wasn't right here. Andy's big bet on the flop followed by a quick check on the turn just didn't quite add up. Unfortunately I didn't listen to my inner voice. Instead I paid way too much attention to the fact that Andy had checked. Andy's check "obviously" meant that my two Sixes were good and therefore I had to bet—*not!*

I bet 330,000 and Andy quickly moves all-in for a total of 1.545M.

I fold.

Bad bet on my part! I was aware that something was wrong but failed to take the time to appropriately decipher the action. Even worse—I had a chance to see the river for free and instead I paid 330,000 not to see the river!

Hand 261

Blinds	My Position	My Hand	My Chip Stack	JF	AB
40K/80K/10K	SB	T♥ 8♥	3.905M	8.625M	2.415M

Andy makes it 250,000 and I call in the SB with T♥ 8♥. Jimmy calls as well and for the first time in a long time we are off to see a three-handed flop. The flop comes:

A very easy flop to play! No matter what happens I am not going to put more money in the pot. I check and Jimmy takes a stab at it betting 500,000.

Andy and I both fold.

Even though my plan is to get Andy out of the picture before I make my move, I have to be a little concerned about the fact that we are letting Jimmy pick up too many uncontested pots.

Hand 262

Blinds	My Position	My Hand	My Chip Stack	JF	AB
40K/80K/10K	BB	K♣ J♥	3.635M	9.095M	2.215M

Jimmy opens for 250,000 and Andy calls in the SB. I am in the BB with KJo and folding is not an option. In fact I am not so sure that calling is a good play, either. Re-raising is a much better idea. I generally love to re-raise pre-flop in short-handed situations but for some reason the cat got my tongue.

I am starting to get very unhappy with my own play in this little private three-handed game we have here. I have made way too many conservative decisions and that is just not the way to win a tournament. I know that the ladder principle has played a big part in my decision-making but right now it is playing a much-too-dominant role in my game.

I call. The flop comes:

Another good holding turned sour by a poor flop. I guess we all felt like that 'cause the flop goes: Check, check, check.

Turn:

Happy to see a picture card, but very unhappy that it is a Queen! Andy and I both check and Jimmy bets 450,000. We both fold.

Just like two hands ago Jimmy wins the pot with a single post-flop bet. I am starting to wonder if Andy and I are just handing Jimmy the victory. Bottom line is, if we both continue with our passive play—no-re-raise, check-fold strategy—it won't be long before Jimmy can lift the trophy.

Hand 263

Blinds	My Position	My Hand	My Chip Stack	JF	AB
40K/80K/10K	SB	J♠ 6♦	3.375M	9.615M	1.995M

Andy limps, I call, and Jimmy checks for a small family pot. The flop comes:

I check, Jimmy checks, and Andy bets 200,000. We both fold.

Hand 264

Blinds	My Position	My Hand	My Chip Stack	JF	AB
40K/80K/10K	Button	K♣ J♠	3.285M	9.525M	2.135M

I open for 250,000 with KJo. Jimmy folds and Andy calls. The flop brings:

A great flop as long as Andy folds to my continuation bet. That's exactly what he did!

After Andy's check I fire 300,000, which is good enough to win the pot.

Hand 265

Blinds	My Position	My Hand	My Chip Stack	JF	AB
40K/80K/10K	BB	Q♥5♣	3.595M	9.475M	1.875M

Jimmy folds, Black bets 220,000, and I call in the BB with Q5*o*. Note that Andy's raise is a little smaller than usual, giving me a slightly better pot odds to continue. Calling 140,000 to win 330,000 in position is trivial no matter what you are holding! Flop:

Andy fires 300,000—basically telling me that he couldn't care less about my position. I fold—basically telling him that I have absolutely nothing.

Hand 266

Blinds	My Position	My Hand	My Chip Stack	JF	AB
40K/80K/10K	BB	K♣8♠	3.305M	9.625M	2.015M

Jimmy opens for 250,000, Andy folds, and I call in the BB with K8*o*. The flop comes:

I check and Jimmy fires 350,000. So what do we have here? A flop with absolutely *no* drawing potential! It is either hit or miss. If Jimmy has a Three he has the lead but not an insurmountable one, a Nine would be ugly, and the Ace put me in a world of pain. But against all the other hands my King-high is usually in the lead. Chances of Jimmy holding a pair is in this case approximately 40%, leaving me with close to a 60% chance of having the best hand. Sixty percent is of course a stretch, but for all I care Jimmy could have just about any two cards, making my computations somewhat believable! What to do?

Folding: As mentioned above my King-high has a pretty good chance of being in the lead—I don't like folding.

Calling: leaves me somewhere in nowhere-land. It fails to define the hand and puts me in a tough spot if Jimmy decides to fire another bullet—don't like that one either.

Check-raising: A much more radical maneuver, treading a more dangerous path—presents some pros and cons. Let us take a look at a few of them:

Cons

Putting a lot more money in the pot drawing somewhere from slim to dead

Pros

Winning the pot right here against a lot of Jimmy's weak holdings!
Bluffing Jimmy out of hands like 55 and KT!
Feeling better about myself after finally making a stand!

Needless to say I didn't have time to go over all the considerations and calculations at the table. To tell you the truth there was only one overwhelming factor that made me go for the check-raise: I just couldn't take it anymore. Having played weak-tight for too many hands and letting Jimmy get away with way too much made me pull the trigger.

I check-raised to 700,000 on my K-high! Jimmy mucked.

Letting your emotions dictate your actions at the poker table is probably single-handedly the worst strategy ever, but nonetheless I see it happen to poker players over and over again.

This time it happened to me! At least there was a little bit of rhyme or reason behind it, and luckily for me the outcome was a pretty good one.

Hand 267

Blinds	My Position	My Hand	My Chip Stack	JF	AB
40K/80K/10K	SB	T♥ 6♥	3.965M	9.015M	1.965M

Andy folds and I decide to follow the aggressive approach that proved successful in the previous hand. I make it 250,000 from the SB with T♥ 6♥. Jimmy calls and the flop comes:

A gut shot and two over cards! No need to slow down with a powerhouse like that! I bet 330,000 and Jimmy moves all-in. I fold.

My aggressive play had taken a hit and I slowly sink back into my chair.

Hand 268

Blinds	My Position	My Hand	My Chip Stack	JF	AB
40K/80K/10K	BB	K♣4♦	3.365M	9.885M	1.695M

Jimmy folds, Andy limps, and I check it right back with my K♣4♦. The flop is:

Andy bets 350,000—a surprisingly big amount for a 190,000 pot—which just makes my decision easier. I fold.

Hand 269

Blinds	My Position	My Hand	My Chip Stack	JF	AB
40K/80K/10K	SB	Q♠8♦	3.275M	9.875M	1.795M

Andy folds and I make it 250,000 from the small blind with Q♠8♦. Jimmy folds—and the same pattern continues. Jimmy is chipping away, I have held my own, and Andy is quietly deteriorating. I can't say I mind as we slowly inch closer to a Gobboboy vs. Hansen confrontation!

Hand 270

Blinds	My Position	My Hand	My Chip Stack	JF	AB
40K/80K/10K	BB	J♦6♠	3.365M	9.885M	1.695M

Jimmy opens on the button for 250,000. Andy folds and I call with my J6o. Looking back, I wish I would have folded a lot of these marginal BB hands or at least re-raised with some of them. My approach the last twenty-plus hands can at best be described as different. The flop shows:

I check another no pair, no draw holding and Jimmy checks behind me. The turn is:

No improvement. I check, Jimmy bets 200,000, and I fold.

Hand 271

Blinds	My Position	My Hand	My Chip Stack	JF	AB
40K/80K/10K	SB	J♥T♦	3.105M	10.195M	1.645M

Andy opens for 250,000 on the button. I have JTo in the SB and contemplate for a second whether to re-raise. I decide against and call, preparing to see a flop. Jimmy wanted it otherwise, though. This was the first time Jimmy had the chance to put both of us under a lot of pressure with a big pre-flop re-raise. It didn't take him long to do so!

Jimmy re-raises to 1.5M and we both fold.

Gobboboy took full advantage of his big-chip lead. It has now become apparent to me that Jimmy knows that both Andy and I are in some kind of a waiting mode. Personally I am hoping that Jimmy will knock out Andy, upgrading me from third to second and a minimum paycheck of one million Australian dollars. There is no doubt in my mind that Andy hopes for the same kind of upgrade.

With the price differential between second and third being AU$ 300,000, it would be foolish for any of us—me especially—to butt heads with Jimmy's massive chip stack. Well played, Jimmy!

Hand 272

Blinds	My Position	My Hand	My Chip Stack	JF	AB
40K/80K/10K	Button	Q♠ 8♣	2.845M	10.715M	1.385M

I make it 250,000 on the button with Q♠ 8♣. Andy and Jimmy both fold.

Hand 273

Blinds	My Position	My Hand	My Chip Stack	JF	AB
40K/80K/10K	BB	Q♥ 2♥	2.985M	10.665M	1.295M

Jimmy opens for 250,000, Andy folds, and I call in the BB with Q♥ 2♥. The flops brings:

Right color, wrong suit! I check, Jimmy bets 350,000 and takes down the pot.

Hand 274

Blinds	My Position	My Hand	My Chip Stack	JF	AB
40K/80K/10K	SB	K♠5♥	2.725M	10.975M	1.245M

Andy folds on the button, I limp in with K5o, and Jimmy checks his BB. The flop comes:

Thinking that my King-high is probably good I bet 80,000 and Jimmy calls. The turn card is the:

Hitting a pair on the turn caught me completely by surprise! So much so that I didn't really know what to do with it. Last time I did it—about twenty hands ago—I played it like an idiot. Hopefully I will do better this time.

I decide to check because of the three diamonds on the board and Jimmy checks behind me. River:

Once again we both check. Jimmy shows 5♣ 5♦ and my pair of Kings wins the pot.

Post-hand comments: What went wrong? Whatever happened to "bet when you think you have the best hand"? Checking the turn seems reasonable with trips and flush possibilities out there. Remember that Jimmy did call my bet on the flop!

Checking the river, on the other hand, was an awful play. Jimmy had throughout the day showed that he was much more likely to call a river bet than actually value bet himself. Jimmy's check on the turn combined with a total blank 2h on the river more than indicated that I had the best hand! A value bet of about 300,000 on the river would have been appropriate.

Maybe it is better for me to stop hitting them pairs because I have already misplayed a couple of them.

Hand 275

Blinds	My Position	My Hand	My Chip Stack	JF	AB
40K/80K/10K	Button	A♥ 8♣	2.905M	10.805M	1.235M

I make it 250,000 on the button with A♥ 8♣. Jimmy folds and Andrew moves all-in for 1.225M total.

First thing to do when facing an all-in bet—unless it is a completely obvious call—is to figure out the pot odds. Second of all, consider the range of hands that you think your opponent might have. Third, make an estimate of how well your own hand will fare against your opponent's various holdings. Fourth, mix all three together, add in your read, and do something!

Go ahead and take as much time as you want, talk to yourself, and act as goofy as you want. Remember it doesn't matter whether or not your opponent gets a read on you. He won't be able to use it for anything.

1. Pot odds: I have to call 975,000 to win 1.545M, close to 3:2 or exactly 38.7%.
2. Andy's range of hands: Any pair, probably any Ace, a bunch of high-card combos, and a couple of I-just-can't-take-it-anymore hands.
3. Estimating my winning chance by considering Andy's possible holdings:
   KK through 88 approximately 30%
   77 through 22 approximately 46%
   AA approximately 7%
   AK through A9 approximately 30%
   A7 though A2 approximately 65%
   Various high card holdings approximately 55%
   I-just-can't-take-it-anymore hands approximately 60%
   Verdict: Average estimate—a little less than 50%!
4. I had absolutely no read on Andy as this was a standard pre-flop raise, re-raise situation. That leaves me with the math: call!

It is of course impossible and too time-consuming to make exact computations at the table but as long as you have some ballpark figures you should be okay.

I call with my A8o and am very happy to see that my "any Ace" category was justified as Andrew shows A♠3♥. I am a 66–34% favorite.

The flop comes:

No Three, but a gut shot for Andy. I'm down to a 62–37% advantage. Turn:

Now it is down 54–45%! I hope it's not a sign. River:

We split the pot with a pair of fours, Ace-high. It would have been nice to knock Andy out, get to heads-up, and not have to worry about any more ladder considerations, but I guess it could have been a lot worse.

We take another short break, as this three-handed match has been going on for quite a while. Five minutes to catch a breath of fresh air.

Hand 276

Blinds	My Position	My Hand	My Chip Stack	JF	AB
50K/100K/10K	BB	T♥8♥	2.77M	10.9M	1.27M

Blinds have increased to 50/100 but the ante is still the same—10k per man.

Jimmy folds, Andy calls, and I check my BB. The flop comes:

Andy checks and I stop for a second to consider my options. I have bottom-pair and an up-and-down straight draw. There is 230k in the pot and Andy has 1.16M left. Checking seems silly with a good, playable hand. There are not a lot of free cards that can hurt me, but still . . .

Making a standard bet of 200k is in my opinion a little goofy. Considering the pot odds I would call an all-in move by Andy anyway. The all-in bet of a million-plus seems to fit my purpose a little bit better. If Andy has me beat I still have a lot of outs, and I might bluff out of the best hand!

Just consider these three holdings—7♣ 4♣, 9♦ 6♦, or K♠ 8♥? Andy would be hard-pressed to call facing elimination, which is exactly what I want! I would obviously love to knock him out of the pot in all three situations. All-in is the best play available, and that is what I do!

I bet 1 million—not quite all-in but close enough. Andy folds.

Hand 277

Blinds	My Position	My Hand	My Chip Stack	JF	AB
50K/100K/10K	SB	4♣ 4♠	2.89M	10.89M	1.16M

Andy folds, I call 50k more with 44, and Jimmy checks his option.

The flop comes:

A pair and an open-ended straight draw in a limped pot, almost exactly the same as last hand. One major difference though—the opposition! This hand will play more deep-stacked than the previous one, and this time I am the one potentially facing elimination. That adds up to an entirely different approach. I check and Jimmy bets 150k. I call! I am not ready to play a big pot—yet.

The turn is:

I check, planning to fold if Jimmy makes a big bet. Luckily he checks.

The river comes:

My pair of Fours has a decent chance to win a showdown, but I am not looking to push the envelope. I check.

Jimmy checks behind and flips over 5♣ 8♣ to beat my pair of Fours.

Post-hand comments: Limping before the flop was intentional. If Jimmy checked behind me we would see a cheap flop, and unless it caught my eye, I could get off the hand for just a tiny investment. If Jimmy raised pre-flop I could go for the true Kamikaze all-in—playing into the strength of my small pair!

Another question comes to mind: "Could I have won the pot if I pushed it hard enough?"

Maybe so, but as it was I'm not too unhappy losing the minimum!

Hand 278

Blinds	My Position	My Hand	My Chip Stack	JF	AB
50K/100K/10K	Button	9♣ 6♥	2.63M	11.16M	1.15M

I fold and Jimmy raises to 350k. Andy announces all-in and after studying for a couple of minutes Jimmy calls. Jimmy holds 5♠ 6♦ vs. Andy's K♦ T♦. The flop comes:

Although Jimmy hits a Five his winning chances dropped to 18.4%. Turn and River brought:

Andy doubles up!

Jimmy's call was on the edge, but reasonable with a considerable amount already in the pot. The initial raise was completely unnecessary, being out of position with 56o. I know that Jimmy has had decent success being the aggressor, but sometimes it is wise just to let one go.

Unfortunately for me the result closed the gap between me and Andy.

Hand 279

Blinds	My Position	My Hand	My Chip Stack	JF	AB
50K/100K/10K	BB	A♥ 2♠	2.62M	10.01M	2.31M

Jimmy opens for 300k on the button, Andy folds, and I call with ace high. A mediocre hand with some good potential—especially if an Ace flops.

The flop comes:

Unfortunately no Ace—I check. Fortunately Jimmy checks behind me.

The turn brings:

My Ace suddenly looks like a mighty big card and I reward it with a 300k bet. Jimmy folds.

Fairly timid play on my part, as I could have been more

aggressive both pre- and post-flop! Remember though: I am still trying to outlast Andy!

Hand 280

Blinds	My Position	My Hand	My Chip Stack	JF	AB
50K/100K/10K	SB	8♥ 5♥	2.99M	9.7M	2.25M

Andy folds and I limp in with 8♥ 5♥. Jimmy checks his BB.

The flop comes:

With endless back-door possibilities it is almost impossible to sit still. To satisfy my craving for the 230k pot I fire 125k. Jimmy folds. Not much to say—insanity prevails!

Hand 281

CRUCIAL HAND 17: Putting Andy Black to the Test with Second Pair

Blinds	My Position	My Hand	My Chip Stack	JF	AB
50K/100K/10K	BB	8♥ 6♠	3.1M	9.35M	2.49M

Jimmy folds, and Andy limps from the small blind. Finally a chance to be a bully! Jimmy has too many chips to be bullied, so this is my best shot. I raise to 320k with my very mediocre Eight-high holding, and needless to say I'm a bit unhappy to see Andy call. I'm not quite sure what to make of Andy's hand at this point, but I have a feeling it is better than mine! The flop comes:

Andy leads out 400k. Decision time! I have middle pair, and Andy must have some kind of hand for his lead-out. I seriously doubt that he would lead out with a powerhouse. It has much more of a probe-bet feel to it.

Probing with a weak-ish hand to get a feel for where your opponent is, is in my opinion an underestimated play, and should therefore be used more often. A lot of times it will win you the pot right there, when your opponent fails to connect. Andy's problem is this time I did connect. My problem is it is not a great connection.

A quick look at the chip stacks also plays a big part in making my decision. Andy has 1.7 million left after his bet, and the pot would contain 1.5 Million. Calling and then making a "good" laydown on the turn doesn't seem to make much sense. I'm going to play the hand on the flop, either by moving all-in or by folding.

If I'm correct in my assumption that Andy is holding a medium-weak hand, an all-in move on my part could very well have the desired effect—a fold by Andy. I didn't fly to Melbourne to fold when I finally flopped a pair, so all-in it is. Andy didn't look too happy about the situation and mucked his hand.

Afterthoughts: When I raised, Andy's facial expression looked like: "Why do they always have a hand when I try to make a move?"

Hand 282

Blinds	My Position	My Hand	My Chip Stack	JF	AB
50K/100K/10K	Button	Q♣5♥	3.78M	9.41M	1.75M

Another equity-up hand for me. I fold the button.

It should be clear to everybody by now that the ladder principle has played a big part in this three-handed encounter! Jimmy has used his big chip lead to bully us both and increase his stack. Andy Black has been waiting around for me to get knocked out, and I for him. But you can only wait so long.

Jimmy opens with a normal raise, 350k from the small blind, and Andy being the "short" guy moves all-in for a total of 1.74M. A very standard play with KQ. Jimmy's play is even more standard as he quickly calls with AQ.

The board:

Followed by a Nine and Ten knocks Andy out of the tournament! Without doing anything I increased my minimum paycheck from 700K to 1M. A nice step up the ladder!

CHAPTER 7

FINAL TABLE—HEADS-UP

Heads-Up Considerations

What's the biggest difference between three-handed and heads-up poker?

1. For starters, the much-talked-about ladder principle is out the window. Leaning back in your chair hoping for somebody else to do your dirty work is not going to do you any good. At best it will get you second place! Having had Andy breathing down my neck for the past couple of hours, I will admit it is nice for a change not to have to look over my shoulder! We were trying to outlast each other to earn a couple of extra bucks. In hindsight it gave room to what under normal circumstances would be some rather suspicious poker decisions. No more apprehensive poker, as my only objective now is to grab hold of all the chips at the table!

2. You go from three players to two players! As mentioned in previous chapters adding or subtracting players will surely change the dynamics of the game. The fewer the players the more extreme the change will be. Needless to say, going from three to two players will have a severe impact on your job description. In a three-handed game you can sort of hide a little bit and let your opponents battle it out. Hiding in a heads-up battle is not going to get you very far.

3. You go from bad cards to lousy cards! You have to play more hands to stay in the hunt, which inevitably will affect the quality. You go from top pair to middle pair, open ended to middle pin, flush draws to back doors, full house to Queen-high! Starting hands like K3, Q6, and T7 can easily become your bread and butter because that is what you will get dealt most of the time. You simply have to know how to deal with "garbage" hands or else you will be a couple of steps behind.

4. Then there are the blinds, Probably the biggest difference of them all. In heads-up you are always in the blinds. You will always have money invested in the hand, giving you lucrative pot odds to continue. Folding too much will very soon leave a brutal impression on your chip stack as your living expenses will slowly wear you down.

No matter what, you have to be more forceful in heads-up play. Patience is still a virtue, but too much patience will leave your stack tiny and useless. Aggression is the name of the game.

I hope I can follow my own advice or else Jimmy will have an easy road to victory. I'm down 3 to 1 in chips and I need something to happen, sooner rather than later.

Back to the Table

Hand 283

Blinds	Chip Count	My Hand	My Position
50K/100K	Gus 3.77M	8♠ 4♣	BB
	Jimmy 11.17M		

Jimmy limps on the button and since the 84*o* wasn't the big hand I was looking for, I check my big blind.

The flop comes:

I could have lead out with my flush draw, but since the 8♠ was the only positive feature about my hand, I voted against. I check, Jimmy bets the minimum 100k, and I call. The turn brings:

We both check. The river is:

No help for me and we are down to the never-ending question: Bluff or no bluff? Jimmy's check on the turn indicated weakness, and betting is my only chance to win the hand, but . . .

There is one important piece of advice that I sometimes unfortunately forget myself. You do *not* have to win each and every hand you play! Especially in a heads-up match where just about 50% will do. It is often much more important to try to win the big pots, and lose the small ones. This was a small pot. After all the cards were out I was still looking at Eight-high. I did not have a good read on Jimmy's hand, so everything is pointing in the same direction. Let Jimmy have this one. I checked, and Jimmy's 200k bet immediately ended the hand.

Hand 284

Blinds	Chip Count	My Hand	My Position
50K/100K	Gus 3.57M	J♠ 6♥	Button
	Jimmy 11.37M		

It seems to me that I am not quite up to full speed yet after my rather timid play when three-handed. Here is another timid play coming up! I limp on the button with J6o. I feel like I should have come out swinging a little harder now when we are heads-up but I still have time to change gears. Jimmy checks behind me. The flop comes:

Jimmy checks and it is time to pick up the bat. I bet 100k into a 200k pot. Jimmy calls and my monster hand doesn't look so strong anymore. The turn is:

Improvement! Now I might suddenly have the best hand since Jimmy could have been calling the flop with a Deuce or a gut-shot straight draw. Jimmy checks again. I wasn't about to give him a free card, making this an obvious bet.

I bet 250k and Jimmy folded.

After-thought: I was thinking about firing a second bullet, even if I didn't help on the turn. Fortunately I didn't have to worry about it when the Six came.

Hand 285

Blinds	Chip Count	My Hand	My Position
50K/100K	Gus 3.77M	Q♠ Q♥	BB
	Jimmy 11.17M		

Jimmy raises to 300k on the button and I have to admit that I am a little bit excited looking down at two Queens. Following the trend from last hand I obviously re-raise and make it 1.2M. A bit of an over-raise on my part but I wanted to make sure that I didn't give myself a chance to fold later in the hand.

Jimmy quickly folds.

The first thought going through my mind after Jimmy's quick release was: "Did I miss an opportunity here?" Quite possibly! This was my first re-raise before the flop in quite some time and with such a strong hand slow-playing could have been the right idea. On the other hand slow-playing pre-flop in No Limit Hold'Em is in my opinion not a very good idea unless you hold the motherload—AA. You can try it with Kings as well, but with QQ you are just facing too many tough post-flop decisions when an Ace or a King hits the board. Not to mention all the times you miss out on the opportunity to get all-in pre-flop against smaller pairs! No slow-play for me—I like my re-raise.

Hand 286

Blinds	Chip Count	My Hand	My Position
50K/100K	Gus 4.07M	9♠ 6♦	Button
	Jimmy 10.87M		

Another limp on the button—I have to admit that I don't know why. Jimmy checks behind me.

The flop comes:

Jimmy bets 150k and with middle pair I think the optimum strategy is to re-raise. Being a little slow on the trigger I call, which is at least the second best play. The turn is:

Not the card I was looking for, especially when Jimmy leads out for another 300k. I have to call 300k to win 800k, almost 3:1 but not even close to being enough if I have to improve. With no straight or flush draws I can only hope for a Nine or a Six, a total of five cards, which means I need 8:1 and not 3:1. I really didn't think he was bluffing, making it an easy fold.

Hand 287

Blinds	Chip Count	My Hand	My Position
50K/100K	Gus 3.82M	K♣ Q♥	BB
	Jimmy 11.12M		

Jimmy folds on the button.

Hand 288

Blinds	Chip Count	My Hand	My Position
50K/100K	Gus 3.87M	5♣ 3♦	Button
	Jimmy 11.07M		

I decided to stray away from my limping mode. Instead I folded.

Hand 289

Blinds	Chip Count	My Hand	My Position
50K/100K	Gus 3.82M	7♥ 3♣	BB
	Jimmy 11.12M		

Jimmy makes it 300k and I fold.

Hand 290

CRUCIAL HAND 18: Turning the Tides with A♠ 2♠

Blinds	Chip Count	My Hand	My Position
50K/100K	Gus 3.72M	A♠ 2♠	Button
	Jimmy 11.22M		

My first raise from the button since we started playing heads-up. It comes a tad bit late, but better late than never. I make it 300k and Jimmy calls. The flop comes:

Top pair! It is always nice to see an Ace in the door when you have raised with a weak Ace. Jimmy checks and I bet 350k into a 600k pot with my pair of Aces. Jimmy calls and the turn is:

Jimmy checks again and I have to decide which approach to take. There is now 1.3M in the pot and I have 3.1M left. With no re-raise before the flop and no check-raise on the flop I am fairly confident that my pair of Aces is the best hand.

I have three options:

1. The check: pretty insane! No matter what Jimmy is holding he has at least a couple of outs, and I therefore cannot let him see the river for free.

2. The 1M bet: definitely puts on some pressure, but has one big flaw. If Jimmy calls there would be 3.3M in the pot, leaving me pot-committed with only 2.1M left. Let us assume that Jimmy has a hand like K♣ 9♣—he would definitely call the 1M bet. In case a King, Nine, or a Club comes on the river, he could bet the remaining 2.1M leaving me with a very tough decision to make. If he doesn't hit, he might be able to get away from the pot. A lot of downsides to this variation.

3. The all-in move: puts maximum pressure on any kind of drawing hand. A bit deceptive as well since a lot of people like to make the all-in move with mediocre holdings and semi-bluffs. I'm known for my "crazy" plays, so this seemed like a good opportunity for such a maneuver. I have a feeling that Jimmy would love to win the tournament on a "great read"—basically enticing him to call.

Needless to say, I move all-in.

Jimmy goes into the tank. After a couple of minutes I was sure my pair of Aces were good! After extensive deliberation he finally called and showed K♥ Q♥. Five outs! No King or Queen and I will be right back in the match.

Nice—I double up to 7.44 million. The gap is closing!

Post-hand thoughts: I believe I made the right play on the turn putting Jimmy on the spot. As for Jimmy's call it is hard to say what I would have done had I been in his shoes. One thing I do know—if I am holding K♥ Q♥ in a heads-up match I am going to re-raise pre-flop!

Hand 291

Blinds	Chip Count	My Hand	My Position
50K/100K	Gus 7.44M	Q♣ T♣	BB
	Jimmy 7.50M		

Jimmy makes it 300k on the button and even though my suited QT has some re-raising potential I opt just to call. The flop comes:

I check and Jimmy bets 400k. I instantly move all-in—a pretty big over-raise moving in for 6.7M more into a 1.4M pot!

Now why did I do that? I guess we will never know. Or will we? An all-in raise about five times the size of the pot seems a bit steep, but it does have some merits.

1. Picking up a lot of pots! What would *you* do with A♦ 7♦ or K♦ 9♦ if somebody moved all-in for 6.7M?
2. Stopping yourself from throwing away the best hand! Same example as above, but changing the dynamics. He bets 400k, you re-raise to 1.2M, he now moves in for 6.8M with A♦ 7♦ or K♦ 9♦. Are you going to call with your QT?
3. Putting your opponent in a tough spot! Is anybody good enough to call with KQ but fold Q9? I don't think so!
4. You might stop your opponent from betting in the future, because he is scared of your crazy all-in move. Getting free cards can win you tournaments!

Let us not forget the devastating downside.

1. He calls your all-in move, turning over hands like QJ, T9, or 88!

I will admit I didn't go through all the relevant and proper computations before I made up my mind. It was more of a spur-of-the-moment kind of thing. I was excited about having doubled up the previous hand, and then I just let it go!

Jimmy looked very surprised at the magnitude of my raise, but after the shockwaves had settled in he quickly discarded his hand. Another successful all-in move and I have now created a little distance between us—1.34 million to be exact!

Hand 292

Blinds	Chip Count	My Hand	My Position
50K/100K	Gus 8.14M	2♣ 3♥	Button
	Jimmy 6.80M		

Having regained the chip lead I wasn't about to go crazy. Even though some people might think that Deuce Trey off-suit is one of my favorite holdings, it is not! I fold.

Hand 293

Blinds	Chip Count	My Hand	My Position
50K/100K	Gus 8.09M	Q♠ T♣	BB
	Jimmy 6.85M		

Jimmy limps on the button. Feeling a bit more confident with my 8 to 7 chip advantage I decide to put in a 300k raise. Jimmy folds.

Hand 294

Blinds	Chip Count	My Hand	My Position
50K/100K	Gus 8.19M	K♦ Q♦	Button
	Jimmy 6.75M		

The tide has turned! I have 1.5M to spare, feeling good about myself, and Gobboboy looks a bit worried. Timing was perfect to push the envelope a bit, maybe creating a big pot when Jimmy was a little out of sync. Instead of the standard 300k raise I make it a total of 400k. Jimmy calls and the flop comes:

Great flop! King-high flush draw and two over cards! As good as it gets, considering I don't even have a pair yet. My only nightmare scenario is A♦-x♦, and if Jimmy happens to have that, well . . .

Jimmy checks, I bet 450k, and to my surprise he check-raises to a total of 1.5M. A pleasant surprise, I might add! I was ready to gamble, so I instantly announced all-in. Jimmy didn't have the same urge to play it big, as he disgustedly threw his hand into the muck.

Post-hand analysis: I played my hand very straightforwardly. Betting with a strong drawing hand after Jimmy's check is a gimme. I am a favorite against most pairs, and even if I should run into a funky J6 I still have 35%.

After Jimmy's check-raise, I guess I could have stopped and thought it over, but considering our stack-sizes it is very hard—and undoubtedly wrong—for anybody to get away from my hand. With Jimmy Gobboboy Fricke sitting at the other end of the table it is impossible! Moving all-in is clearly the superior play. Jimmy's insta-fold led me to believe that I had encountered yet another imaginative play from the young lad!

Banking almost 2 million on our last transaction, I had crossed the 10-million barrier for the first time!

Hand 295

Blinds	Chip Count	My Hand	My Position
50K/100K	Gus 10.09M	T♠ 6♦	BB
	Jimmy 4.85M		

Jimmy folds.

Hand 296

Blinds	Chip Count	My Hand	My Position
50K/100K	Gus 10.14M	9♠ 2♣	Button
	Jimmy 4.80M		

I fold.

Hand 297

Blinds	Chip Count	My Hand	My Position
50K/100K	Gus 10.09M	K♣ 5♥	BB
	Jimmy 4.85M		

Jimmy raises to 300k and I'm holding K♣ 5♥. Which way to go? There is a tendency in NHL to fall in love with Aces, or should I say a single Ace. I can't really say that I disagree, since the Ace is the strongest card in the deck. What about a King? A King cannot be that much worse, or can it? In a ring-game yes, since somebody is probably holding an Ace! This is not a ring-game situation—this is heads-up.

Over the years I can remember plenty of heads-up hands where I opened on the button only to get re-raised all-in by an A-*x* hand. In the final hand of the inaugural Poker Superstar Invitational, blinds were very high, which is pretty much inevitable at the end of a tournament, and I called Johnny Chan's all-in re-raise with my JT. In the inaugural European Poker Masters stacks were a little deeper, so I decided to fold my Q9, when Marc Goodwin moved all-in. Both times I got re-raised by an A2. Admittedly both times it was the best hand, but so would a K-*x* have been! All this just to state the fact that in short-handed, short-stacked No Limit Hold' em high cards are very valuable, and it doesn't have to be an Ace!

This time stacks are much bigger, and I see no need to go absolutely crazy with my King-high, so no re-raise. On the other hand folding seems a bit weak, considering it might very well be the best hand right now. This leaves calling as the only alternative and the best one to boot.

The flop comes:

I check and Jimmy checks behind. The turn:

Check, check.

River:

Pairing the board and for some odd reason I bet 350k into a 600k pot. Jimmy quickly calls with a pair of fours and takes down the pot. So what was I thinking? That's the problem—I didn't think. He was never folding a pair. Judging from previous hands and the texture of the board he wasn't going fold an Ace either!

He wasn't calling with J-high or worse, so it couldn't really be considered a value-bet. And then there were the Kings. I think I would have bluffed him out of half the pot if he was holding K-*x* and maybe even the entire pot against KJ. Needless to say, it was a bad bet. The upside was very small and the downside . . . well, you saw what happened!

Hand 298

Blinds	Chip Count	My Hand	My Position
50K/100K	Gus 9.44M	8♠ 7♥	Button
	Jimmy 5.5M		

I open on the button 350k with 8♠ 7♥, trying to pick up the blinds. I had been limping a couple of times. Hopefully Jimmy had noticed and would give me credit for a hand. But Jimmy didn't care! He quickly re-raised to 1.2M, and my 87 suddenly looked a little bit bleak. I only have to call 850k to win 1.55M, about 9 to 5, but this wasn't the time or the place to get fancy. I folded and Jimmy took down another pot.

Side note: Had we both been very deep stacked I definitely would have considered calling. Furthermore, this was the first time Jimmy re-raised pre-flop, so I had to give him some credit.

Hand 299

Blinds	Chip Count	My Hand	My Position
50K/100K	Gus 9.09M	9♥ 8♠	BB
	Jimmy 5.85M		

Jimmy folds.

Hand 300

Blinds	Chip Count	My Hand	My Position
50K/100K	Gus 9.14M	7♦ 4♦	Button
	Jimmy 5.8M		

Last time I raised on the button I got re-raised and didn't even get to see the flop. I wasn't going to let that happen this time. The nature of my hand, suited, semi-connected low cards, was more of a let-us-see-the-flop kind of hand than a pre-flop-raising-war kind of hand anyway. I call and Jimmy raises to 350k. I have to call 250k more to win 450k, exactly 9 to 5. I have heard that song before!

Note that the math is almost exactly the same in hand 298 and this hand. I'm getting 9 to 5 on a pre-flop call and I'm in the same lucrative position on the button. I folded the first one and really want to call the second. Why is that? Is the 74 suited really that much better than 87o?

The strength of the hands is actually very comparable, so it has to be something else. Two things! In the first hand it was a re-raise I was looking at, indicating a lot more strength than an initial raise. Just as important is the amount I have to call compared to the stack-sizes!

If I call this hand, I still have some room to maneuver depending on the flop. On the other hand, because of the already significant pot size, I might be forced to play an all-in pot with something like second pair or a straight-draw. Not an enviable spot to be in, and it should therefore be avoided. Bottom line: It makes much more sense to call this hand than in hand 298. I call.

The flop comes:

Not bad for a let-us-see-the-flop kind of hand!

Jimmy surprisingly checks! I had expected a continuation bet, and the check totally ruined my all-in plans. Time to reconsider! If Jimmy checked two high cards like AJ or KQ, I could afford to check it back, letting him catch up a little. If he trap-checked with a big pair all the money would probably go in the pot at some point anyway. Unless of course the dreaded Nine would show up on the turn, counterfeiting my two pair, in which case I could get away a little cheaper. To sum it all up: I didn't want to lose my customer—checking is superior. I check.

Turn:

A little straighty and a little flushy, but unless Jimmy showed up with T 8, 8 5, or 5 3, all three pretty close to impossible holdings, I was still in control.

This time Jimmy led out 500k into a 700k pot. Again a little bit surprising, since the Six did not figure to help him. I slow-played the flop, but with his bet the pot is getting too big to fool around anymore! Only remaining question is: "How much to raise?"

No surprise here—I like to go for it all! When I think I have the best hand, but my opponent has a number of unknown outs, I like to avoid paralyzing decisions in the near future. I wouldn't know what to do if a Six, Nine, Eight, Five, or spade showed up. If you don't know exactly what you are up against, you are often better off letting your opponent do the guessing. By moving all-in you put him or her to the test. Furthermore you also eliminate any mistakes you might make later on in the hand.

With a pot-sized raise I could leave myself somewhere in Nowhere Land. Jimmy would have good implied odds on some strong drawing hands like A♠ T♠, 8♠ 8♣ etc. Ultimately giving me a very tough decision if he fired the last 3.2M on a scary river card!

All those "ugly scenarios" could be avoided by one simple statement: "All-in!"

Jimmy gave it a huff and a puff, but did not seem to be interested in ending it all right here and now. Jimmy folded!

Epilogue: When pots reach a certain size you have to consider your options very carefully. More often than not the all-in play has some substantial merits that the other more in-between plays can't compete with.

1. Maximum pressure.
2. Your opponent has to have a hand to even consider calling.
3. You will never get bluffed.
4. It might be a mistake pushing all-in, but at least it's gonna be the last one you make.

I pick up 850k on my two small pairs, and once again I'm at the 10M mark.

Hand 301

Blinds	Chip Count	My Hand	My Position
50K/100K	Gus 9.99M	J♠ 3♠	BB
	Jimmy 4.95M		

Jimmy limps and I check my J♠ 3♠ behind.

Flop comes:

Although I flopped an open-ended straight draw, it is not exactly something to be too proud of. Straight draws that only involve one card from your hand and three from the table are not that lucrative. If you are lucky enough to hit a King or an Eight, you are not going to win a big pot anyway since everybody can see that it only takes a Jack to complete the straight. Pairing the J is not too hot either because now both the King and Eight make a straight. Realizing that my hand is not very good, I'm not really looking to push it. I'd rather keep the pot small and then pick up the speed if something good develops. I check and Jimmy checks behind me.

Turn comes:

We both go through the same checking motion.

River comes:

Nothing good ever happened, and with only 200k in the pot I see no reason to try anything. We both check and actually split the pot with Jack high. J6 for Jimmy but fortunately the kicker doesn't play.

It was a similar situation to the one in hand fifteen where I made a hopeless bluff with my King-high. Or was it?

From playing with a lot of players over the years, I have noticed that they are a little bit wary of betting their draws! They check because they don't want to get re-raised out of the pot. I played my draw in this hand very carefully too—a good indicator that Jimmy was holding the same Jack as me, or maybe a King with no kicker.

Pairs weren't easy to come by. Checking the flop and turn a Queen, Ten, or Nine was not likely to be in Jimmy's hand. An Ace was unlikely because of the pre-flop limp, and with small cards 45, 46 he might have taken a stab on the flop. Again a King or a Jack made the most sense. He wouldn't call with a Jack and he really would have to dig deep to call with a King.

This would therefore have been a good small bluff risking 100k–150k. Picking up 100k against a Jack and 200k against a King! Avoiding getting bluffed by an 86 would also have earned me 200k. Even though it was a small pot you should always look for opportunities to add money to your stack.

Hand 302

Blinds	Chip Count	My Hand	My Position
50K/100K	Gus 9.99M	J♠ 3♠	Button
	Jimmy 4.95M		

It is not a misprint! I did actually have J♠ 3♠ in two consecutive hands. I limp on the button and Jimmy checks as well. The flop comes:

Jimmy bets 150k and I flopped a flush-draw! Folding is out. I could definitely put some pressure on by raising—if called I would still have plenty of outs. If he folded to my raise, perfect, but what if he re-raised? It would be a tough call since I wasn't about to double him up in an un-raised pot with a Jack-high flush-draw! Clearly I would have to fold to a big re-raise. I have to admit it would be a shame to raise myself out of a hand that potentially could win me a big pot.

Being in position also favors the more timid call. I have the luxury of dissecting his actions, thereby making a more informed decision before committing too much money to the pot. I like to just call. Turn comes:

Really bad! On a scale from 1 to 10, 10 being the worst, the 4♣ was definitely a 10! A Jack would have been nice, a Five very good, and a spade of course excellent!

Jimmy bets out another 400k and this would have been a very good time to depart with the hand. The board just paired, Jimmy obviously liked his hand, and I had no idea what he was holding. Remember, this was a limped hand! Jimmy could have any two-card combination out there: 4 2, 5 3, K 7, 6♠ 5♠, 9 4 were all in the mix. Some were very strong hands, some mediocre, and there were a couple of drawing hands! More important, my hand was slowly deteriorating. My flush-draw had certainly lost some of its zest, and a river-hit on my part could possibly result in further damage to my stack. In case I improved to what in professional terms are known as "second best hand."

I think I was just being a little stubborn. Calling 400k to win 900 was not at all justifiable with Jack-high. Even though a case could be made for some implied odds, it was simply a bad call! I called.

River was the:

Jimmy's 700k river-bet easily knocked me out of the hand.

Aftermath: I should have escaped a bit cheaper on this hand. Being stubborn is definitely not one of the qualities you want to develop as a poker player.

Hand 303

Blinds	Chip Count	My Hand	My Position
50K/100K	Gus 9.39M	Q♥ 4♦	BB
	Jimmy 5.55M		

What was perceived as being an aggressive heads-up battle has turned into a little bit of a limping contest. Jimmy beats me into the pot with another limp. Maybe it was because of some mediocre holdings or maybe we just both thought that we could outplay the other guy post-flop. No matter what, I limp right back. The flop comes:

Good flop. Top pair, no kicker! Not quite sure in what direction to take this hand, I decide to check. Jimmy checks behind me. The turn is:

Bad turn. I bet 100,000 as a strange case of opposite poker! Checking top pair on the flop and firing 100k when your worst nightmare appears is hardly recommended. The fact remains I just did it. Jimmy calls.

The river comes:

There is now a four-flush on the board, so my betting days are definitely over. My calling days are probably coming to an end, too. I check and Jimmy checks behind me.

Showdown:

Me: Q♥ 4♦—still top pair, no kicker.
Jimmy: 5♠ 6♦—bottom two.

Once again Mr. Fricke had taken down a pot with a imaginative call on the turn. At least this time it was a small one.

Hand 304

Blinds	Chip Count	My Hand	My Position
50K/100K	Gus 9.19M	Q♦ 6♠	Button
	Jimmy 5.75M		

Getting tired of the limping game I make it 350k with my
beautiful Q♦ 6♠. Fortunately that was the last decision I had to
make with that skimpy holding. Gobboboy folds.

Hand 305

Blinds	Chip Count	My Hand	My Position
50K/100K	Gus 9.29M	A♥ 6♣	BB
	Jimmy 5.65M		

Jimmy limps from the button and I decide to kick it up a
notch with A♥ 6♦. I make it 350k to go. Jimmy calls. The flop
comes

I bet 375,000 with my middle pair and again Jimmy calls.
On a connecting flop Jimmy could have just about anything,

therefore I am not going to waste too much time and energy trying to figure it out. Instead I will try to gain more information on the subsequent streets. Turn:

I do have the key card 6♦, the only diamond that actually pairs the board. Apart from that not too much to cheer for. I check and Jimmy checks. I love when Jimmy checks behind me! That was exactly all the information I needed! Being as aggressive as he is, Jimmy would "never" just call the flop and then check the turn behind me with anything that could beat A 6. A blank on the river and I should be home free. River:

Pretty blank! Apart from fading a random King, I should win this pot. I am not sure that Jimmy has anything to call with so I opt for the check-call. Jimmy bets 400,000 and I quickly call. Jimmy taps the table, announcing "I play the board." I turn over the 6♦ and take down a nice 2.25 million pot!

Hand 306

Blinds	Chip Count	My Hand	My Position
60K/120K	Gus 10.415M	Q♦ Q♣	Button
	Jimmy 4.525M		

Coming back from the break I am sensing that Jimmy is still a little bit steamed. He hasn't won too many hands since we started the heads-up battle and has gone from almost 11M in chips down to 4.5M.

He seems very eager to get the chip lead back. If I can pick up a big hand or two this might be my chance to go for the final blow. The best way to deal with an opponent eager to play a huge pot is simply to play your big hands very straightforwardly.

Looking down at two Queens I might have an opportunity to end it right here and now. I raise to 400k obviously praying for a re-raise, but no such luck—Jimmy just calls.

The flop comes:

I do not have the Queen of hearts. Jimmy checks, I bet 450k, and Jimmy quickly announces all-in. Oops! Right back in my face!

This was the first time that a hand had played out this way—Jimmy check-raising me all-in! At first I had no idea what hand to put Jimmy on. There was a flush draw out there, some possible straight draws, and as always in Hold'em a lot of pair draws. I could handle a lot of them, but was of course afraid of him holding the devastating Ace.

After thinking it over for a while I decided I did not need to surrender my solid chip lead on what could turn out to be an ugly two outer for me. I folded.

Post-Hand Analysis

Pre-flop: The hand played itself.

On the flop: Jimmy checks and it is now up to me to decide what to do. There is 800k in the pot and Jimmy is holding approximately 4M. I was ready to play for all of his money before the flop, but with the Ace showing my two Queens have turned into a more mediocre holding. This was a good situation for a check, since giving a free card was very unlikely to hurt me. If Jimmy was holding a K9 I was of course giving him a free chance to beat me with a King. He could also be holding a JT where I actually want to give him a chance to catch up and not knock him out of the hand. Another problem with betting the flop is that it plays right into the strength of all the drawing hands. Leading out for 450k gives Jimmy a perfect opportunity to check-raise all-in with holdings such as 86, 64, 43, and any flush draw, leaving me in a very difficult spot with my two Queens.

Now let us look at the fold: I have to call 3.6M to win 5.3M. If I do so successfully the match is over. I need approximately 40% winning chance to call. The only card I am really afraid of is the Ace. As mentioned above there are a ton of drawing hands that Jimmy could have. Hands like 87 and K5 are also very much in play. It is the perfect time to semi-bluff with a scary Ace lurking out there. It all adds up to one very bad scenario and a dozen lucrative ones.

Was I really so scared of the Ace that I had to fold what looked like a very playable hand? I guess so! In hindsight I shouldn't have been. What Ace could he possibly be holding? If he had AK through A8, I think he would have re-raised before the flop. A7 and A5 are such powerful holdings that he would have slow-played. That leaves us with A6, A4, A3, and A2. Not really that many! I think I folded the best hand! Given the circumstances—the pot odds and Jimmy's steam factor—it was just a horrible laydown.

This might turn out to be a good fold when I see it on TV but if there was one hand I could play over this would be it.

Hand 307

Blinds	Chip Count	My Hand	My Position
60K/120K	Gus 9.565M	A♦ 8♦	BB
	Jimmy 5.325M		

Let us go back to the previous hand, which is still lurking at the back of my mind! I'm not so sure the bet on the flop was wrong, in fact I'm starting to like it more and more. It is the combination of a lead-out-bet followed by a fold that sets me on fire! Realizing that I probably could have ended it all last hand made me wanna throw up. I think it is fair to say that I had built up a little steam myself!

Holding A♦ 8♦ I was definitely not looking to just call, I was re-raising! I didn't get the chance, as Jimmy quietly folded.

Hand 308

CRUCIAL HAND 19: Big Call—Bad Beat with A♥ K♥

Blinds	Chip Count	My Hand	My Position
60K/120K	Gus 9.615M	A♥ K♥	Button
	Jimmy 5.325M		

I pick up yet another great hand on the button—A♥ K♥. It seems like my hands are really picking up speed here in the heads-up battle. I make it 425k and once again I am praying for a re-raise. Jimmy calls and the flop comes:

Jimmy checks and I bet 500k. Immediately Jimmy moves all-in and I have another big decision to make. The first thing that entered my mind was: "Why weren't the two flops reversed?" A75 to my AK and JTT to my two Queens. It would have made it all a lot easier! Nonetheless I had to deal with the situation at hand. Let's take a look at his possible holdings.

First of all I was discarding all total bluffs like the 6♣ 7♣. That leaves us with semi-bluffs, good hands, and powerhouses.

Semi-bluffs—on a flop like this the semi-bluffs seem endless: Any two diamonds, the KQ, the Q9, the 98, the AQ, but discarding the 97 and the 87.

Good hands: Any Jack fits into that category.

Powerhouses: Any Ten and especially QT since the Queen is blocking my straight draw. JT is discarded as well. I don't know anybody who would check-raise all-in with that hand in this situation.

So what to do? I have to call 4.35M to win 6.2M which means I need exactly 41.2% to call.

Against the semi-bluffs I am doing very well. It is only the straight-flush draws that are a favorite against my hand. Against the various other flush draws and weak straight draws I am ranging from a 51% to a 75% favorite. Against the Jacks I have between 28% and 40% depending on his kicker. Against the powerhouses I have 17% unless it is a QT where I am looking at a measly 3.7%.

How do you add all this up at the table? The answer is very simple, you don't! You make an estimated calculation, add in your read and then you close your eyes and call. Just kidding! My read was solely based on the fact that Jimmy did not have a Ten. I didn't believe that he would push so hard with such a strong holding. Suddenly the equation becomes a little simpler since I am only looking at the Jacks and the various drawing hands. With my hand winning percentage ranging from 28% to 75% against those hands the call becomes pretty clear.

I called and was very happy to see Jimmy turn over K♠ Q♦. He did have the Queen of diamonds, but I was still a 70% favorite to win the tournament right here and now!

The turn:

Now Jimmy is down to only 21.6%. The river is:

Ouch! I usually stay pretty calm at the table, but I have to admit that 9♣ did fuck me up! Jimmy doubles up and now he has well over 10M and I'm back in the 4M range.

Hand 309

Blinds	Chip Count	My Hand	My Position
60K/120K	Gus 4.3M	J♠8♠	BB
	Jimmy 10.64M		

Trying to regain my composure from a vicious blow to the head, I'm looking to lay low. I have a general rule that I want to stay out of trouble after losing a huge pot. I don't want to face any big decisions with my head still spinning. On the other hand I don't want to throw away perfectly good playable hands just because I had a little misfortune. Jimmy makes it 400k from the button giving me an excuse to fold! I believe that the J♠8♠ is too good of a hand to fold in a heads-up battle, so I decide to call anyway!

The flop comes:

A good time to lead out!

Probably the most common mistake in poker is the "check to the raiser." Unfortunately I have to admit that I'm guilty too. Sometimes it happens automatically, almost subconsciously, because it is so ingrained in the poker culture, but let me warn you it is, plain and simple, bad poker! Here is a list of some of the downsides when checking blindly.

1. You give away the initiative.
2. You gain no information.
3. You give away free cards.
4. You over-commit yourself when check-raising.

Needless to say I'm not a big fan—I like to lead out. I guess I am a little discombobulated because I couldn't even follow my own directions! I foolishly checked and Jimmy checked behind me. Turn:

I was still holding top pair and I had just added a flush draw to the equation. The likelihood of Jimmy checking a Seven on the flop was slim to none, so I wasn't really worried about the straight. Time to lead out again! I bet 500k and Jimmy quickly mucks.

Epilogue: I gave Jimmy a free look at between three and ten outs depending on his holding. He didn't hit it this time, but if you give your opponent too many complimentary chances it will end up costing you.

Hand 310

Blinds	Chip Count	My Hand	My Position
60K/120K	Gus 4.7M	Q♠ J♥	Button
	Jimmy 10.24M		

I make it 400k on the button. Jimmy folds.

Hand 311

Blinds	Chip Count	My Hand	My Position
60K/120K	Gus 4.8M	5♥ 2♣	BB
	Jimmy 10.014M		

Jimmy raises to 400k on the button. With 5♥ 2♣ even I have to throw in the towel—I fold!

Hand 312

Blinds	Chip Count	My Hand	My Position
60K/120K	Gus 4.7M	T♥ 7♦	Button
	Jimmy 10.24M		

I limp on the button with T♥ 7♦ and Jimmy checks behind me. The flop comes:

Jimmy leads out 150k and I quickly fold. Nothing to it.

Hand 313

Blinds	Chip Count	My Hand	My Position
60K/120K	Gus 4.58M	Q♣ 8♣	BB
	Jimmy 10.36M		

Jimmy folds.

Hand 314

Blinds	Chip Count	My Hand	My Position
60K/120K	Gus 4.64M	A♠ 9♥	Button
	Jimmy 10.3M		

I raise to 400k and Jimmy folds.

Hand 315

Blinds	Chip Count	My Hand	My Position
60K/120K	Gus 4.74M	K♥ T♠	BB
	Jimmy 10.2M		

Jimmy calls on the button, which makes my KT looks like a mighty fine hand. If one of us is dominated it is going to be him! It is very hard to out-kick my King if he has a Ten in his hand, and if he is holding a King my Ten kicker still looks awfully good. Even though I am first to act throughout the remainder of the hand, raising has a very appealing feel to it. I raise 350K more to a total of 470K, and Jimmy calls without hesitation. Flop comes down:

Top pair and judging from my little intro, a practically unbeatable kicker! I bet 500k and again Jimmy quickly pushes all-in. I call even more quickly. I guess I should have thought about it. This was going to be a very significant hand in determining the Aussie Million Winner, so I could at least have spent the mandatory five seconds on my decision! In my pre-flop evaluation I put him on an inferior holding and since I had just flopped top pair it was very unlikely he had me beat. His only chance was a random K6 or J6, in which case I would have had to come up with some serious drawing power. I guess it wouldn't have been the first time.

Instead it was Jimmy who had to take a deep breath. My KT was just about as bad as it could get for him. Jimmy was holding the Q♣ 9♦ and only had a 12.7% winning chance! Curiously enough had I been holding KK for top set, Jimmy would have been better off with a whopping 13.7% winning chance! Fortunately for me no miracles occurred with a Five and Six on the turn and river, and suddenly the chip stacks were reversed again.

My decisions in the hand were all very simple. A good holding pre-flop, a very good one post-flop, both played accordingly with normal-sized bets. The call was a complete no-brainer.

What about Jimmy's decision to push all-in? Had he lost his mind? Looking at my KT it certainly looked that way. Jimmy's move was definitely on the aggressive side, especially if we consider my pre-flop raise out of position. Not an option I had exercised a lot, so the KJ on the flop figured to be in my range. A case can of course always be made for bluffing. Admittedly I would be hard-pressed to call with hands like A9 and 55, but then again if your main objective is to bluff why not go all-in all the time. There has to be some rhyme or reason behind it or else it just becomes an all-in fest. Jimmy's play was too crazy for me, and I think it is fair to say his timing was a little off!

Hand 316

CRUCIAL HAND 20: Gus in Wonderland

Blinds	Chip Count	My Hand	My Position
60K/120K	Gus 9.48M	2♠ 2♥	Button
	Jimmy 5.46M		

I decide to just call on the button with two Deuces, a strange play since it probably plays worse than any other hand post-flop. Unless you flop a set there are always three over cards to worry about, making it hard to proceed properly.

It is much better to raise hoping to win it pre-flop, and if not maybe take it down with a continuation bet on the flop. If you get really lucky you flop a set, top pair for your opponent and you win it all right there. *Dream on.* Never happens!

The flop comes:

Not too bad! My original plan was to win a small pot, and since it is highly unlikely that Jimmy connected with a pair on the board, we can soon move forward to the next hand. After he checks, a small bet from my side should be sufficient to win it against his random Ten-high. He disrupts my plan by betting out 150K. Was that allowed? No matter what, since he wasn't going to bet out with a King or a Five, I still had the best hand. The call was trivial and for now better than the raise, indicating that I was probably slow-playing a King or a Five.

Turn brought the:

Jimmy now bet 400k. Again, same easy read: No King, no Five, and why on earth would he be betting a Nine? To make it even easier for me he placed the bet in such a manner that I was sure indicated weakness. I called again preserving the best for last. The river:

Didn't change anything—and yet he still fired the million-river-bullet. Well I had to give it to him. He was being mighty stubborn, pulling the trigger for the third time with absolutely nothing! Although the doubt was slowly creeping into my mind, I just couldn't let him steal a big pot like this. Furthermore a fold would erase all my great efforts and reads from the previous betting rounds. Raising seemed to be the best play, knocking him out of contention just in case he was bluffing with the best hand. Then again, how much money could I possibly put into the pot with my two "mighty" Deuces? No need to raise! He didn't have a pair, and just in case I had misinterpreted something along the way I opted for the "safe" call. He turned over Q5 for an easy winner! Oops! All my "great" calls went quickly down the drain.

So where did I go wrong? From the beginning to the end adding insult to injury on all four streets dipping into my dwindling stack! I obviously played the entire hand in Wonderland!

Instead of playing "normal" poker, I came up with three imaginary reads costing me a lot of money.

Recap: I managed to lose 1.67 million on a stupid hand, on a fucked-up flop, trying to be a hero. Can we please just forget about this hand?

Hand 317

Blinds	Chip Count	My Hand	My Position
60K/120K	Gus 7.81M	Q♣ 6♦	BB
	Jimmy 7.13M		

Jimmy raises to 400k on the button and I am holding one of those mediocre hands that got me into a lot of trouble when we were three-handed. Calling pre-flop raises out of position with non-suited, non-connected hands like K5, Q6, or J7 is not going to make you a lot of money. Being as math-happy as I am, I don't like to fold any two cards in the big blind to a standard raise. Here I am risking 280k to win 520k, which means I need an exactly 35% winning chance to call.

We haven't even seen the flop yet, so I call.

Mind you, in hold'em the flop represents 43% of your entire hand—3 cards out of 7. A lot of times, especially when you already have money invested in the pot as in the Big Blind, it is worth it to pay a little extra to see those three cards.

The flop comes:

The 43% of my hand that the flop represents didn't help me one bit. I still have Q high or as some might say KQ high.

I check, Jimmy bets 500k, and I fold.

Hand 318

Blinds	Chip Count	My Hand	My Position
60K/120K	Gus 7.41M	J♣ 8♣	Button
	Jimmy 7.52M		

I make it 400k on the button with J♣ 8♣. As always when you raise with Jack high you are happy to see your opponent fold. Jimmy folds.

Hand 319

Blinds	Chip Count	My Hand	My Position
60K/120K	Gus 7.53M	5♣ 5♦	BB
	Jimmy 7.41M		

Jimmy folds on the button.

Hand 320

Blinds	Chip Count	My Hand	My Position
60K/120K	Gus 7.59M	5♣ 6♦	Button
	Jimmy 7.36M		

I limp on the button with 5♣ 6♦. Jimmy checks behind and the flop comes:

Middle pair, opposition checks, obvious bet! I make it 150,000 and Jimmy folds.

Hand 321

Blinds	Chip Count	My Hand	My Position
60K/120K	Gus 7.71M	2♥ 4♥	BB
	Jimmy 7.23M		

In my opinion poker players in general put way too much emphasis on one thing: the cards being suited. A lot of players will happily play the K♣ 5♣ only to throw away K9o in the next hand, which does seem a bit strange since K9o is obviously a better hand. So why are suited cards so attractive? Is it the percentage of times where you actually make a flush? Or is it because it plays so much better? I think it is the latter. The fact that you can put pressure on your opponent without having a made hand and pick up pots by semi-bluffing adds a lot of value to suited cards.

Jimmy raises on the button to 400k and I decide to call 280k more with my beautifully suited one-gapper 2♥ 4♥. The flop comes:

I check and Jimmy bets 500k. An obvious spot for a check-raise with a straight flush draw and if it hadn't been for the two Aces, I would have done so. I tend to play my straight and flush draws a little bit more carefully when there are pairs on the board. If I raised and Jimmy had an Ace, he would re-raise and I would have to make a decision for all of my chips before even seeing the turn, not a pleasant scenario. Even if he was holding a medium to big pair I thought he might be capable of making the same all-in move. Another unpleasant scenario!

The hand reminds me a little bit of a hand played against my good friend Howard Lederer in the inaugural Poker Superstar invitational. Seated in order at the four-handed table were Howard Lederer, T.J. Cloutier, Johnny Chan, and me. Howard opens in first position, T.J. and Chan fold, and I call in the big blind with 6♦ 4♦. The flop comes:

I'm looking at a beautiful straight-flush draw. I check, Howard bets, I check-raise, and before I can rake in the pot Howard moves all-in. Oops, that didn't go as planned. I needed 40% to call, and after a long deliberation I decided to fold.

Why did I fold such a nice-looking draw?

1. I was sure Howard had a very strong hand as I didn't think he thought I was gonna fold.
2. And then there was the pair on the board. If I hit my hand he would always have full house re-draws against me. When deciding to fold I put Howard on a minimum of two Queens.

T.J. and Johnny asked me after the hand what I had, since it took me so long to fold. I quickly answered 4♦ 6♦ because I knew they would never believe me. They both started laughing since I'm not exactly known for my big laydowns. I learned afterward that Howard was holding A♣ 3♣, giving me a 43% winning chance, making my fold slightly incorrect.

I raised myself out of the pot against Howard. I'd made a costly mistake, not even getting a chance to hit my "pretty" draw! Time to try something different!

In the current situation my hand is also much weaker. I only have a gut-shot draw and Jimmy is much more likely to be holding an Ace than Howard a Trey. The call seemed like the best play. The turn comes, a pretty-looking:

I checked and Jimmy quickly checked behind me. The river brought:

Again I checked, hoping to induce a bluff as I thought Jimmy had absolutely nothing. Jimmy checked behind me, confirming my suspicions. Very curious about his holding, I patiently waited for him to either muck or turn over his cards—he showed J♣ 5♥.

I took down the pot with my flush.

Post-hand analysis: Having checked the turn I actually liked the check on the river as I felt quite sure that Jimmy had total air. Having said that, I think my check on the turn was weak. I was only holding the Four-high flush. Jimmy could easily have a higher heart, a Trey, a Ten, or even a random pair, in which case I was giving him 4–7 outs for free. Hands he would never call with facing a substantial bet.

If Jimmy had an Ace I think my chances of getting all his money would have been better by leading out. If Jimmy has an Ace with a big heart all the money is going in no matter what I do. Of course I miss out on a bluff opportunity from Jimmy by leading out, but nonetheless I think checking the turn was the wrong play.

Hand 322

Blinds	Chip Count	My Hand	My Position
60K/120K	Gus 8.61M	J♠ T♣	Button
	Jimmy 6.33M		

Limping on the button has always seemed kind of odd to me as I feel it goes against general poker principles. I know Phil Hellmuth loves to do it and personally I have been experimenting more with it lately. I haven't made a final conclusion. Let me try it one more time!

Jimmy checks behind and the flop comes:

Jimmy checks and I bet 150k with my up-and-down straight draw. Jimmy calls and the pot now contains 540k. The turn is:

Great card! Contemplating what to bet, Jimmy surprisingly bets out 500k. The lead-out changed the dynamics of the hand completely since the considerable size of the pot, already over a million, might make me able to go for the kill. This was definitely a situation where I needed to take some time to consider the available plays:

The Fold: Usually not recommended when holding the nuts.

The Call: A trap play, hoping for another lead-out on the river and then going for the big raise. If Jimmy doesn't lead out, I would, then opt for a big-value bet. There are two problems with the trap play. First of all, I don't like trap plays. The other problem is the two flush draws on the board, which means that there are nine spades, nine diamonds, eight cards pairing the board, and an off-suit Jack or Ten that could freeze the action. That's a whopping twenty-eight cards out of the remaining forty-four that change the complection of the board. Not that I am ever going to fold my hand, but it might stop Jimmy from betting, consequently winning me a smaller pot. There is an upside, though. He might be drawing dead, thus folding to a raise on the turn.

The Raise: A good solid poker play following the standard guideline "Raise when you have the best hand!"

The All-in Move: A little steep for the situation at hand since Jimmy still has 5.44M left. And there is only 1.54M in the pot after my call.

I decide to call. The river brings:

I'm happy to see that I am still holding the nuts, but unhappy to see Jimmy looking a bit disgusted with the Ace! Jimmy checks. Oops!

In my call analysis I forgot to think about the Aces. If Jimmy was leading out on the turn with a random King, an "Ace on the river" (Barry Greenstein's well-renowned book) could also freeze the action. I still had to decide what to bet, though. I bet 1.1M into the 1.54M pot. Jimmy called fairly quickly and I'm guessing he was holding a pretty good King.

I think I missed an opportunity to win a bigger pot! Had I

instead made a normal raise on the turn we might have gone to war. Considering the texture of the board it was also a much better poker play. The main reason I decided to just call was the fact that I had made very few trap plays at the final table. I wanted to give Jimmy a different look. In hindsight the timing was wrong—no more trap plays for me!

Hand 323

Blinds	Chip Count	My Hand	My Position
60K/120K	Gus 10.60M	T♠6♠	BB
	Jimmy 4.34M		

Jimmy calls on the button and I check out of position with T♠6♠. The flop comes:

I check and he bets 150k. I fold. No need to get fancy.

Hand 324

Blinds	Chip Count	My Hand	My Position
60K/120K	Gus 10.48M	Q♣9♥	Button
	Jimmy 4.46M		

Another funky limp on the button with an above-average holding!

I limp on the button and Jimmy raises 350k more. I call and the pot now contains 940k.

The flop is:

Jimmy fires 600k and it is time to stop and analyze the situation.

The Fold: Seems reasonable considering I didn't connect on the flop and am still holding Queen high. Although I have a gut shot there is also a pair on the board, making straight draws less lucrative. This was also one of the few times Jimmy had raised me after limping on the button, indicating strength on his part.

The Call: Also very reasonable. I do have a gut shot, the Queen is probably a winner, and the Nine could be as well. With all my cards live I could be looking at up to ten outs twice going into the turn. Don't forget I do have position and I can see whether Jimmy is willing to fire a second bullet.

The Mini-Raise: Luring him into playing a really big pot, a play that I might very well have made with a KJ or a 87! This play has proven itself to be very successful over the years and both Jimmy and I have used it at least once at this final table. Why not try it with a Q9?

The All-in Raise: The ultimate pressure play, but strangely enough it is often perceived as weaker than the mini-raise. Thinking ten hands back, the gut-shot all-in move didn't work very successfully for GobboBoy. I don't like this play.

I end up folding my hand.
In retrospect I would have liked to play this hand differently.

I feel like I chickened out and folded. Analyzing the hand away from the table, my top choice would have been to call.

Hand 325

Blinds	Chip Count	My Hand	My Position
60K/120K	Gus 10.01M	J♠T♦	BB
	Jimmy 4.93M		

Jimmy calls on the button and although J♠T♦ is definitely an above-average hand in a heads-up situation I choose to check behind him. The raise is marginal at best. Keeping the pots small out of position seems to be a sound heads-up, No Limit Hold'em strategy. The flop comes:

I could bet my pair of Tens, which is likely the best hand, but if he has me beat a bet on my part accomplishes nothing and if I indeed have the best hand he is probably drawing absolutely dead. The only holdings he can have where he has a chance to possibly draw out on me are a random King or the 98 where the gut-shot Jack can beat me.

Best course of action is to check. Jimmy bets 150k and I of course call. The turn is:

With the blank Five it appears that the thought process I went through on the flop is still valid, so I check again. Jimmy checks behind me and by now I don't really have a clear picture of what Jimmy is holding since he could be checking Aces, Queens, Tens, or absolutely nothing. I will say that nothing is the overwhelming favorite. The river brings:

It appears like my three Tens with a Jack kicker is the absolute "nuts." Throughout the match my value bets have been more successful than the induce-a-bluff check, so I opt for the value bet and lead out 500k into a 540k pot. Jimmy folds quickly and my guess is that he had something in the range of Nine-high. In retrospect I think I should have given him one more chance to fire at it!

Hand 326

Blinds	Chip Count	My Hand	My Position
60K/120K	Gus 10.28M	T♣ 6♦	Button
	Jimmy 4.66M		

I limp on the button trying to see a cheap flop in position. T♣ 6♦ is of course not much of a hand, but you have to remember that this is heads-up. Most of the time you will start out with mediocre-to-poor hands! Jimmy checks and the flop comes:

Jimmy checks and I check, not wanting to get involved in a small pot with Ten high.

The turn:

Jimmy checks and suddenly my hand has a bit of potential with a flush draw and a gut-shot straight draw. I might take the pot away with my Ten-high, as Jimmy's two checks indicate he doesn't have too much either, but I decide to check and see if I can make my hand. If Jimmy checks again on the river and I miss, I might go for the small bluff. The river brings:

Jimmy checks again and now my 6♦ looks like a mighty big card. I bet 150k for value, Jimmy calls, and my flush is good. I take down the 540k pot. I don't really know what Jimmy called me with, but it could very well have been a tiny diamond.

Hand 327

Blinds	Chip Count	My Hand	My Position
60K/120K	Gus 10.55M	4♦ 5♣	BB
	Jimmy 4.39M		

Jimmy raises to 400k. A very marginal decision with 4♦ 5♣, but since I have turned into such a conservative player I decide to fold!

Hand 328

Blinds	Chip Count	My Hand	My Position
60K/120K	Gus 10.43M	8♣ 7♣	Button
	Jimmy 4.51M		

Limping with 8♣7♣ on the button in a heads-up game is just plain tight! In fact I feel certain it is as tight as you will ever see me play! I didn't want to get into a raise/re-raise scenario before the flop, so I guess the limp is actually quite all right!

Jimmy checked his BB and the flop came:

Jimmy checks and I bet the minimum 120k with my second pair. Mind, you at this point the pot only holds 240k so the 120k is consistent with a continuation bet of approximately 50%. Not that a flop bet in a limped pot can really be considered a continuation bet, but nonetheless. Jimmy calls. The turn card is:

Jimmy checks and, not wanting to face a check-raise with third pair, I check behind him. My pair of Sevens could very well be the best hand, but for now I wanted to keep the pot small. The river brings:

Not a bad card! My mediocre hand had suddenly turned into a powerful holding. Jimmy unfortunately still checks. I was hoping to cash in big, but at least I still have a chance to extract something with a decent-sized value bet.

My general tendency is to value bet big and bluff a little bit smaller. It seems to me that people do not pay enough attention to the size of the bet. Either they pay you off or they don't. So in this case, if Jimmy had something he was probably going to pay me off regardless of whether I bet 300k or 400k. I obviously opted for the latter and bet 400k. Jimmy, who probably had his usual Jack-high, folded rather quickly.

I am now at my all-time high with 10,670,000 in chips, and I'm sensing that Jimmy is getting a little frustrated with his lack of cards!

Hand 329
CRUCIAL HAND 21: Victory—Aces Hold Up!

Blinds	Chip Count	My Hand	My Position
60K/120K	Gus 10.67M	A♣ A♦	BB
	Jimmy 4.27M		

With a substantial chip lead and an aggressive opponent at the other side of the table I am at this point definitely looking for a hand with which I can deliver the final blow.

Jimmy limps on the button and I look down only to find the biggest hand of them all: AA! AA is such a powerhouse in a heads-up confrontation! The first thing that enters my mind is how to extract as much money as possible from Jimmy's stack. So far Jimmy hadn't folded to any of my raises when he limped on the button, so there was definitely no reason to take it easy. The plan was to build a large-enough pot so that if Jimmy caught any piece of the flop he would be in all-in territory. It was obvious to me by now that if Jimmy had so much as a gut shot he was liable to make a big move at the pot.

I raise to 450k, a little bit of an over-raise but that was the way we had been playing so far, and I saw no reason to change gears now.

As expected he called and the flop comes:

A flop with a lot of drawing potential, which is what I was hoping for since I knew Jimmy was going to be loose on the trigger. I made my usual continuation bet of a little more than half the pot, firing 500k. Jimmy immediately announced all-in, and without hesitation I called. He looked at me in disbelief, moaning, "Did you flop top pair again?" I of course shook my head as I turned over my two Aces. I was hoping for Jimmy to turn over a random T8o giving him an approximately 24% chance to win the hand. Unfortunately he turned over 9♣ 7♣, giving him an up-and-down straight draw and a back-door club draw with a winning chance of 36.4%.

Showdown

My Hand   **Jimmy's Hand**

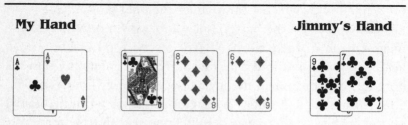

The turn brought the 2♣ and even though this card gave Jimmy a flush draw on top of his straight draw his winning chances actually dipped to 31.8%.

For some strange reason his strong drawing hand didn't seem to bother me a bit. I felt this might be the end of the tournament!

River:

My Aces held up and it was all over!

CHAPTER 8

STATS AND TIPS

I am a sucker for numbers, stats, and fancy computations. In this chapter you will find details about hand categories, number of hands played, uncontested pots, continuation-bets, limping, all-ins, and bluffing.

Intro

As far as I am concerned, "stats" is a fairly new word in the poker dictionary. I doubt it was used much in the good old days, but with the coming of internet poker, stats have made their entry onto the poker stage. Most internet players with respect for themselves keep stats on their day-to-day rivals. Furthermore and probably most important of all, they also keep track of their results, their own mannerisms and their behavioral tendencies. I don't! This is surely a mistake on my part which puts me at a disadvantage against my internet foes. Using poker analytic software will constantly keep you up to date on how you are doing against different opponents, give you an idea of whether you are calling too much, raising too little and last but not least tell you if you or your opponents' patterns are too predictable. To put it another way: stats is the modern approach to get tells on your opponent—and if you ask me a pretty good substitute for the old-fashioned Phil Hellmuth technique of staring into your soul. Used properly, it's probably also a tad more precise.

Don't get me wrong. I am not trying to diminish the conventional over-the-table reading ability. I actually believe it played a big part in my success here Down Under. I am just stating the obvious: "Reads are imperfect and numbers don't lie."

Every time you are at a crossroad and have to make a big decision at the poker table you have to rely on intuition, instinct, poker know-how and whatever read you have on your opponent. Just imagine if you could back up the decision with some healthy stats and security in numbers. I bet you would notice a slight increase in enjoyable bank statements.

Unfortunately you can't, as this is all internet talk and there is basically no way to get stats from live games. You have to keep meticulous record for the stats to have any meaning, then process the data to have some answers ready for next time you play live. Although I am sure it would boost your results significantly, I don't know of anyone who goes to those lengths to improve their game. I have tried to do so once or twice in a cash game situation but for some reason it seems to work much better for me in a tournament setting. Getting up from the table every three to five minutes, taking notes by talking into my little gadget and keeping track of as much as possible while the impressions are still fresh in my mind has almost become a routine of mine. Then I can work it all out from the recordings when I have more time.

But that is al in the past, the tournament is over, the 329 hands are written and all that is left is to turn my attention to the numbers. Invent some never before seen stat categories, display my strengths and weaknesses and give you a behind the scenes look at what I think really happened throughout the tournament. It is solely to give you as well as myself a better understanding of which hands work well under different circumstances and which types of plays turn a profit in the long run. It will obviously be a very mathematical, number-crunching way of looking at it, as I am basically dissecting the entire five days with my little calculator.

Hand Categories

So how did I win it? Well for starters I played a lot of hands—329 to be exact. Did I really have 329 premium hands, just winning the tournament because of superior card holdings? Well, see for yourself. Below is a chart showing what I have decided to call category one (Top-Notch), category two (Good), category three (Medium) and category four (Don't Try This at Home) hands.

HAND CATEGORIES		
No. of hands dealt = 850	*No. of hands played = 329*	
Hand Categories		**Number of Hands**
Top-Notch	AA	3
	KK	0
	QQ	4 TOTAL = 22
	JJ	3
	AK	10
	AQs	2
Good Hands	TT, 99, 88, 77, 66	
	AQ*o*	
	AJ	
	ATs	52
	KQ	
	KJs	
	KTs	
	QJs	
	QTs	
	JTs	

	55, 44, 33, 22	
	ATo, KJo, QJo, JTo	
	AX, KXs, QXs, JXs	
	KTo, K9o, K8o, K7o, K6o	
Medium	QTo, Q9o, Q8o, Q7o	166
Hands	JTo, J9o, J8o	
	T9o, T8o, 98o	
	T9s, T8s, T7s, T6s	
	98s, 97s, 96s, 95s	
	87s, 86s, 85s	
Don't Try This at Home	Remaining hands	89

This chart is somewhat different than your standard seven-eight category chart, but I find it hard to distinguish between K♦ 5♦ and T♠ 8♠ or 7♥ 7♣ and Q♣ J♣. I can't with firm conviction in my voice tell you that one is better than the other or vice versa. I therefore obviously put them all in the same category.

Group 4 is all the discombobulated hands that deserve some attention even though they fall outside the customary categories. I pretty much believe any two-card holding could be playable in the right setting—mostly from the button or defending the big blind. The top-notch hands haven't really changed since Doyle Brunson was a kid, and are all fairly well represented apart from the "slumping" Kings—I guess "The Cowboys" never made it to Australia.

This chart is made from the 329 hands I played but you should note that I was dealt approximately 850 hands. You can rest assured that the 521 (850 − 329) hands I did not play with 99% certainty were all in the two bottom categories. I played precisely 255 medium to less attractive two-card-combinations and made some serious pocket change with a lot of them. Given the right circumstances—position, profiling, and good timing—a wide range of them actually are extremely profitable.

I know a lot of people out there who disagree and therefore do not enter any pots with less than premium holdings. They try to win tournaments with Aces versus Kings, always being on the right side of the cold-deck and the coin-flip and hoping for somewhere in between eight to fifteen double-ups to lift the trophy. Playing that way is to me a lost cause—you need miracles to pull that one through. It could work, but probably only does so about 1 in 2000 in a 500 player field. I for one like to see my winning chances increase instead of having them hit rock-bottom. Although patience has its moments, too much of it will most likely leave you high and dry. Exclusively depending on patience as your main source of income will according to my homemade estimates reduce your chances of winning a tournament by two to four times compared to the average field. Let me repeat: the game is called Poker, not "waiting for the nuts." In order to accumulate chips and make something happen you have to do exactly that: Play Poker!

In most of the following sections I have discarded the hands from three-handed and heads-up play as they would give an erroneous picture to the stats.

Number of hands

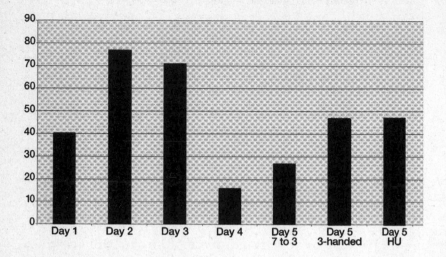

Up until only Andy, Jimmy, and myself were left, I had been dealt 754 hands and played 235 of them. Just about 31% in what should be considered an on-average seven-handed game. 31% is probably more than most other people would ever dream of playing but it is actually not that insane. Going by my own guideline in chapter 3 (page 118) where I recommend playing 30% of all hands in a six-handed game, it should be no surprise that I am located in the higher regions of the scale. It definitely shouldn't be a revelation to anyone that tournaments in most cases are won by people being loose on the trigger. It can be hard to change your ways, follow a more aggressive path and play more hands. But I strongly recommend you to do so if you want to find yourself on top of the tournament ranks.

Uncontested Pots

How to proceed with all these mediocre hands I'm urging everybody to play? The first step is to raise and then see what happens. Sometimes that is all the action required. I personally picked up fifty-five pots throughout the course of the tournament meeting absolutely no resistance. Let me repeat. I managed to pick up fifty-five uncontested pots with a very loose image. Think about what damage can be made with a tight image, kicking your pre-flop raising frequency into gear?

And that's not all! I picked up another fifteen pots pre-flop by re-raising the initial raiser. Some of them with a firm belief that I was holding the best hand, but quite a few funk-balls snuck in there. In order of strength:

The Span of My Re-raising Hands													
AK	AK	AK	JJ	99	99	88	77	55	A8o	K7o	QTo	76o	54o

I don't exactly have to have picture cards or better to put a lot of money in the pot. Sensing some hesitation or reluctance on your opponent's part is sometimes all you need. It is worth noticing though that in all the cases where I re-raised with weak holdings I was facing a late position raiser. Apart from your actual holding, picking your spots carefully is the single most important factor when deciding whether to re-raise or not.

I won a total of seventy pots without ever seeing a flop. I love to see flops but in 29% of all hands nobody would let me. ☺

Continuation Bet

So what happened in all those pots where I raised pre-flop and met some resistance? I gave up on fourteen of them due to some violent behavior on my opponents' part. The rest of them, thirty-eight pots, I was given the chance to perform the exercise known as the continuation bet. Even though I like his style, I didn't quite live up to his standards. The name is Barry Greenstein and as far as I am concerned one of the most fierce continuation betters out there—I think he is as close to 100% as possible. I was up there in the same range a couple of years ago, but with my newfound tight and conservative approach I'm settling for a little less. Although it is extremely important to constantly keep your opponent under pressure I feel I have slightly better results by staying around 80%. I made thirty attempts, which is exactly 79% of the time and right where I want to be. Some stabs were more successful than others, but at least I managed to get fourteen checkmarks in the beautiful hands-won-post-flop-without-a-pair column. A category you won't be able to visit unless you are the aggressor. And that is what it's all about. Keep swinging as your opponent will only flop a pair 34% of the time. Continuously taking aim at pot after pot will eventually break down even the toughest of opponents, and most likely leave a gorgeous pile of chips right in front of you.

I'm not saying that you should aimlessly follow the Barry Greenstein model as this takes years of practice and loads of experience to master, but chances are if you only make a continuation bet 50% of the time you are playing too tight and predictable.

Limping

I limped nineteen times in 235 hands. A surprisingly high number if you ask me—especially if you consider the following. I never limp on the button, 1 off the button, in super high ante structures, with high cards, when it is my birthday, when I'm drunk and I could go on. Bottom line: I'm not a big fan of limping.

So where did the nineteen limps come from? Well, I do limp in the first couple of levels, with small pairs, with limpers in front of me and when it is somebody else's birthday. Maybe limping isn't that bad after all. It really depends on your objective. If you feel you can outplay your opponent with good solid post-flop decisions, limping and keeping the pot small is okay. If you want to play Ram & Jam style limping doesn't really seem to fit the picture. However you want to play, you should make sure that your initial decision follows that trail.

Beware though—limping has one big flaw. It doesn't give you a chance to pick up uncontested pots. As we saw in one of the previous sections, I had a lot of success doing just that—picking up uncontested pots. As a matter of fact I believe it was one of my major sources of income throughout the tournament. No matter who you are you can not afford to give up on equity like that.

I for one have no doubts! Limping in general is a mistake! You are basically making a small error in the hopes of your opponent making a blunder later on in the hand. Be careful when you tread those waters. Ante-stealing is a crucial element in winning tournament strategy, and can only be obtained by raising, so keep your limps to a minimum. Limping should only be used sporadically as a decoy or when your hand, your position, and the structure dictates it. It should never ever be your main technique for entering pots.

All-ins

Someone once told me that in order to win the 1995 WSOP main event Dan Harrington moved all-in forty-one times. Sometimes with the best hand, sometimes as an underdog, sometimes as a semi-bluff and of course there were also a couple of stone-cold bluffs in the mix. It wasn't part of the story but of course he didn't get called all the time.

Therefore it is hard to say exactly how many times he actually was all-in with his tournament life on the line. All I do know is that I don't really like to be all-in. I try to avoid it as much as possible. You can't play scared, but you can of course try to steer the action in the direction you want.

ALL-IN HANDS

Hand No.	Gus All-in (G)/ Opponent All-in (O)	Potentially Devastating Hand	Opponent	Winning Chance When the Money Gets In	Win (W)/ Loss (L)/ Tie (T)
14	G	X	Unknown	90.9%	W
17	G	X	Unknown	77.3%	W
30	O		Unknown	67.5%	L
63	O	X	Jeff Madsen	75.1%	W
75	O		Unknown	40.2%	W
76	O		Unknown	28.8%	L
82	O		Unknown	66.0%	W
83	O		Unknown	43.7%	L
84	O	X	Unknown	45.2%	W
87	O		Unknown	54.7%	W
120	O		Alvin Barron	35.4%	L
131	O		Kostas Varoxis	54.0%	L
133	O	X	Lee Nelson	76.9%	W
140	O		Paul Wasicka	18.7%	L
141	O		Ross Boatman	31.5%	L
154	O		Paul Wasicka	38.7%	T
155	O		Ross Boatman	92.9%	W
184	O		Robert Goldfarb	36.4%	L
186	O		K. Atkins/R. Goldfarb	35.1%	W (3-way)
190	O		Patrick Fletcher	52.3%	L
193	O	X	Patrik Antonius	75.0%	W
215	O		Kristy Gazes	52.9%	W

220	O		Hans Martin Vogl	31.5%	L
232	O		Julius Colman	43.9%	T
275	O		Andrew Black	66.0%	T
290	G	X	Jimmy Fricke	88.6%	W
308	O	X	Jimmy Fricke	66.9%	L
315	G	X	Jimmy Fricke	87.3%	W
329	O		Jimmy Fricke	63.6%	W

In this tournament I managed to be all-in a whopping four times—needless to say I won them all. All four times as a huge favorite having respectively 91%, 77%, 89% and 87% winning chance. I had twenty-two different opponents all-in on twenty-five different occasions. With an average win percentage of 52.2% once the money got in the middle it seemed like a very fair outcome that I won eleven of them, lost eleven and had three ties. I definitely over-performed in the absolutely crucial situations as I could have been knocked down with a 6 count or sent packing on nine different occasions.

Let's put the luck-factor aside, since you have absolutely no way of controlling the outcome of the coin-flips. What you can control is whether to butt heads with the big stacks, punish the small stacks, or maybe do a bit of both. My best advice is to accumulate a lot of chips early, become the chip-leader and stay there. That way you will never have to face an all-in decision for the rest of the tournament. ☺

Bluffing

Let me start out by defining the term "bluff" as I see it: A bluff is not a continuation bet on the flop with A♠ 8♠ or Q♦ T♦ on a raggedy flop as your opponent might have 9♥ 7♥ and missed the flop as well. A bluff is not betting some kind of big draw on the turn with 8-high. A stone-cold bluff is when you bet with what is knowingly the worst hand and have little to no chance of improving. Given the circumstances you don't believe your opponent to be able to call your bet and therefore you make the play. That is going to be my definition but before we dip into the actual stats let me give you a little pre-stat story.

During a recent interview I was asked about my internet performance but especially how I thought I was perceived by some of my competitors. I have to admit that I still have to get used to play on the internet as it is somewhat of a different beast than playing live. I therefore have a lot of improvements to make. I try too much and play too many tables at the same time thereby neglecting to take notes on my opponents. Following that trail I do not have a good idea of how they see me. Failing to come up with a reasonable answer it was displayed to me in the form of a blog on one of the many internet forums. I'm not going to tire you with all the ins and outs of what the bulletin said but stick to the most interesting comment. Brian Townsend, aka Sbrugby, very explicitly explained: "Gus never bluffs!" As you can see Sbrugby used the in-poker-terms inadmissible word "Never." A pretty strong statement if you ask me. "Could he possibly be right?" Let me re-phrase: "What the fuck is going on here?" A player with a reputation for being one of the big bluffers in the game never bluffs! Have I just had a good PR woman? Is it because I only bluff on TV for everybody to see? Is it all just a big hoax on my part? Well let's take a look on the "Big Bluff" category.

BLUFFING ENDEAVORS

Day 1	The only two cracks I made were at an early stage in hand 6 and 10. By the way both attempts failed. I failed to make an obvious bluff in hand 21.
Day 2	Two small successful stabs were taken on the flop in hand 70 and 73. In both hands I was knowingly beat and had very little chance of improving. Not knowing I had made the back-door the nut-flush in hand 94, I tried a hopeless bluff. My bluff failed but I won the hand because I didn't know what I had.
Day 3	Hand 132: Fired a second barrel with Queen high knowing that my opponent would fold. Hand 135: Moved all-in on the flop against Ross Boatman's short stack. Both winners.
Day 4	Hand 208: Bet into four people on a paired board with King high.
Day 5	Hand 212: Check-raised the flop with Ace high and followed it up with another bullet on the turn. Hand 266: Same check-raise this time with King high.

Not a very impressive rap sheet. I actually limp more than I bluff.

Back to the question at hand: Sbrugby is mistaken—but not by a lot. I do bluff—just not very often. He was right in profiling me in that category as it is not a big part of my game. I have of course pulled some stunts over the years, and since quite a few of them have been on TV I guess it has stuck in people's minds. I prefer the stab and the occasional re-raise and basically do not consider myself a big bluffer! There you have it, the cat is out of the bag or maybe this section is just another big bluff!

CHAPTER 9

AFTERTHOUGHTS

I started out with limited optimism due to my mediocre tournament results in 2006, but five days and 746 players later, I have a slightly different view. Higher confidence level, positive attitude, and a big smile on my face. ☺

After all, what you strive for is to play your best and ultimately join Bruce Willis in the ranks of "Last Man Standing." I felt pretty good about achieving the most significant goal— winning the tournament. As far as my level of play goes, overall I am very happy with my performance but it is all on paper right in front of you so I'll let you be the judge.

I have revealed everything. My hands, my thoughts, my observations, basically everything that happened in those past five days—pokerwise that is. Everything that could fit into my little tape-recorder—and most of the things that didn't—has been dissected and commented on. To the best of my abilities I have added my insights and analysis, explaining the ins and outs of my decision-making process. Sometimes unfortunately falling short because I had to admit that I had no idea what the heck I was thinking! I have been brutally honest every step of the way, not trying to cover up anything—including my own shortcomings.

My deepest apologies for any discrepancies that might have occurred within this book. I have tried my best to keep every hand, all chip counts and every character as accurate as possible. With my tape recorder and my memory as my only gizmos, it is a definite possibility that I might have missed something along the way. Remember, I did try to play poker while keeping track of everything and everyone surrounding me. Nonetheless I hope you have enjoyed this five-day poker diary and that my ideas on how to approach a tournament and my insights on how to execute those ideas have given you a little food for thought. Maybe even inspired you to work on your game, improve your batting-average, reduce your mistakes and ultimately achieve your goals.

Personally I always try to minimize my own mistakes. Looking back on this past week I am generally happy with the outcome apart from one major blunder:

Day 1, Table 1, Hand 1. I had an opportunity to make a substantial side-bet with Mr. Phil Ivey. Failing to negotiate the right price could very well have cost me AU$ 1,500,000! Had I been man enough to cross-book the entire tournament Phil would probably have paid a little more attention to the final table. Well, maybe next time?

On a different note, one question sneaked into this book-writing process time and time again. Mostly from poker-interested friends of mine but also from several top-notch poker pros: *"Why would you display your style of play, your secrets, basically your entire game for everyone to see?"* Although it is true that I have exposed myself by showing everything that happened throughout this week's play, it doesn't mean that I left myself totally defenseless.

The main thing that identifies all top poker players is that they are able to vary their game, change gears and stay unpredictable. The fact that most people have labeled me as somewhat of a crazy lunatic hasn't hurt my results over the past years and I doubt this book will. But in case I am wrong and this book is going to be the end of my tournament career because everybody knows how to read me and pinpoint my weaknesses, I guess I have brought it on myself. Or to state the obvious: then I don't belong among the ranks of the top players! If I am not able to randomize my play and keep people guessing after a little bit of exposure I'll be looking for a different career pretty soon. So go ahead—challenge my ability to change my ways, personally I am looking forward to see the outcome!

Good Luck.